**Richard C. Schwartz, Ph.D., developer of the IFS model, and adjunct faculty, Department of Psychiatry, Harvard Medical School.**

Ever wonder how IFS (Internal Family Systems) fits with the philosophies of such luminaries as James, Freud, Jung, Jesus, Buddha, Damasio, Goethe, or Winnicott? Marcel Duclos, an IFS therapist and former professor of psychology and philosophy, takes us on a fascinating, nonlinear tour of those great minds and more, focusing on how the essence of their thinking connects to IFS.

**Susan McConnell, MA, Senior Lead Trainer, IFS Institute, and author of the forthcoming book *A Practitioner's Guide to Somatic IFS.***

The concept of "Self" has indeed eluded my attempts as an IFS trainer to explain or define with words. Before reading this book, I had primarily relied on guiding my students to experience this foundational aspect of the Model. Duclos collects the viewpoints of theologians, philosophers, scholars, psychotherapists, and mystics along with his poems, his sacred moments with patients, and his defining personal moments to reveal the incarnated and transcendent trinity of our core nature. He illuminates how the self is transformed by the SELF into the Self, our essential nature that fosters healing and harmony within the multiple aspects of the psyche. This embodied relational trinity reveals the unity of the psyche, soma, and spirit, and it will inform my teaching. This book takes its place as an essential contribution to the IFS Model as well as to the field of philosophy, psychology, and spirituality.

**Martha Sweezy, Ph.D., Assistant Professor at Harvard Medical School and co-author of *Internal Family Systems Therapy,* second edition, with Richard Schwartz, Ph.D.**

In this erudite telling of his career, Marcel Duclos, religious scholar, psychologist, and psychotherapist, takes us on a deep dive into the lectures of William James on religion, spirituality, and mysticism; Bettelheim's insights on Freud; Damasio's view on Spinoza and James; and Jung's take on psychology and religion, all the while interweaving his own experience as an internal family systems (IFS) therapist. Readers who want a handy reference for how James and Jung relate to IFS will value having this book on the shelf. Readers who wish to learn more about the roots of psychotherapies that focus on the healing power of consciousness will value the history Duclos presents here. And those looking for narrative will enjoy the story of the author's journey through psychotherapy into old age.

**Julien Olivier, D. Min., BCCC Clinical Chaplain, Fellow in Hospice and Palliative Care**

Facing disease and death, the patient is forced to reflect on the unthinkable: *I am no more what I was. I may soon not even be.* It is the task of the chaplain to be present and with the person on that core journey. *The Elusive Self* challenges the reader to think about the mystery which is the Self. Its pages contain a lifetime of scholarship and reflection, bringing together the fields of psychotherapy, psychology, philosophy, theology, as well as the arts, literature, and science. The question, "Who am I?" is universal. Marcel Duclos's essays are encyclopedic in their spiral endeavor to respond. Although perhaps best suited to the psychotherapist or the IFS therapist, this book will reward the chaplain who has the courage to pursue its dense pages to glean a deepened appreciation of the Self who suffers.

**Amy Jelliffe, M.D., Board Certified Psychiatrist, Certified Yoga Teacher**

Marcel Duclos, psychotherapist, philosopher, poet, teacher, friend, and colleague has inspired and moved me with his words and works. His book embodies elements of what makes him such a wonderful therapist and person. Anyone who knows him is lucky to know his tender touch, attentive ear, and wealth of knowledge. As a psychiatrist, I would have loved to have had him as a teacher and mentor in order to long ago expand my understanding and experience of the "Elusive SELF."

# THE ELUSIVE SELF:

# REFLECTIONS OF AN INTERNAL FAMILY

# SYSTEMS THERAPIST

**Marcel Aimé Duclos**

Black Forest Publishing
10665 Arrowgrass Loop
Peyton, Colorado, 80131

Cover Photo—The SELF
(Oil on canvas by the author)

# THE ELUSIVE SELF

*Psychology and religion are thus in perfect harmony up to a point, since both admit that there are forces seemingly outside of the conscious individual that brings redemption to his life.*

**—William James,** *The Varieties of Religious Experiences*

# DEDICATION

To all the patients
who have graced me
with their presence,
their trust,
their courage.

*The inner self is reached by deep introspection,*
*which leads us to grasp our inner states*
*as living things constantly* becoming.

—Henri Bergson in Mae-Wan Ho, 1993,
*The Rainbow and the Worm*

*She had trained herself to look for answers at eye level*
*but they were lower, they were changing all the time.*

—Jenny Xie, 2018, "Ongoing," in *Eye Level*

# CONTENTS

i

*Homo sum: Humani nil a me alienum puto.*
*(I am a man: Nothing human is alien to me.)*
　　　　—Terence (Publius Terentius Afer) (c. 195 BCE)


## FOREWORD

Absent the premise of the multiplicity of the mind, the entire structure and function of Internal Family Systems (IFS) therapy fails its
avowed mission—the promotion of Self Leadership.

For eons, humans have experienced and left evidence of their colloquy with internal entities as being both helpful and harmful to their survival. Great and small global and local cultures, as seen in carvings,
drawings, paintings, writings, oral lore, customs and rituals, myths and
legends, reveal the welcomed and unwelcomed intrusions and experiences of all manner of multiplicity. Who among us cannot recall some
early childhood moment when an internal yes and no struggled to gain
ascendency?

I grew up in a Franco-American milieu colored by the narrow
Jancenistic Catholicism of my Quebecois ancestors. It was a world of
defined opposites: good and bad, right and wrong, virtue and sin, salvation and damnation. Angels and devils were real. The forces of good
and evil were real. A battle for the life of the soul was playing out in
the inner and outer world. During those World War II years, danger
lurked everywhere. The battle against Nazi and Japanese aggression
was proof positive of demonic possession. How else could we explain
such wanton and destructive cruelty amid the deafening silence of
nighttime blackouts along the militarized New England coast?

To the mind of a first grader, God, as proclaimed by priests and
taught by nuns, could not be the *real* God. To me, the real God, as creator of all that is, also created those who did good and those who did
evil. More than that, He provided for them both, gave them both rain

and food, but He caused disasters, illness, and death. God was not all good.

I kept my thoughts to myself, but on a daily basis, I talked to my Guardian Angel, who lived on my right shoulder and promoted good deeds. The Devil assigned to me, as tempter to evil deeds, resided on my left shoulder. Within this dichotomy was an inner polarity, I made deals with both.

The Devil hated me when I chose to do good, and he redoubled his efforts to win me to his side. My Guardian Angel never wavered in his friendship. He never scolded, never put me down when I veered in the other direction. He waited for my return and soothed my guilt and shame, seeming to understand my problem with the GOD of the Church. As I matured, I came to recognize my angel as the *gnostic heretic* side of myself striving to liberate me from a fear-based orthodoxy. As a man, I discovered a much larger chorus of parts that constituted my inner world. I also discovered a center, a core, a source that even went *beyond* the beyond.

Eventually, I found the Archetypal Psychology of Carl Gustave Jung, a psychology that illumined my study of the soul as a philosopher and theologian into a new orbit—that of the cosmic field of archetypes and complexes, inner figures and energies of their own origins. These manifested among and were influenced by the parts of myself that I could trace to my own personal biography and to the figures inhabiting the far reaches of my unconscious.

Along with Jung, Sigmund Freud and Wilhelm Reich also helped me navigate through the planetary sphere governing the orbits swirling around in all that makes up the multiplicity of my personality. In time, these teachings helped refine my understanding and further influenced the negotiations with my inner and outer worlds. My study of Objects Relations Theory, Self-Psychology, Psychosynthesis, and the Systemic/Structural/Strategic schools of Family Therapy further shaped my thinking. These models, among others, supported my earlier acceptance of the reality of multiple personalities; that is, of Dissociation as the ultimate defense against the chaos of trauma, as reflected in both childhood and adult onset, with all of its permutations as the origin of ingested, introjected, and replicated burdens locked in mind and body (The Incarnated Psyche). The practical contributions of Body Psychotherapy rounded out this query. The world of applied neuroscience affirmed the validity of the body-mind functional unity in the reality of multiplicity and, therein, IFS therapy. The conviction of the centrality of the *SELF* in IFS found a solid place in my philosophy and practice of psychotherapy.

The body of IFS literature continues to increase. Practitioners and therapists, trainers and researchers advance the validity and reliability of this therapeutic approach, and IFS is now recognized as a best practice with professional training firmly in place. The refined techniques are replicable. The conceptual language is described and defined. What continues to elude us, and probably always will, is a language to express the individual's felt understanding of the *Elusive SELF*. The Carmelite mystic Teresa of Avila hinted as much in her writings. To understand SELF would be to understand GOD: both an impossibility. The finite cannot comprehend the infinite. William James paid attention to her thought.

Journeying into James's Gifford lectures is an attempt to move the discussion more openly to what some might call a metaphysical approach to the geometry and landscape of the self (the ego, the I, the me), the Self (the I transformed by the qualities of the SELF), the SELF (the archetypal living image of the source of our being), and that OTHER (the sustaining source of our being, of our conscious, sentient, emerging, and evolving awareness of SELF). To me, James offers, through a circumambulation of his insightful pragmatism as applied to the world of soul (let us say Psyche), a workable thesaurus of terms, concepts, and hypotheses grounded in documented experience.

ix

Once we leave the domain of the physically measurable, the language passed down through the ages to symbolize what might be metaphysical in origin but psychological and physical in experience is full of potentially clarifying insights and blinding confusion. Seekers of practical wisdom—philosophers, theologians, spiritual leaders of great renown and heroic dedication, physicists, astronomers, mystics, poets, and prophets (and we must not forget our ancient ancestors who populated the communities of seekers before recorded time)—devoted their lifetimes to this endeavor for the good of humanity.

If you are reading this modest book (this trying out, this tentative effort), you have already encountered the language of SOUL and SELF, of the *I* and the *Me* and the *Non-Me* from the past and present cultures across our planet. In this *essai,* in the search for the Elusive SELF, we will stand on the shoulders of William James as we consult other sources. I join you as we explore this communal voyage. May we all arrive safely home to our own Center where we bathe in the same living waters.

## ACKNOWLEDGMENT

To my students, supervisees, and patients
who, over the years, have journeyed with me
on the byways of the multiple mind
into the domain of all things trinity
in search of the SELF
energizing our evolving Selves;
to you who have challenged me at every step,
I bow and say *Namaste.*
To my friends and colleagues at home and abroad,
I thank you for the community.
To Vaughn Neeld, generous and demanding editor,
my gratitude for her patience and humor.
To my wife who guards the sanctuary of my study
with her ferocious love;
I look into her eyes and smile.

## INTRODUCTION

In the style of William James (a style of his age), I will interweave the words of the man as we circumambulate selected sections of the text of his lectures that focus on the experiential definitions of the Elusive SELF. James interlaces psychological, philosophical, and spiritual language throughout his extended exposition of what was for him a most personal case history of a man who feared insanity and had considered suicide. We know that he has company in facing one's demons.

When you read the text, be aware that words in **bold italics** indicate my way of highlighting the connections between James's understanding of the Elusive SELF, the insights of selected sources, and the operational IFS concepts related to the self, the Self, and the SELF. I will proceed in the same manner throughout Part Two as well as in the Appendices.

As we follow James's discussions and those of others we will differentiate between multiple concepts of the self/Self/SELF, visit the qualities of actionable Self-led skills, reflect on the various understandings of personal integration, and welcome differing understandings of life-guiding functional truths.

I accept that the SELF will always elude us, and as it is with the sun, we must approach it with utmost respect while welcoming its life-giving warmth and while knowing that, like Daedalus and Icarus, were we to give in to our juvenile hubris and fly too close to the sun we would burn and plunge to our death in the deep waters of the unconscious. I welcome the admonitions of the anonymous fourteenth-century English monk and author of *The Cloud of Unknowing*, translated by James Walsh, in this endeavor. I also am grateful to Richard Elliott Friedman's brilliant 1995 book, *The Hidden Face of God*, which can be taken as a metaphor for what I call The Elusive SELF. As with *The Cloud of Unknowing*, Friedman's book remains in the background, shedding light on the twist and turns I take in the meandering reflections that have eventually led to this book.

*Truly you are a God who hides.*

—Isaiah 45:15

# PART ONE: WILLIAM JAMES'S GIFFORD LECTURES

## CHAPTER ONE: ON THE SHOULDERS OF WILLIAM JAMES

The spirit of William James lives in cosmopolitan Boston where the religious, the spiritual, the psychological, and the scientific find a home. The psychotherapy community is cognizant of past and present figures who are knowingly or unknowingly of the Jamesian tradition. The worlds of Mindfulness and Internal Family Systems (IFS) therapy both have deep Jamesian undertones.

In the 2015 January/February *Psychotherapy Networker,* Ronald D. Siegel and Richard C. Schwartz address what they call "The Fiction of the Self" in their discussion of "The Paradox of Mindfulness in Clinical Practice." They evince the development of "a coherent sense of self," depending on the definition of the term and the lived experience of therapist and client, and they challenge the work of psychotherapy "to the degree that we no longer believe in the self," suggesting that it can up-end our psychotherapy practice. They offer the Buddhist's realization of the non-self and the deceptively simple mindfulness practice that leads to *anatta.*

I am reminded of the Latin saying *nihil novi sub sole*—nothing new under the sun—as well as the maxim "the more things change, the more they stay the same." The feelings I had when, as a young theology student in New England, I first discovered Carl Jung's analytical psychology still resonate to the meditation process that invites one to try to accept whatever arises, whether pleasant or unpleasant. The time-honored Eastern and Western monastic tradition of examining one's

1

conscience exposes the practitioner to the "flux of mental content" of every imaginable and unimaginable array of opposites.

The literature of the near east, and of the psalms, songs, and poems of praise for the awesome and awful display that energy manifests as perceivable mass, evokes a felt sense of oneness and separateness with all that *is*—known and unknown. Ronald Siegel and Schwartz add that the contemporary cognitive sciences validate the Buddhist description of the flux out of which "we create our sense of self and our understanding of the world around us."

As a student and professor of psychology and philosophy, I recall, with a lingering smile Aristotle's (384-322 BCE) teaching, quoted approvingly by the medieval scholar Thomas Aquinas, that truth is the *adequatio mens cum re;* truth is the unequivocal relationship of the mental with the object of the senses. Yet the science of psychology, from that of early European experimentalists to today's neuroscientists, shows how sensory input and the subject's perception of the same are not identical. At best, there is no absolute equation, only a reliable relative correlation between what we, as persons, experience and what exists, including our experience of our selves.

I witnessed the disconcerting, even shattering, realizations expressed by thoughtful undergraduates at the fragility of their certainties. Later, I took note of comparable unsettling insights by graduate and doctoral counseling students and interns. Therapists and clients who are partners in the psychotherapeutic process are subject to this shared and humbling state of human affairs in the self-to-self interaction during therapy sessions. Ronald Siegel and Schwartz describe it in this way: "It all begins with sense contact. Sensations are then immediately organized into perceptions, conditioned by language, personal history, and culture." Therefore, think about feeling tones, intentions, habits of intention (the old concept of *habitus*)—dispositions that lead to "important elements of our identities."

All of the assertions—I am this; you are that—clutter and cloud our judgment of our personal self and of each other, and they find their origin in our organismic structure as humans. Michael C. Heller, the renown Swiss Psychologist and Body Psychotherapist, has quite scholarly explored this understanding in his 2012 pivotal book *Body Psychotherapy: History, Concepts, and Methods*, a seminal tome that I had the privilege of translating for W. W. Norton from the original French edition published by Debroeck Publishing in Belgium.

Thus, it is that we actually create our identity—the *I,* or better said, the *Me* (the word Freud chose from common German that we use to identify who we are). We even find it plausible that we are made up of parts, ego-states, personae, subpersonalities, masks, and social roles. We concur with the premise that we participate in the multiplicity of the mind and brain, reaching down to our cellular biochemistry and to the postures, gestures, and movements of our bodies; that the continuum of dissociation is our common defense against the accumulated threats to our sense of self, which can lead to encapsulated *alters* in the extreme. Heller might well agree with Ronald Siegel and Schwartz that "our cherished divisions between 'me' and the rest of the ecosystem in which we reside fall(s) apart." Indeed, it dies.

I was introduced to Greek, Roman, and Germanic mythologies while in high school. At that time, I was too immature to grasp the significance of that world. I recall being bored by all that make-believe. Only later, when I studied biblical literature and found the archetypal world through the works of Jung, did I discover to what extent, back then and likewise today, mythological figures were the result of human projections. It made so much sense to me that wisdom required that whatsoever we asserted about the divine, we needed to immediately deny.

Daniel Siegel, M. D., Director of the Mindsight Institute (not to be confused with Ronald Siegel), makes reference to personality structures and dynamics presented by Sigmund Freud, Carl G. Jung, Roberto Assagioli, and Richard C. Schwartz, the founder of Internal Family

Systems (IFS), when he states succinctly, in a discussion between Schwartz and himself in an article titled "The Colors of Tomorrow" in the 2015 May/June issue of *Psychotherapy Networker,* that IFS therapy "helps clients identify a pantheon of internal parts and uses insights from system treatment to help these parts get along better with one another."

In 1996, during my first Core Energetics Therapy training session, John Pierrakos (1921-2001) unambiguously told me to drop my mask of serenity and to become better acquainted with the qualities lurking in my lower self. From both Jungian trainers and Jungian analysts, I have studied and explored not only my *anima, animus,* and *persona,* but also my *shadow,* which in "The Fiction of the Self," Ronald Siegel and Richard Schwartz call "split-off elements of the personality that aren't acknowledged as part of our conscious identity." The experiential learning continues. My pantheon is fathomless; I am not unique.

We are animals—rational, emotional, spiritual mammals—after all. If we lived our lives as healthy, undomesticated sentient beings, imagine the increased amount of truth we might live and exhibit. I think of Peter Levine's Somatic Experiencing and his referenced analogies to the animals in the wild who literally shake off the metabolic implications of an immediate real threat of death and then continue to graze— an action I witnessed at dusk in the Zambian wild of the Luangwa Valley.

Heller agrees with Daniel Siegel when he says that "different aspects of our human nature [are] just parts of the fluid organism" that we are. Brilliant and courageous biochemist and geneticist Mae-Wan Ho (1993), author of *The Rainbow and the Worm: The Physics of Organisms*, has referred, both in her writings and in a personal conversation with me at a Jungian conference in Assisi (late 1990s), to humans as multifaceted *liquid crystals.* She courageously refused to do research with the stained cells of dead organisms and risked her status as a rising star in the international field of biology in her opposition to unitary and

4

single-dimension research. I offer the 1980s view of an equally clear and daring practitioner/researcher, psychiatrist Colin A. Ross, who resisted a unitary approach to the psyche, that dissociation and the formation of *alters* happens to us—that dissociation is our fundamental defense, that we are multiples in our organized state.

We would find it disingenuous if we disagreed with the premise that we all have the capacity, in Ronald Siegel and Schwartz's words, "to accept a full range of impulses [to choose] not to act on the harmful one." It is at this point that I ask, Who chooses to act or not to act? Someone? The person? The I? The me? The not I? Some aspect of us? Parts of us of our own making? Parts of us that emerge from ancient and perennial chambers of the psyche? Separate personalities? Subpersonalities? Unknown others? The answer must wait. James will have his say—and so will many others.

Of course, the more we allow aspects of our shadow into awareness without identifying with it, we are less likely to enact them. This statement would need no additional reflections, no further considerations were the shadow to contain only the nefarious parts of our embodied psyche. To our great benefit and redemption, what also lives in the shadow blesses our humanity. Jungian analyst Edgar Herzog (2001) explores this blessing in *Psyche and Death: Death-Demons in Folklore, Myths and Modern Dreams.* He says that it is not only Thanatos and his minions who threaten to do us in, to overtake us into destructive delusions and runaway acting out, but also Eros, in his full display of creative connectedness, who resides outside the bounds of consciousness, out of our line of sight. Note that the two previous statements are incomplete when described as fully distinct energetic entities. Eros and Thanatos, life and death, the orientation to connection and to separation, are joined opposites fueling the process and the endpoint Jung calls the Union of Opposites. Plus and minus equals zero, the emptiness necessary for fullness, the death needed for life, vice in need of virtue, virtue in need of vice, the saint and sinner as one. This is *radical hope.* (See

5

J. Lear, 2008, *Radical Hope: Ethics in the Face of Cultural Devastation.* I will further explore this concept in a subsequent chapter.)

We can also agree with Daniel Siegel that the pursuit of self-esteem is a losing proposition if we are seeking self-glorification. But, if it is the realization of a Self through the energies of the Elusive SELF and the cessation of the pursuit of self-aggrandizement that we seek, then to esteem the Elusive SELF is humility to the core, integrity welcomed, a fitting end, a *causa finalis* par excellence.

Do we not see self-compassion in this, to follow my understanding of Daniel Siegel's thinking expressed in his language? We seek to be present to and to be with all that reveals itself to us. Richard Schwartz teaches, repeatedly and tirelessly, that *all parts are welcome.* Our parts, your parts, their parts, all parts of our common humanity are welcomed. This short phrase is easy to say, but it demands a profoundly challenging and revolutionary vow to execute. In my view, there are no *others,* no *foreigners,* no *aliens,* no *unwanted ones*, no *misunderstood ones*. There are only parts to be welcomed into a mutual and loving dialogue *within* as belonging to the *whole.*

Sensations, emotions, feelings, perceptions, cognitions, and actions are all body-inclusive phenomena that reveal the process of being in this manifest moment, but they do not define any one of us. All is happening to each one of us, and we observe the phenomena as much as we react to it, respond to it, direct it—all of us so energetically alike were it not for mass—the miraculous gift that makes differentiation possible.

Ronald Siegel and Schwartz fill their article, "The Fiction of the Self," with enhanced gems that challenge us to engage in mindfulness as we meditate on our experience of self (of the Me, of the I). They speak of practicing "being with," of "develop[ing] the capacity to tolerate, even embrace, the bodily sensations of strong emotion" or, I add, the *emotions* of strong sensations, "to [be open] to whatever may be happening in the moment," accepting what is; "see[ing] that our

6

emotions are just a mix of bodily sensations, words, and images, [noticing that a] life is just a series of moments." And then they drop this precious gem: "All you have to do is embrace your insignificance [and] enjoy the present moment without so much judgment and fear." Ronald Siegel and Schwartz's final thrust is to invite the reader to allow egocentricity to fall by the wayside as "not only illusory but remarkably painful and constraining" as they send this parting shot across the bow, advocating that there is no self.

It is at this point that I decided, back in 2015, to consult the thoughts of William James, whose 1902 book, *The Varieties of Religious Experience: A Study in Human Nature*, I had not sufficiently perused in the past and had not specifically searched for his understanding of the Elusive Self. I sought to respond to Ronald Siegel and Schwartz with the words of a giant who, I like to imagine, is smiling on the further articulation of some of his revered intellectual and personal realizations centered these days in the hospitable soil of greater Boston and the IFS adventure of Self-Leadership.

James offers his discussion on the varieties of religious experience as an empirically grounded speculation—a *conceptional itinerary,* to borrow the words of Robert Kegan. I am reminded of Richard Rohr, the founder and director of the Center for Action and Contemplation in Albuquerque, New Mexico, who does not let us forget that our first word is a breath, as is our last one; that we are the breath of the One who is breath. And who is this One?

The content of James's lectures strongly suggests that the reader drop down into a Self-state and invite the source of Self-Leadership to energize the individual "I" that we are. A breathing exercise of one's choice offers the probability of greater centering. We may follow our breath in and out. We may engage in one of many progressive relaxation strategies. We might find our safe place and settle into that quiet zone. Whatever approach we choose, we must invite that letting go and letting be that promotes finding the ground of our being.

**James's *Selected Writings:* A Brief Discussion**

The discussions in this section are based on *William James: Selected Writings,* published in 1997 by the Book-of-the-Month Club (BOMC). The book includes an introduction by Robert Coles as well as an essay by James titled "What Pragmatism Means." Were it not for Coles' introduction to these selected writings, a contemporary reader might relegate the Gifford Lectures on "The Varieties of Religious Experience" to the dustbin of turn-of-the-century thought, but truly, it is otherwise. Even when James's language is of the late-Victorian era, it reveals an honest struggle to make sense of experience when contemporary concepts are insufficient to hold emerging understandings. How then do we proceed?

First, we extract thoughtful guidance from Coles in his introduction. We then consider the import of James's conviction of the value of a pragmatic attitude toward all of life. And, with that preparation, we follow, well aware of personal choices, the elements of James's thoughts that manifest as ***antecedents*** to the rich geology and geography of the inner world we navigate in Internal Family Systems therapy. Since this book is not an exposition of IFS, I will limit myself to a minimal amount of overt signaling to IFS reference points in the exegesis of James's text.

My preferred approach is to explore all sides of an issue, of a subject, of a phenomenon, to view it from as many vantage points as it is willing to reveal itself to me and as I am able to take in. I walk around it in a concentric spiral and come to a respectful halt if its brilliance sears my vision. An unhurried circumambulation is my lifelong approach to the investigation of a topic. Here, and in all the other chapters, I will allow referenced authors to speak in their own voice. James's words are indicated in quotation marks followed by page references to the 1997 BOMC edition.

I do not pretend to be an expert on William James, who humbly confessed how much he has learned from his predecessors—East and West. I am a learner in awe of James's broad shoulders.

8

**Robert Coles' Introduction to *William James: Selected Writings***

Coles reminds us that James wanted no cult of personality. In fact, James "hailed Freud as the one to whom the future beckoned," adding that "James's prophesy proved correct, though only for a while, since each future is destined to become part of a past succeeded inevitably by yet another of time's demanding intellectual waves" (pp. xvii, xviii). James was "ever prepared to ask and ask again, to wonder, to describe, but [he] let the reader decide, to reverse direction, to acknowledge hesitations, doubts, second thoughts, to await what will be shown by others, to call upon what has already been offered by others, to delight in the mind's booming, buzzing confusion" (p. xix). James abhorred simplification. Coles describes James as a thinker "who knew to wait before pouncing with certitude, [one who waits] to inform his readers, his moral intelligence a guide that can help us look around, look within, look ahead" (p. xix).

Through the findings in what follows, I hope to be able to determine whether or not James's understanding of the Elusive Self presents a deeply rooted basis for the SELF as referenced in IFS. But, first, we need to determine what Pragmatism means.

**James's Pragmatic Method**

What does James have to tell us about his pragmatic approach to the life of the self, which in his day was expressed as that of the psyche, the soul. In *Pragmatism: A New Name for some Old Ways of Thinking,* James (1907) explains what has become known as The Pragmatic Method.

Whenever a dispute is serious, we ought to be able to show some practical difference that must follow from one side or the other's being right. . . . The whole function of philosophy ought to be to find out what definite difference it will make to you and to me, at definite instants of our [lives], if this world formula or that world formula be the true one. . . . A pragmatist turns his back resolutely and once and

9

for all upon a lot of inveterate habits dear to professional philosophers. He turns away from abstractions and insufficiency, from verbal solutions, from bad *a priori* reasons, from fixed principles,
closed systems, and pretended absolutes and origins. He turns toward concreteness and adequacy, toward facts, toward action, and
toward power. . . . It means the open air and possibilities of nature,
as against dogma, artificiality, and the pretense of finality in truth.
(pp. 2, 5)

James insists that the pragmatic method "does not stand for any special results. It is a method only. . . (p. 6). He states, "Theories thus became instruments, not answers to enigmas, in which we can rest" (p. 6).
"The pragmatist cling[s] to facts and concreteness, observe[s] truth at
its work in particular cases, and generalize[s]. Truth, for him, becomes
a class-name for all sorts of definite working-values in experience"
(p. 14). And James reminds us that "Pragmatism is uncomfortable away
from facts [and that] Rationalism is comfortable only in the presence of
abstractions" (p. 14). Pragmatism may be a happy harmonizer of the
empiricists' way of thinking, with the more religious demands of human
beings. . . (p.15)." We must not forget that when James uses the term
"religion," we ought to think of the present term "spiritual" or the old
Latin term *"religio"* (linked together again, united, integrated, the one
union of opposites).

James is dedicated to view the latitude and longitude of any and all
topics, including the topic at hand. "Now pragmatism," he writes, "devoted though she be to facts, has no such materialistic bias as ordinary
empiricism labors under. . . . She has no *a priori* prejudices against theology. If theological ideas prove to have a value for concrete life, they
will be true, for pragmatism, in the sense of being good [for so many]"
(p. 17). This is authentic cultural sensitivity and competence.

In his lectures, James admits, "[I am] well aware how odd it must
seem to some [who] hear me say that an idea is true so long as to believe
it is profitable to our lives" (p. 18). James's doctrine was that truth is

10

one species of the good; that certain ideas are "helpful in life's practical struggles" (p. 19). "Pragmatism is a mediator and reconciler . . . ; she will entertain any hypothesis, she will consider any evidence" (p. 21). She is . . .

> willing to take anything, to follow either logic or the senses, and to count the humblest and the most personal experiences. She will count mystical experiences if they have practical consequences. . . . Her only test of probable truth is what works best in a way of leading us, what fits every part of life best, and combines with the collectivity of experience's demands, nothing being omitted. . . . What other kind of truth could there be, for her, than all this agreement with concrete reality? (p. 21)

I hear a prefigured IFS therapeutic pragmatism in James's words. I can only imagine a colloquy between William James and Richard Schwartz.

Thus, the guide to practical life is what works, promotes wholeness, heals, reconciles, witnesses what was and what is, retrieves what is lost, unburdens, and resources. It can be said that this is the pragmatist's personal and professional code of conduct. IFS belongs to this tradition.

What James has to tell us in his deeply personal and extensive discussion of the varieties of religious experience leads us to posit that he prepared the future universe of ideas in the *anima mundi,* the world soul that begot what he hoped would be the eventual healing modalities that were not available to him in his long, tortuous, organismic personal struggles. I find that it is worth following his meandering discourse to gain a glimpse of a singular pair of Self-led shoulders on which IFS practitioners may well stand. Here, again, in his Gifford Lectures, James speaks directly to us from a century ago.

### The Varieties of Religious Experience in a Self-led Life

My premise is that what James presents as the religious life is a description of a Self-led life (Self-leadership as advanced by IFS) as expressed in the language of an early 20th-century New England pioneer

11

philosopher-psychologist. In this section, I give only the essence of James's lectures as they relate to our search to further grasp a pragmatic understanding of the self/Self/SELF trinity in the language of IFS.

### *Lecture I. Religion and Neurology*

James moved up in his academic career, from being an instructor of Anatomy and Physiology before turning to Experimental Psychology and then turning to Philosophy. In his first lecture, he asserts that "there is not a single one of our states of mind, high or low, healthy or morbid, that does not have some organic process in its condition" (p. 36). He affirms that "our thoughts and feelings . . . scientific doctrines, our disbeliefs . . . flow from the state of their possessor's body" (p. 36). The history, concepts, and methods of body psychotherapy attest to this. (See Heller, 2012, *Body Psychotherapy*.)

I find it difficult to argue against James's body-based understanding of all behavior to which he adds his pragmatic criterion: "By their fruits ye shall know them, not by their roots" (p. 42). Speaking of the religious life, he says, "You must be ready now to judge the religious life by its results exclusively. . . . To understand a thing rightly we need to see it both out of its environment and in it, and to have acquaintance with the whole range of its variations" (pp. 43-44). He continues, "Few of us are not in some way infirm, or even diseased; and our infirmities help us unexpectedly" (p. 44). The Jungian analyst, Alfred J. Ziegler spoke of this in his 1983 book, *Archetypal Medicine.*

### *Lecture II. Circumscription of the Topic*

James encourages the study of opposites—the entire range of variations, the borders of things, personality—if we want to be people of action. He defines Religion as "the feelings, acts, and experiences of individual[s] . . . in their solitude, so far as they apprehend themselves to stand in relation to whatever they may consider divine" (p. 53). It "is [an individual's] total reaction upon life. . . " (p. 57).

James quotes Marcus Aurelius: "And so accept everything which happens, even if it seems disagreeable, because it leads to this, the health of the universe. . ." (p. 65). He quotes the unknown author (c. 14th century) of the *Theologia Germanica:* "Enlightened men . . . are in a state of freedom, because they have lost the fear of pain or hell, and the hope of reward or heaven. . ." (p. 65). It is difficult not to think of James making reference to the philosopher, historian, and economist David Hume, who vowed to face death without the soporifics of conventional religion. James references Thomas à Kempis (c. 15th century), author of *The Imitation of Christ,* who wrote: "Do with me as thou knowest best" (James, p. 66). (Keep in mind the "SELF within" when James makes reference to God.) Speaking of his personal experience with infirmities, James seems to sigh when he writes, "Well we are all such helpless failures in the last resort. The sanest and best of us are of one clay with lunatics and prison inmates, and death finally runs the best of us down" (p. 69).

James suffered bouts of depression and knew suicidality. He faced them, interfaced with them, but he adds, with a tinge of optimism, that in a religious state "the time for tension in our soul is over, and that of happy relaxation, of calm deep breathing, of an eternal present, with no discordant future to be anxious about, has arrived, a gift of our organism, the physiologist will tell us, a gift of God's grace, the theologians say. . . . Religious feeling is thus an absolute addition to the Subject's range of life" (pp. 69-70). He reminds us that "a solemn state of mind is never crude or simple; it seems to contain a certain measure of its own opposite in solution. A solemn joy preserves a hint of bitter in its sweetness; a solemn sorrow is one of which we intimately consent. For when it is all said and done, we are in the end absolutely dependent on the universe" (p. 73). The IFS therapist would say that in the end the individual who is under the sway of the SELF's leadership is blessed with calm in the abiding present.

### Lecture III. The Reality of the Unseen

The characteristic of the life of religion, James states, "consists of the belief that there is an unseen order, and our supreme good lies in harmoniously adjusting ourselves thereto" (p. 75). But what is this unseen order? James reminds us that "the unreasoned and immediate assurance is the deep thing in us, the reasoned argument is but a reasoned exhibition. Instinct leads; intelligence does but follow" (p. 96). Is this not a premonition of what we express today as the bottom-up/backfront processes of the brain? (See M. Solms and O. Turnbull, 2002, *The Brain and the Inner World.*) James says, that in the religious realm, "the subconscious and non-rational holds primacy . . . as a matter of fact" (p. 96). Note that James's use of his contemporary term "subconscious" refers to the entire unconscious, the entire inner world: personal and universal (collective). As an IFS therapist, I would add the inner world of multiplicity, the world of personal and universal parts and subparts.

### Lectures IV and V. The Religion of Healthy-Mindedness

James is a critic of the unabashed fantasy of perfect health in all dimensions of the human organism. There is, he insists, no perfection, no completion in this world. He asserts that "the great central fact in human life is the coming into a conscious vital realization of our oneness with Infinite Life" (p. 123). His statement, "Give up the feeling of responsibility, let go of your hold . . . pass into nothing," reminds me of the Gospel proclamation of the need to die in order to live, of the Jungian ego's need to yield to the primacy of the Self as a faithful servant of the SELF (p. 132). James says it clearly: "To get to it [the SELF], a critical point must usually be passed, a corner turned within oneself. . . . What divides the religious from the merely moralistic character [is that] *they know*; for they have actually *felt* the higher powers in giving up the tension of their personal will" (p. 132). Might this be the harmonizing of conflict-laden parts who willingly bow to the leadership of the SELF?

14

In this section of his lectures, James admonishes those who might see health and happiness as the endpoint of religion. He speaks of "re-generation by relaxing, by letting go" (p. 133). He pointedly, and with a vaguely disguised sense of humor, says, "It is but giving your little private convulsive self a rest and finding that a greater Self is there" (p. 133). He advocated for a time apart for silent meditation, for enter-ing into the silence. He borrows a Roman Catholic phrase of his time, that of "re-collection," an entering into the presence of God (pp. 137-138). We can interpret this as being in the presence of the Ar-chetypal OTHER beyond the Elusive SELF. (In Part 2, Chapter Four, I will speak of the Ein Sof of the Kabbalah.)

Making the point that there are many religious systems that promote the fruits of a full life, James argues against sectarian scientists: "What, in the end, are all our verifications but experiences that agree with more or less isolated systems of ideas [conceptual systems] that our minds have framed? But why, in the name of common sense, need we assume that only one system of ideas can be true" (p. 144)? James is open to what works. I add that linear thinking and the experimental method, the offspring of duality, have limits to their merit. There is no logical access to the SELF; only an experiential approach.

### Lectures VI and VII. The Sick Soul

In his strong language, James puts forth his conclusion that "evil is a disease; and worry over disease is itself an additional form of dis-ease. . . . The best repentance is to up and act for righteousness and forget that you ever had relations with sin" (p. 149). He understands Baruch Spinoza's (1632-1677) philosophy as having "this sort of healthy-mindedness woven into the heart of it" (p. 149). I imagine James's delight were he to have been around to read Antonio Damasio's (2003) book, *Looking for Spinoza: Joy, Sorrow, and the Feeling Brain*.

James makes reference to the practice of the Examination of Con-science and of "the Catholic practice of confession and absolution [as a

15

way to] start the clean page with no old debts inscribed" (p. 150). What an unburdening, what a resourcing after compassionate witnessing! *This is what happened to you. Now you are here. You fell in with burdened parts of you. You are not your sin. You acted out under a well-intentioned misguided extreme protector. You have the right and the ability to request and be granted an internal agreement to heal imperfectly.* This, IFS firmly believes.

James insists that "there is no rationally deducible connection between any outer fact and the sentiment it may happen to provoke . . . since the same fact will inspire entirely different feelings in different persons and at different times in the same person" (p. 172). He is further emphatic that changes in religious sentiment "depends almost always upon non-logical, often organic conditions" (p. 173). It is here that Adolf Guggenbuhl-Craig's thoughts on the nature of the psychopath could be helpful to understand James's view of the suffering soul, the soul in need of deliverance. (See A. Guggenbuhl-Craig, 1980, *Eros on Crutches: Reflections on Amorality and Psychopathy.*)

James ends this lecture by referring to Buddhism and Christianity as the religions "in which the pessimistic elements are best developed" (p. 187). Essentially, they are religions of deliverance: Man must die to an unreal life before he can be born into the real life. James promises that he will try to discuss some of the psychological conditions of this second birth, and he adds that it will be a "more cheerful" subject.

### *Lecture VIII. The Divided Self and the Process of Its Unification*

James asserts that "there are two lives, the natural and the spiritual, and that we must lose the one before we can participate in the other" (pp. 189-190). He makes reference to the French novelist Alphonse Daudet, who exclaims, *"Homo duplex, homo duplex!"* (Man is double, man is double!) Daudet experienced his duality at the occasion of his brother's death when he experienced part of himself weeping and part of him thinking of the reason for his weeping (p. 189).

16

In *Memories, Dreams, and Reflections* (1957), Carl Jung also speaks of his adolescent realization of having a first and second personality. In addition, James notes that in Frédéric Paulhan's 1909 book, **Les Caractères** *(The Characters* or *Character Structures),* there is an example of the "recent works on the psychology of characters" that has had "much to say about this point" (p. 190). In Paulhan's psychic types, we see different parts of the personality, when in 1894 he contrasted *les Équilibres* (the even-tempered/balanced), *les Unifiés* (the unified/ integrated), with *les Inquiets* (the worried), *les Contrariants* (the annoying personalities), *les Incohérents* (the incoherent ones), and especially *les Émiettés* (the fragmented/fractured/split-up/crumbled/fragmented personalities (James, note 2, p. 190). All of these can be understood as parts of an individual's organismic internal system. (IFS therapy is one of those organismic psychological models of psychotherapy [Heller, p. 571].)

James strongly hints at something more than just a duality between a Higher Self and a Lower Self as described in the language of Core Energetics Theory founder John Pierrakos, a student of Wilhelm Reich and Reich's collaborator, Alexander Lowen. James says,

Now in all of us, however constituted, but to a degree the greater in proportion as we are intense and sensitive to diversified temptations, and to the greatest possible degree if we are decidedly psychopathic (suffering in our soul), does the normal evolution of character chiefly consist in the straightening out and unifying of the inner *self.* ***The higher and lower feelings, the useful and the erring impulses, begin by being a comparative chaos within us—they must end by forming a stable system of functions in right subordination"*** [Emphasis added]. (p. 192)

It behooves us to interpret "subordination" not as a servile subservience but as one that is ordered and integrated under the leadership of the Self energized by the SELF.

James identifies this phenomenon as connected to what he calls "the life of the subconscious self." It seems to me that, here again, James's use of the term "subconscious" is akin to Jung's concept of the personal and collective unconscious. "The man's interior is a battleground for what he feels to be between two hostile selves, one actual, the other ideal" (James, p. 193). Augustine (354-430 CE) spoke of being caught in and by both sides of himself, a reference James points out. The goal of the battle is to gather in these two polarities. We hear in this idea a still-persisting simplistic polarity. When James mentions the phenomenon of Being Born Again, he tells us that "in all of these instances, we have precisely the same psychological form or event—a firmness, stability, and equilibrium succeeding a period of storm and stress and inconsistency" (p. 198). Multiplicity, in its fullest display as the natural state of the psyche, was not the understanding of the day, and for the ensuing decades.

James, the physician, psychiatrist, psychologist, and philosopher, increases his use of theological language to express his psychological understanding by borrowing words from Leo Tolstoy, who after having quested for three years to find a way to live rightly, wrote, "Why do I look farther? A voice within me asked. He is there: He without whom one cannot live. To acknowledge God and to live are one and the same thing. God is what life is. Well, then! Live, seek God, and there will be no life without him" (James, p. 207). James interprets Tolstoy's experience in this way: "His crisis was the business of setting his soul in order, the discovery of its genuine habitat and vocation, the escape from the falsehood into what for him were ways of truth" (p. 208). Soul, I submit, is James's alternative word for Self. Perhaps a subsequent foray into the practice of mystical Judaism will gift us with another vantage point from which we can enrich our foggy portrait of the SELF.

### Lecture IX. Conversion
James boldly begins this lecture by revealing how he understands the meaning of conversion. He speaks from what he calls a religious perspective:

18

> To be converted, to be regenerated, to receive grace, to experience religion, to gain assurance, are so many phrases which denote the process, gradual or sudden, by which a self, hitherto divided, and consciously wrong, inferior and unhappy, becomes unified and consciously right, superior and happy, in consequence of its firmer hold upon religious realities. (p. 211)

We hear in his words the phenomenon of brokenness, fragmentation, internal oppositions. Then he explains that . . .

> if you open the chapter on Associations, of any treatise on Psychology, you will read that a man's ideas, aims, and objects form diverse internal groups and systems, relatively independent of one another. Each "aim" which he follows awakens a certain kind of interested excitement and gathers a group of ideas together in subordination to its associates; and if the aims and excitements are distinct in kind, their groups of ideas may have little in common. When one group is present and engrosses the interest, all the ideas connected with other groups may be excluded from the mental field. (p. 215)

With this statement, James reveals his familiarity with what we now refer to as the multiplicity of the mind and the polarity of parts. He continues,

> Our ordinary alterations of character, as we pass from one aim to another, are not commonly transformations, because each of them is so rapidly succeeded by another in the reverse direction; but whenever one aim grows so stable as to expel definitely its previous rivals from the individual's life, we tend to speak of the phenomenon, and perhaps wonder at it, as a "transformation." (p. 216)

As it was in James's time, and as it is still to a great extent today, the internal world of the psyche was thought of in terms of a combat between competing dynamics that will be resolved only if one party vanquishes the other. To me, it seems that Jung opened the door to a less adversarial terrain with his understanding of the archetypes and their related complexes. Surely, it is here that IFS has fermented an alchemy

19

of hospitality and deep amity in ways hinted at, but not realized, in James's day, and not so fully or differently evolved and developed by other approaches familiar with, for example, concepts such as ego states or subpersonalities. (See J. G. Watkins and H. H. Watkins, 1997, *Ego States.*)

James says, "These alterations are the completest of the way in which a self may be divided. A less complete way is the simultaneous coexistence of two or more different groups of aims, of which one practically holds the right of way and instigates activity, whilst the others are only pious wishes, and never practically come to anything" (James, p. 216). Then he adds more, specifically the following, which I take to be a decisive nod to the formulation of an internal family system: "Such fleeting aspirations are mere *velleitates,* whimsies. They exist on the remoter outskirts of the mind, and the real self of the man, the center of his energies, is occupied with an entirely different system" (p. 216).

Permit me to refer to this "entirely different system" as the Psyche's system centered by the Elusive SELF, at least as potentially so. As we know, James lived his intellectual curiosity widely and deeply. He searched far and wide, within and without, to understand his own challenging physical, psychological, and spiritual human condition. He was sympathetic to Buddhism. In this, his ninth lecture, he challenges his listeners with the following: "For [Buddhists], the soul is only a succession of fields of consciousness: yet there is found in each field a part, or subfield, which figures as focal and contains excitement, and from which, as from a center, the aim seems to be taken" (p. 217). James speaks of centers of energy in the plural—of parts and subparts of the psyche.

Later James discusses self-surrender, making reference to a higher helper. Here one can hear the future language of a Higher Power as expressed by Alcoholics Anonymous influenced by Jung's ineffable OTHER behind the archetypal SELF; also of the Higher Self in the language of Core Energetics.

20

James quotes from his contemporary Edward D. Starbuck's 1911 book, *The Psychology of Religion:* "To exercise the personal will is still to live in the region where the imperfect self is the thing most emphasized. Where, on the contrary, the subconscious forces take the lead, it is more probably the better self *in posse* [in the realm of the possible] which directs the operation. Instead of being clumsily and vaguely aimed at from without, it is then itself the organizing principle. What then must the person do" (James, pp. 231-232)? James continues Starbuck's thought:

> He must relax . . . , fall back on the larger Power that makes for righteousness, which has been welling up in his own being. . . . The act of yielding, in this point of view, is giving one's self over to a new life, making it the center of a new personality, and living from within, the truth of it which had before been viewed objectively."
> (James, p. 232)

For James, "Psychology and religion are thus in perfect harmony . . . , since both admit that there are forces seemingly outside of the conscious individual that bring redemption to his life" (p. 233). Forces, we say, enlivening the center of consciousness—transforming the ME, the self, the I, into the Self.

James speaks of the psychology of self-surrender in this way: "We cannot create a belief out of whole cloth when our perception actively assures us of the opposite" (p. 234). Thus, James proposes that there are two ways of getting rid of undesirable affects: (a) let opposite affections overpower us, take us over, or (b) let ourselves become exhausted; that is, suffer from activation or collapse (mania or depression). The continuum of affective disorders flashes before me in the dance of exiles, managers, and protectors open to witnessing, retrieval, and unburdening. IFS therapy offers an "overpowering" through the power of compassionate conviction—an enterprise James would support.

21

### *Lecture X. Conversion (Concluded)*

James concludes his reflection on the phenomenon of conversion by speaking of the divided mind. He states that generalizations must be based on particulars, that "man's liability to sudden and complete conversion [is] one of his most curious peculiarities" (p. 252). He remarks that "the expression 'field of consciousness' has but recently come into vogue in psychology books," noting that the mind, the mental state, is not a unit but, rather, an "entire wave of consciousness" (p. 253). Then he asserts, "Our mental fields succeed one another, each has its center of interest, around which the objects of which we are less and less attentively conscious fade to a margin so faint that its limits are unassignable" (p. 253).

James is speaking of the border, of the line, of the liminal space and place that forty or so years ago became known as the borderline zone. This concept was then incorporated into the nosology of the third edition (1980) of the *Diagnostic and Statistical Manual of Mental Disorders-III* (DSM-III) by the American Psychiatric Association. One might also equate this to Jung's "personal unconscious" and/or Freud's "subconscious."

James continues: "In certain diseased conditions, consciousness is a mere spark, without memory of the past or thought of the future, and with the present narrowed down to some one single emotion or sensation of the body" (pp. 253-254). We might say overcome, blended. "Our whole past store of memories floats beyond this margin, ready at a touch to come in; and the entire mass of residual powers, impulses, and knowledges that constitutes our *empirical self* stretches continuously beyond it" (p. 254).

Referring to the previous lecture, James underscores the reality that "those who first laid stress upon these phenomena could not know the facts as we know them" (p. 254). He is aware of and accepts the evolution of our understanding of ourselves. With a strong emphasis, he tells his audience,

I cannot but think that the most important step forward that has occurred in psychology since I have been a student of that science is
the discovery, first made in 1886, that, in certain subjects at least,
there is not only the consciousness of the ordinary field, with its
usual center and margin, but in addition thereto in the shape of a set
of memories, thoughts, and feelings which are extra-marginal and
outside of the primary consciousness altogether, but yet must be
classed as conscious facts of some sort, able to reveal their presence
in unmistakable signs. I call this the most important step forward
because, unlike the other advances which psychology has made, this
discovery has revealed to us an entirely unsuspected peculiarity in
the constitution of human nature. (p. 255)

James suggests Alfred Binet's 1892 book, *Alterations of Personality,*
to his audience, aware that Binet could not provide evidence of such a
consciousness. James was referring to hysteria, or what we might asso-
ciate with the residuals of developmental trauma. He borrows the term
"automatism" from Frederic W. Myers, founder of the Society of Psy-
chical Research, to speak of "the sensory or motor, emotional or
intellectual . . . whole sphere of effects . . . due to 'up-rushes' into the
ordinary consciousness of energies originating in the subliminal parts
of the mind" (p. 256).

James reminds his audience of what we now know as post-traumatic
ego states. He notes the contributions of not only Binet but also of Pierre
Janet, Eugen Bleuler, Sigmund Freud, George Mason, Morton Prince,
and others. Thanks to them, he says, "We have revealed to us whole
systems of underground life in the shape of memories of a painful sort
which lead a parasitic existence, buried outside of the primary fields of
consciousness. . ." (p. 256). James seems to pick up speed at this point:

Whenever we meet with a phenomenon of automatism, be it motor
impulses, or [an] obsessive idea, or [an] unaccountable caprice or
delusion, or [a] hallucination, we are bound first of all to make
search whether it be not an explosion into the fields of ordinary

23

consciousness, of ideas elaborated outside of those fields in subliminal regions of the mind. (p. 257)

I would suggest that we understand James's ideas, not as concepts, but as living entities in the personal and collective unconscious.

In the hysteric cases (think of disorders of body and mind such as conversion and somatoform disorders, all manner of somatization for instance), James proffers that "the memories, which are the source, have to be extracted from the patient's Subliminal by a number of ingenious methods, for an account of which you must consult the books" (p. 257). James was referring to the books of his day that were hinting strongly toward the phenomena of dissociation. "Alter or abolish by suggestion these subconscious memories, and the patient immediately gets well" (p. 257). This is what he knew. I can only imagine James's agreement if he could have experienced the gentle and hospitable IFS approach of witnessing, unburdening, and resourcing. Would he not also celebrate other modalities dedicated to the treatment of all manner of trauma such as Eye Movement Desensitization and Reprocessing (EMDR), Trauma Incident Reduction, Sensorimotor Therapy, and Somatic Experiencing, just to name a few?

Remembering that James is making his argument in the context of and in the language of the psychology of religion of his day, he states that a religious conversion "must be decided on empirical grounds exclusively" (p. 259). And then he makes a statement that evokes a possible antecedent to the IFS concept of Self-Energy: "When we touch our own upper limit and live in our own highest center of energy, we may call ourselves saved . . ." (p. 261).

James then quotes from *The Spiritual Life: Studies in the Science of Religion,* written by American psychologist George A. Coe (1900). "The ultimate test of religious values is nothing psychological, nothing definable in terms of *how it happens,* but something ethical, definable only in terms of *what is attained"* (James, p. 263). James then adds the following:

24

As we proceed farther in our inquiry we shall see that what is attained is often an altogether new level of spiritual vitality, a relatively heroic level, in which impossible things have become possible, and new **energies** *and* new endurances are shown. The personality is changed, the man *is* born anew, whether or not his psychological idiosyncrasies are what give the particular shape to his metamorphosis. . . . Sanctification is the technical name of this result. . . . Just as our primary wide-awake consciousness throws open our senses to the touch of things material, so it is logically conceivable that *if there be* higher spiritual agencies that can directly touch us, the psychological condition of their doing so *might be* our possession of a subconscious region which alone should yield access to them. (pp. 263-264)

But, always the pragmatist, James states that "in any case the *value* of these forces would have to be determined by their effects . . ." (p. 265). James is mightily interested in criteria and measurable fruits of such a sanctification, a holiness, a balance-making phenomenon, an integration.

### *Lectures XI, XII, and XIII. Saintliness*

In his three lectures on Saintliness, James first reminds his audience of the "movingly happy conversions" of the reliable people he referenced in his previous lecture. But, again, his pragmatism leads the way. He asks, "What may the practical fruits for life have been for such individuals and for ourselves?" He answers: "Saintliness." To explain himself, he discusses what he means by "character." Today we might say "personality." He suggests that character is "something distinguished from intellect. . . . [We all differ] chiefly in our *differing susceptibilities of emotional excitement* and in the differing impulses and inhibitions which these bring in their train" (p. 283). "Sometimes no emotional state is sovereign, but many contrary ones are mixed together" (p. 284). He compares irascibility and earnestness as the

25

difference between "susceptibility to wrath" and "the willingness to live with energy, though energy brings pain" (p. 286). And, "The great thing which the higher excitabilities give is *courage* . . ." (p. 287). James moves on to present "those fruits of the religious state . . ." (p. 289):

The man who lives in his religious center of personal energy, and is activated by spiritual enthusiasms, differs from his previous carnal self. . . . Magnanimities once impossible are now easy. . . . The stone wall inside of him has fallen, the hardness of his heart has broken down. . . . The collective name for the ripe fruits of religion in a character is Saintliness. (p. 289)

James declares that he is hesitant to use such a term because of its "certain flavor of 'sanctimoniousness.'" But he does say that saintliness "is the character for which spiritual emotions are the habitual center of the personal energy. . ." (p. 295). It is the same in all religions. His list, in brief, includes the following:

1. A feeling of being in a wider life than that of this world's selfish little interest;
2. A sense of friendly continuity of the ideal power with our own life, and a willing self-surrender to its control;
3. An immense elation and freedom, as the outlines of the confining selfhood melts down;
4. A shifting of the emotional center toward loving and harmonious affections. (p. 295)

He continues:

"These fundamental inner conditions have characteristic practical consequences:

(a) the 'asceticism' necessary to remain loyal 'to the higher power';
(b) the 'strength of soul that allows fears and anxieties [to] go, and blissful equanimity takes their place';
(c) 'the shifting of the emotional center [that] brings with it [an] increase in purity'; that is, 'sensitiveness to spiritual discords [and]

26

the cleansing of existence from brutal and sensual imperatives'; and

(d) 'the shifting of the emotional center brings [an] increase in charity, tenderness for fellow-creatures.'" (pp. 294-296)

The ultimate increase in tenderness for all of our burdened and overworked parts finds expression in the IFS classic question, "How do you feel toward this part?" Compassion is at the heart of the healing process in IFS therapy.

James adds his personal experience of episodes of physical illness, depression, and anxiety to his intellectual conviction of the following:

The transition from tenseness, self-responsibility, and worry, to equanimity and peace is the most wonderful of all those shiftings of inner equilibrium, those changes of the **personal center of energy** which I have analyzed so often; and the chief wonder of it is that it so often comes about, not by doing, but by simply **relaxing** and **throwing the burden down**. This abandonment of self-responsibility seems to be the fundamental act in specifically religious, as distinguished from, moral practice. It antedates theologies and is independent of philosophies. (p. 311)

This is the beautiful spiritual discipline that the healing methods of IFS therapy facilitate.

Based on longstanding spiritual traditions and referencing Catherine of Genoa (1447-1510), James asserts that to live fully responsive to the exigencies of the *present moment* is essential to leading an authentic spiritual life. Jean-Pierre de Caussade, SJ (1675-1751), taught this spiritual philosophy in his book, *The Sacrament of the Present Moment.* The therapeutic approach of the here and now has long roots into antiquity, in both the East and the West.

Further along in his extended lectures on saintliness, James comes to the point of stating the following:

1. "Only those who have no private interests can follow an ideal straight away" (p. 341). (This is equivalent to saying that the self

27

or the me, infused by the energy of the SELF, has no agenda other than that of faithfully becoming a Self on the way back home to the SELF.)

2. "A man possesses of learning only so much as comes out of him in action" (p. 342).

3. "There is in the desire of having, something profounder still. . . , the satisfaction found in absolute surrender to the larger powers" (p. 342).

James expands on these statements:

> Really to give up anything on which we have relied, to give it up definitely, "for good and all," and forever, signified one of those radical alterations of character which came under our notice in the lectures on conversion. . . . In it, the inner man rolls over into an entirely different position of equilibrium, lives in a *new center of energy* from this time on, and the turning-point and hinge of all such operations seems usually to involve the sincere acceptance of certain nakedness and destitution. . . . Only when the sacrifice is ruthless and reckless will the higher safety really arrive. (p. 343)

One could substitute SELF for "new center of energy." One could think of the I, Me, Ego that lives in, with, and by the SELF, or by the Anointed One—the Cosmic Christ within—as some in the Christian mystical tradition say.

In his next two lectures, James, as a dedicated pragmatist, devotes himself to expounding on the operational value of saintliness.

### Lectures XIV and XV. The Value of Saintliness

James boldly tells his audience that he espouses empiricist principles in these religious spiritual matters and that he proposes "to test saintliness by common sense, to use human standards to help us decide how far religious life commends itself as an ideal kind of human activity. . . . If we claim only reasonable probability, it will be as much as men who love the truth can ever at any moment hope to have within

28

their grasp. . . . The religious experience which we are studying is that which lives itself out within the private breast" (pp. 353-357). He explains:

A genuine first-hand religious experience is bound to be a heterodoxy to its witnesses, the prophet appearing as a mere lonely madman. If his doctrine prove contagious enough to spread to any others, it becomes a definite and labeled heresy. But if it then still prove contagious enough to triumph over persecution, it becomes itself an orthodoxy; and when a religion has become an orthodoxy, *its day of inwardness is over*: the faithful live at second hand exclusively and stone the prophets in their turn. The new church, in spite of whatever human goodness it may foster, can be henceforth counted on as a staunch ally at every attempt to stifle the spontaneous religious spirit, and to stop all later bubblings of the fountain from which in purer days it drew its own supply of inspiration. (p. 359)

These wise, forceful, polite admonitions apply to all healing of the human soul, but James is no naïve bystander: "The fruits of religion . . . are, like all human products, liable to corruption by excess" (p. 361). "If balance exists, no one faculty can possibly be too strong—we only get the stronger all-around character" (p. 362).

James asserts his certainty with regard to the value of saintliness: (a) "helpfulness in human affairs," and (b) "to be of some public or private use is also reckoned as a species of divine service" (p. 376). Ever a realist, James insists that "it is better that a life should contract many a dirt-mark than to forfeit usefulness in its efforts to remain unspotted" (p. 376). Life is lived in a natural and human world full of cruelty and injustice, but all the same, in need of loving stewardship and compassion. This is the IFS dictum: All Parts Are Welcome. All parts have a role to play. All parts intend to do good even when they are blind to compassion.

Applicable to the practical demands of his professions, as a practicing philosopher and psychologist, James acknowledges the pragmatic

29

need to balance the reality of two opposite approaches to human life: (a) an eye for an eye, as a way to resist the powers of darkness in the world, and (b) the golden rule, which he describes in this way:

Were there no one prompt to help his brother first and find out afterwards whether he was worthy; no one willing to drown his private wrongs in pity for the wronger's person; no one ready to be duped many a time rather than live always on suspicion; no one glad to treat individuals passionately and impulsively rather than by the general rule of prudence, the world would be an infinitely worst place than it is now to live in. (p. 378)

It seems to me that James would agree with Damasio's understanding of Spinoza. James appears to be advocating for Johann Goethe's well-known admonition: "Treat people as if they were what they ought to be, and you help them become what they are capable of becoming."

According to James, saints are . . .

authors, *auctores,* increasers of goodness. . . . We know not the complexities of personality, the smoldering emotional fires, the other facets of the character . . . , the resources of the subliminal region. . . . One fire kindles another; and without that over-trust in human worth which they [the saints] show, the rest of us would lie in spiritual stagnation. . . . No one who is not willing to try charity, to try non-resistance as the saint is always willing, can tell whether these methods will or will not succeed. (pp. 379-380)

What a statement in favor of hospitality and hope! This encapsulates and foreshadows the Sanctuary Model of Care.

James was not much for externally imposed rules and norms. He is philosophically an antinomian. I see him as a revolutionary, a heretic. I think here of the IFS invitation to be merchants of hope. He stays with this theme and continues:

[When these methods] do succeed, they are far more powerfully successful than force or worldly prudence. Force destroys enemies; and the best that can be said of prudence is that it keeps what we already have in safety. But non-resistance, when successful, turns enemies into friends, and charity regenerates its objects. These saintly methods are . . . creative energies. . . . (p. 380)

Inclined to use examples from real life, creditable testimony, and the maxims of the wise, James's words remind me of one of Augustine's convictions, expressed somewhere in his confessions, a belief that has stayed with me since my early college years: that if we only love God enough, we may safely follow all our inclinations. (See M. Boulding, Trans., 1997, *The Confessions of Saint Augustine of Hippo.*) It is not such a stretch to say that if we love SELF enough, we can follow its creative energies; that if Self loves self enough, self will yield to the imperfect transformative love of SELF.

At this point in his lecture, James refers to the Buddha's middle way and quotes from Hermann Oldenberg's *Buddha,* translated by William Hoey in 1882: "The only perfect life . . . is that of inner wisdom, which makes one thing as indifferent to us as another, and thus leads to rest, to peace, to Nirvana" (p. 383-384). In short, James makes a long argument for balance, harmony, and equilibrium.

### *Lectures XVI and XVII. Mysticism*

James tells his audience: "One may say truly . . . that religious experience has its root and center in mystical states of consciousness; so for us, who in these lectures are treating personal experience as the exclusive subject of our study, such states . . . ought to form the vital chapter from which other chapters get their light" (p. 401). James further advances the idea that personal experience can be considered mystical when (a) the feeling defies expression, (b) "the states of insight into depths of truth [remain] unplumbed by the discursive intellect," (c) the state "cannot be sustained for long," and (d) the individual feels "as if he were grasped and held by a superior power" (pp. 402-403). For individuals who experience such a mystical moment, "some memory of their content always remains [along with] a profound sense of their importance" (p. 403).

James refers back to a principle he stated in his first lecture: "Phenomena are best understood when placed within their series, studied in their germ and in their over-ripe decay, and compared with their exaggerated and degenerated kindred" (p. 404). James welcomes the full spectrum of human experience. He freely quotes John A. Symonds from H. F. Brown's 1895 biography, *John Addington Symonds,* and appropriates the descriptive definition of mystical consciousness:

> [The mood] consisted in a gradual but swiftly progressive obliteration of space and time, sensation, and the multitudinous factors of experience which seem to qualify what we are pleased to call *Self.* In proportion as these conditions of ordinary consciousness were subtracted, the sense of an underlying consciousness acquired intensity. At last nothing remained but a pure, absolute, abstract *Self.* The universe became without form and void of content. But *Self* persisted, formidable in its vivid keenness, feeling the most poignant doubt about reality, ready, as it seemed, to find existence break as breaks a bubble round it. And what then? The apprehension of a coming dissolution, the grim conviction of this state was the last state of the *conscious Self,* the sense that I had followed the last thread of being to the verge of the abyss. . . . Often, I have asked myself with anguish, on waking from that formless state of denuded, keenly sentient being, Which is the unreality?—the trance of fiery, vacant, apprehensive, skeptical *Self* from which I issue, or these surrounding phenomena and habits which veil the *inner Self* and build a *self* of flesh-and-blood conventionality? What would happen if the final stage of the trance were reached? (pp. 407-408)

This statement, and other considerations, led James to the following unshakable conclusion:

**Our normal waking consciousness, rational consciousness as we call it, is but one special kind of consciousness, whilst all about it,**

32

*parted from it by the filmiest of screens, there lie potential forms*
*of consciousness entirely different.* (p. 410)

And one of these potential forms of consciousness "is as if the opposites of the world, whose contradictoriness and conflict make all our difficulties and troubles, were melted into unity" (p. 410). What a powerful metaphor for Jung's "union of opposites" and the IFS welcoming of apparently disparate and opposing parts, of temporal and non-temporal origins.

At this point, James introduces his understanding of the ancient training in mystical insight that is Yoga, based on the 19th-century sources available to him. He refers to Yoga as the "experimental union of the individual with the divine. . . . The yogi, or disciple, [is the one] who has . . . overcome the obscurations of his lower nature sufficiently and comes face to face with facts which no instinct or reason can ever know" (p. 422).

Availing himself of a Vedantic understanding [that is, all reality is a single principle], James dares to further expose his audience to the mystical with its source in the superconscious state, the "above consciousness." (See Swami Vivekananda, 1896, "Raja Yoga.") In such a state,

there is no feeling of *I*, and yet the mind works, desireless, free from restlessness, objectless, bodiless. Then the Truth shines in its full effulgence, and we know ourselves . . . for what we truly are, free, immortal, omnipotent, loosed from the finite, and its contrasts of good and evil altogether, and identical with the . . . Universal Soul. (p. 422)

Such an experience must meet the empirical test: Its fruits must be good for life; there must be a character change; and there must be a life change. It is not a wild-eyed jump to think of Jung's statement in "Archetypes and the Collective Unconscious" in which he says,

The meeting with oneself is, at first, the meeting with one's shadow. The shadow is a tight passage, a narrow door, whose painful constriction no one is spared who goes down to the deep well. But one must learn to know oneself in order to know who one is. For what comes after the door is, surprisingly enough, a boundless expanse full of uncertainty, with apparently no inside and no outside, no above and no below, no here and no there, no mine and no thine, no good and no bad. It is the world of water, where all life floats in suspension; where the realm of the sympathetic system, the soul of everything living, begins; where I am indivisibly this and that; where **I** experience the *other* in myself and the *other-than-myself* experiences me. (Jung, *The Collected Works of,* v. 9, p. 27)

In this realm, only poetic language lets us into the ineffable. Yet, in this physical world, we are still in need of practical ways to identify the stages of becoming contemplative. James borrows the language of Buddhism's four stages: 1. No desire; 2. A satisfied sense of unity; 3. Indifference; 4. Ideas and perceptions stop, and the practitioner is able to say, "There exists absolutely nothing" (James, p. 423). This evokes the via negativa of the gnostic Christian spiritual traditions and the unutterable name of the One who is not whatever we might say the One is— the *One without a name,* the ONE energizing the self, the MULTIPLE ONE manifesting through the archetype of the OTHER. (I will return to this theme in more detail in Chapter Four: Mystical Judaism and IFS.)

James makes mention of what he has read of the Sufis on the matter. The soul is "detached from the world. The heart is purged entirely of all that is not God. There is a total absorption in God. Sight [is] illumined by a light which uncovers hidden things and objects the intellect fails to reach" (pp. 426-427).

There is in this mystical transport, an "incommunicableness." The experience is beyond sensation but not beyond immediate feeling, which James highly values. He seems to anticipate Damasio, given that he is familiar with Spinoza. He discusses the method called Orison— profound contemplative prayer in the Western monastic traditions. He mentions Ignatius of Loyola (1491-1556), John of the Cross (1542-

1591), and Teresa of Avila (1515-1582) as his sources. Such a contemplation is "a union of love [that] exceeds the senses, both inner and outer, and imposes silence upon them. . . . The soul then feels as if it is placed in a vast and profound solitude, to which no created thing has access, in an immense and boundless desert, [a] desert the more delicious the more solitary it is" (p. 429). According to John of the Cross, it is an "abyss of wisdom." Teresa of Avila writes that "the soul is fully awake as regards to God, but wholly asleep as regards things of this world and in respect of herself" (p. 430). James interprets the words of this mystic by saying, "In short, she is utterly dead to the things of this world and lives solely in God . . ." (p. 431). The self no longer lives. The Self now lives in and by and through the SELF. Teresa of Avila would say in and by and through the Anointed One, the *Christos,* the *Alpha et Omega.*

Once again, James returns to a familiar theme. How do we evaluate the validity of these experiences? He answers, "To pass a spiritual judgment upon these states, we must not content ourselves with superficial medical talk, but inquire into their fruits for life" (p. 435). He affirms that Ignatius was a mystic, but "his mysticism made him assuredly one of the most powerfully practical human engines that ever lived" (p. 435).

James concluded that Teresa's mysticism accounts for the "formation of a new center of spiritual energy." And, the optimism that drove both Ignatius and Teresa, as well as others of disparate spiritual traditions over the years, is a key ingredient of a truthful mysticism. "Furthermore, it is the awareness that the Ultimate is a No! according to the Upanishads" (p. 438). And it is Dionysius the Areopagite (c. 1st century), the fountainhead of Christian Mysticism, who describes the absolute truth by negatives exclusively" (p. 438). We can add that all that we state about the Absolute, all that we say about the archetypal OTHER and its image (the SELF), we must immediately deny, for it is beyond our relative understanding.

A Jungian might say that the Ultimate is the boundless *OTHER of which the SELF is the living symbol.* James sees this as a "denial made on behalf of a deeper yes" (p. 435). He does so, as do the mystics Meister Eckhart (1260-1328) and Jakob Boehme (1575-1624), because the Ultimate infinitely exceeds what can be said of it. "Like [Georg] Hegel in his logic, Mystics journey towards the positive pole of truth only by the *'Methode der Absoluten Negativitat'*" (Method of Absolute Negation) (James, p. 439).

James is also familiar, as is his audience, with the language of Paul of Tarsus. He says, "In Paul's language, I live, yet not I, but Christ liveth in me. Only when I become as nothing can God enter in and no difference between his life and mine remain outstanding. . . " (p. 440). James says, "In mystic states we both become one with the Absolute and we become aware of our oneness" (pp. 440-441). James again quotes the Vedantists: "As pure water poured into pure water remains the same, thus, O Gautama, is the *Self* of a thinker who knows. Water in water, fire in fire, ether in ether, no one can distinguish them; likewise, a man whose mind has entered into the *Self*" (pp. 441-442).

This reminds me of the elderly Jung in the famous 1957 BBC interview with Dr. Richard Evans when, to the question, "Do you believe in God?" Jung takes a few puffs of his omnipresent pipe, holds the moment silent, and then answers with an emphatic "NO." He returns to his pipe and a loud silence fills his study before he professes: "I KNOW." ("Jung on Film: The Richard Evans Interview," BBC, 1957.) It was as if, as so aptly described by the West Coast Jungian Analyst Edward F. Edinger, individuation manifests when the Ego, **the self, returns to SELF as an evolved Self at the end of life.** (See Edinger, 1972, *Ego and Archetype.*)

In this life, James notes, the experience of the Self finds expression in poetry, and he quotes phrases from mystical literature, such as "dazzling obscurity," "whispering silence," "teeming desert" (p. 442). He

36

further quotes from Helena P. Blavatsky's 1889 book, *The Voice of Silence:*

> For then the soul will hear and will remember. And then to the inner ear will speak THE VOICE OF THE SILENCE. . . . And now the *Self* is lost in **SELF**, *thyself* into **THYSELF**, merged in that **SELF** from which thou first didst radiate. . . . Behold! thou has become the Light, thou has become the Sound, thou art thy Master and thy God. Thou art THYSELF the object of thy search. . . . Thou art the voice OF THE SILENCE. (James, p. 443)

James, the pragmatist, wants to reassure his audience: "Our senses, namely, have assured us of certain states of fact; but mystical experiences are as direct perceptions of fact for those who have them as any sensations ever were to us. . ." (pp. 445-446). In short,

> The mystic is *invulnerable,* and must be left, whether we relish it or not, in undisturbed enjoyment of his creed. . . . It is evident that from the point of their psychological mechanism, the classical mysticism and . . . lower mysticism (as such delusions) spring from the same mental level, from that great subliminal or trans-marginal region of which science is beginning to admit the existence, but of which so little is really known. (p. 448)

The value of mystical experiences "is to be ascertained by empirical methods so long as we are not mystics ourselves" (p. 449). And he adds that there is a place in all of this for religious philosophy, the topic of his next lecture.

### Lecture XVIII. Philosophy

Never one to relegate reason to the trash heap, James admits the following: "I do believe that *feeling* is the deeper source of religion, and that philosophic and theological formulas are secondary products, like translation of a text into another tongue. . . . Feeling is private and dumb, and unable to give account of itself" (pp. 453-454). It is not surprising then that "religious experience . . . spontaneously and inevitably

37

engenders myths, superstitions, dogmas, creeds, metaphysical theologies, and criticisms of one set of these by the adherents of another" (p. 455). Furthermore, he disagrees with the statement that "what enters the heart must first be discerned by the intelligence to be *true*" (p. 456). He disagrees with the renowned English theologian Cardinal John Henry Newman. James politely says,

What God has joined together, let no man put asunder. The Continental schools of philosophy have too often overlooked the fact that man's ***thinking is organically connected with his conduct.*** [It seems to me] to be the chief glory of English and Scottish thinkers to have kept the organic connection in view. The guiding principle of British philosophy has in fact been that every difference must *make* a difference, every theoretical difference somewhere issues in a practical difference, and that the best method of discussing points of theory is to begin by ascertaining what practical difference would result from one alternative or the other being true. (pp. 464-465)

James reminds his audience that it is in this way that "[John] Locke [1632-1704] takes up the question of personal identity. What you mean by it is just your chain of particular memories. . ." (p. 465). I am what I remember myself to be in the past in this immediate present, which is one way of stating it. So, also, is stating that I am what I will be in the emerging future at the end of my evolution and return to the original SELF.

James pays his respects to Charles Sanders Pierce, who he describes as "an American philosopher of eminent originality" and credits him for having provided the "principle of *pragmatism*" (p. 466):

Thought in movement has for its only conceivable motive the attainment of belief or thought at rest. Only when our thought about a subject has found its rest in belief can our action on the subject firmly and solidly begin. Beliefs, in short, are rules for action; and the whole function of thinking is but one step in the production of active habits. (p. 466)

James agrees that if a belief serves the good life, it is to be valued in and for itself. He does not see a value in dogma. "We must," he says, "bid a definitive goodbye to dogmatic theology. In all sincerity, our faith must do without that warrant" (p. 470). James's statement reminds me of Hume's similar position when he was reported to have reaffirmed, at the end of his life, that he would die without the hand of belief. (I am grateful to Michael Heller for this information from a conversation while we were collaborating in the translation of his *magnum opus*. See References.)

When James makes reference to Immanuel Kant (1724-1804), he appreciates the man's successors who "convert . . . abstract consciousness into an infinite concrete self-consciousness which is the soul of the world, and in which our sundry personal self-consciousnesses have their being" (p. 471). James refers to John Caird, the author of the 1880 book, *An Introduction to the Philosophy of Religion,* when he says, "It is only in communion with [the] absolute Spirit or Intelligence that the finite Spirit can realize itself"; and that "to acknowledge [our] limits is in essence to be beyond them" (p. 472). On the Center for Action and Contemplation website invitation to the 2018 CONSPIRE Conference, Rohr puts it this way: "The path of descent is the path of transformation." Caird, quoted by James, further explains himself:

As a thinking being, it is possible for me to suppress and quell in my consciousness every movement of self-assertion, every notion and opinion that is merely mine, every desire that belongs to me as this particular **Self,** and to become the pure medium of a thought that is universal—in one word, to live no more my own life, but let my consciousness be possessed and suffused by the Infinite and Eternal life of spirit. *And yet it is just in this renunciation of self that I truly gain myself, or realize the highest possibilities of my own nature, for whilst in one sense we give up self to live the universal and absolute life of reason, yet that to which we thus surrender ourselves is in reality our truer self.* (p. 473)

39

This is at the heart of all practical wisdom found in all of the pragmatic spiritual traditions in the world. James ends this lecture by saying,

> The science of religions would depend for its original material on facts of personal experience and would have to square itself with personal experience through all of its critical reconstructions. It could never get away from concrete life, or work in a conceptual vacuum. . . . In the religious sphere, in particular, belief that formulas are "true" can never wholly take the place of personal experience. (pp. 478-479)

In IFS, the concrete personal experience of relational therapy is what reliably validates the theory that emerges from the practice. Richard Schwartz intimates that it is not a spiritual method that allows us to exercise the practice of compassion for our own repulsive and reptilian parts, as well as those of others, but that it is the hospitality we extend to the **SELF** and the unmerited visit of the same *ELUSIVE SELF* that transforms the phenomena of hate and fear to that of love and trust in the members of our individual internal and external families. (See R. C. Schwartz, 2015 September-October, "Facing Our Dark Sides: Some Forms of Self-Compassion are Harder than Others," *Psychotherapy Networker.)*

### *Lecture XIX. Other Characteristics*

James returns to the central theme in his discussion of the varieties of religious experience—"the use of religion, its uses to the individual who has it, and the use of the individual himself to the world, are the best arguments that truth is in it" (p. 480). He counts on empirical philosophy: "The true is what works well, even though the qualification *'on the whole'* may always have to be added" (p. 480). He warns us that we over-intellectualize our religious experiences (p. 480). He stops for a moment to reflect on the psychological value of confession. (He could have substituted the value of candid, clear, and courageous revelations in therapy.) He notes: "It is part of the general system of purgation and cleansing which one feels oneself in need of in order to be in right relation to one's deity" (p. 480). Can we not substitute here one's Higher Self, one's Core Self, one's Center, the Nameless Other reflected by the SELF? James continues: "For him who confesses, shams are over and realities have begun; he has exteriorized his rottenness. If he has not actually got rid of it, he at least no longer smears it over with hypocritical show of virtue—he lives at least upon a basis of veracity" (pp. 484-485). Jung said the same. He preferred the manifestations of the Shadow to that of the Persona. Pierrakos. embraced the manifestations of the Lower Self out of which would emerge the Higher Self. Again, we see the theme of descent before the assent, of death to the old life before resurrection to a new life. Religion and psychology are in tandem. The great *Exultet* at the Easter Vigil ends with the verse: "The night will be clear as day: it will become my light, my joy."

For James, "Prayer is religion in act; that is, prayer is real religion. . . . [It is] the very movement itself of the soul, putting itself in a personal relation of contact with the mysterious power of which it feels the presence. . ." (p. 486). "The conviction that something is genuinely transacted in this consciousness is the very core of living religion. . . . Through prayer, religion insists, things which cannot be realized in any other manner come about: *energy which but for prayer would be bound is by prayer set free and operates in some part, be it objective or subjective, of the world of facts"* (p. 488).

James quotes Myers: "*Prayer* is the general name of that attitude of open and honest expectancy" (p. 489). This is just what the IFS therapist fosters during therapy. James continues:

So, when one's affections keep in touch with the divinity of the world's authorship, fear and egotism fall away; and the equanimity that follows, one finds in the hours, as they succeed each other, a series of purely benignant opportunities. It is as if all doors were open, and all paths freshly smoothed. We meet a new world when

41

we meet the old world in the spirit which this kind of prayer infuses.
(p. 496)

James bows to Marcus Aurelius and to Epictetus (50-135 CE), whom he quotes: "Any one thing in the creation is sufficient to demonstrate a Providence, to a humble and grateful mind" (p. 496).

Boldly, James tells his audience that they "will, in point of fact, hardly find a religious leader of any kind in whose life there is no record of automatism, [that] beliefs are strengthened wherever automatisms corroborate them" (p. 500), and that "we cannot . . . avoid the conclusion that in religion we have a department of human nature with unusually close relations to the trans-marginal or subliminal region" [by any other name] (p. 505). The region of personality . . .

is obviously the larger part of each of us, for it is the abode of everything that is latent and the reservoir of everything that passes unrecorded or unobserved. It contains, for example, such things as all of our momentarily inactive memories, and it harbors the springs of all of our obscurely motivated passions, impulses, likes, dislikes, and prejudices. Our intuitions, hypotheses, fancies, superstitions, persuasions, convictions, and in general, all of our non-rational operations, come from it. It is the source of our dreams, and apparently, they may return to it. (pp. 505-506)

This is the fertile ground of the Internal Family System with all of its parts, none excluded, all welcomed.

### *Lecture XX. Conclusions*

In his 20th and final lecture, James summarizes his findings. He details the three beliefs that result from spiritual judgment about the religious life; findings, he warns, that "cannot be as sharp as dogmatic conclusions" (p. 507). These beliefs are:

1. That the visible world is part of a more spiritual universe from which it draws its chief significance;

42

2. That union and harmonious relations with that higher universe is our true end;

3. That prayer or inner communication with the spirit thereof—be that spirit "God" or "law"—is a process wherein work is really done, and spiritual energy flows in and produces effects, psychological or material, within the phenomenal world. (p. 508)

James adds, "Religion includes also the following psychological characteristics:

- A new zest which adds itself like a gift to life and takes the form either of lyrical enchantment or of appeal to earnestness and heroism;
- An assurance of safety and a temper of peace, and, in relation to others, a preponderance of loving affections." (pp. 507-508)

James is not shy to state that in what he calls the "above way" of life there are some dangers and that "no two of us have identical difficulties, nor should we expect to work out identical solutions" (p. 509). "We must frankly recognize the fact that *we live in partial systems, and that parts are not interchangeable in the spiritual life"* (p. 509). He insists that it is surely best for "each man to stay in his own experience, whate'er it be, and for others to tolerate him there" (p. 510). *"Our private lives are like those bubbles . . . on the foam which coats a stormy sea . . . floating episodes, made and unmade by the forces of wind and water . . . , epiphenomena . . . "* (p. 521). "Our inner state is our very experience itself; its reality and that of our experience are one" (p. 521). Allow me to quote James at greater length:

A conscious field *plus* its object as felt or thought of *plus* a sense of self to whom the attitude belongs—such a concrete bit of personal experience may be a small bit, but it is a small bit as long as it lasts; not hollow, not a mere abstract element of experience, such as the "object" is when taken all alone. It is *full* fact, even though it be an insignificant fact; it is of the *kind* to which all realities whatsoever must belong; the motor currents of the world run through the like of

43

it; it is on the line connecting real events to real events. *That unshareable feeling which each one of us has of the pinch of his individual destiny as he privately feels it rolling out on fortune's wheel may be disparaged for its egotism, may be sneered at as unscientific, but it is the one thing that fills up the measure of our concrete actuality, and any would-be existent that should lack such a feeling, or its analogue, would be a piece of reality only half made up.* (p. 521)

James is personally and intellectually convinced that "individuality is founded on feeling; and the recesses of feeling, the darker, blinder strata of character, are the only places in the world in which we catch real fact in the making, and directly perceive how events happen, and how work is actually done" (pp. 523-524). His analysis of the matter is that . . .

both thought and feeling are determinants of conduct, and the same conduct may be determined either by feeling or thought. When we survey the whole field of religion, we find a great variety in the thoughts that have prevailed there; but the feelings on the one hand and the conduct on the other are almost always the same, for Stoic, Christian, and Buddhist saints are practically indistinguishable in their lives. (p. 526)

A faith-state "is a biological as well as a psychological condition," and James reminds us that "Tolstoy is absolutely accurate in classing faith among the forces *by which men* live. The total absence of it, *anhedonia,* means collapse," and "a faith-state may hold a very minimum of intellectual content" (p. 527). Now it is "not God, but life, more life, a larger, richer, more satisfying life, which is in the last analysis, the end of religion" (p. 529). And this is the endpoint, the omega of a body, inclusive in IFS therapy. It is that *"more... with which our own higher self appears* in the experience to come into harmonious working relation" (p. 532). There is *"more life in our total soul* than we are at any time aware of" (p. 433). James hints at the fact that *the subconscious*

44

[unconscious] *self is exceedingly of greater vastness than the conscious self can imagine.* He again quotes Myers:

> Each of us is in reality an abiding psychical entity far more extensive than he knows—an individuality which can never express itself completely through any corporeal manifestation. The *Self* manifests through the organism; but there is always some part of the *Self* unmanifested; and always, as it seems, some power of organic expression in abeyance or reserve. (p. 534)

James continues: "But in it many of the performances of genius (as well as behaviors of the disordered) seem also to have their origin; and in our study of conversion, of mystical experience, and of prayer, we have seen how striking a part invasion from this region plays in religious life" (p. 534). Then he adds, "Let me then propose, as a hypothesis, that whatever it may be on its *farther* side, the 'more' with which in religious experience we feel ourselves connected, is on the *'hither'* side the subconscious [unconscious] continuation of our conscious life" (p. 534).

James wonders "how far our transmarginal consciousness carries us if we follow it on its remoter side" (p. 536). When he adopts what he calls a "monistic interpretation," he sees it as telling "us that the finite self rejoins the absolute self [SELF], for it was always one with God and identical with the soul of the world" (p. 535). This view does not necessarily contradict the experience and phenomena of the multiplicity of the mind and body. It is close to Jung's understanding of the psyche in its archetypal dimensions and complexes. (Edinger masterfully explicates this reality in *Ego and Archetype.)*

In italics, James emphasizes *"the fact that the conscious person is continuous with a wider self through which saving experiences* [religious/spiritual experiences] *come literally and objectively true as far as it goes"* (p. 537). It seems to him that the "further limits of our being plunge into an altogether other dimension of existence from the sensible and merely 'understandable' world" (p. 537). "We belong to it in a more

45

intimate sense than that in which we belong to the visible world. . . .
Yet the unseen region in question is not merely ideal, for it produces
effects in this world" (p. 538).

> We and God have business with each other; and in opening ourselves
> to his influence our deepest destiny is fulfilled. The universe, at
> those parts of it which our personal being constitutes, takes a turn
> genuinely for the worst or for the better in proportion as each one of
> us fulfills or evades God's demands. As far as this goes, I probably
> have you with me, for I only translate into schematic language what
> I may call the instinctive belief of mankind: God is real since he
> produces real effects. (pp. 538-539)

The I and the SELF, as well as all of our other subpersonalities, have
business with each other. SELF is real because it produces real effects.
And these real effects "are exerted on the personal centers of energy"
(p. 539). The SELF energizes the self and its parts into a functional Self.

Ever the scientist, James insists that religious experience is in need
of a *real hypothesis"* (p. 539). And for him,

> a good hypothesis in science must have other properties than those
> of the phenomenon it is immediately involved to explain, otherwise
> it is not prolific enough. [Thus, he submits,] the pragmatic way of
> taking religion [is] the deeper way. It gives it body as well as soul.
> [He affirms that] the whole drift of [his] education goes to persuade
> [him] that the world of our present consciousness is only one out of
> many worlds of consciousness that exist, and that those other worlds
> must contain experiences that have a meaning for our lives also; and
> that although in the main their experiences and those of this world
> keep discreet, yet the two become continuous at certain points, and
> *higher energies filter in.* (p. 541)

### James's Postscript

James admits that his views about religion and spirituality are not
the accepted view of his day. "The current of thought in academic

circles runs against me, and I feel like a man who must set his back against an open door quickly if he does not wish to see it closed and locked" (p. 544). "Nevertheless," he asserts, "religious experience, as we have studied it . . . testifies to [the fact] that we can experience union with *something* larger than ourselves and in that union find our greater peace" (p. 547). In an even bolder manner, he states:

All that the facts require is that the power should be both other and larger than our conscious selves. Anything larger will do, if only it be large enough to trust for the next step. It need not be infinite, it need not be solitary. It might conceivably even be only a larger and more **godlike self,** of which the **present self** would then be but a mutilated expression, and the universe might conceivably be a collection of such selves, of different degrees of inclusiveness, with no absolute unity realized in it all. (p. 547)

From the religious and spiritual world of soul, which has been the essence of his lectures on the varieties of religious experience, James makes mention that "polytheism . . . has always been the real religion of common people and is still so today. . ." (p. 548). And this brings me back to the great myths of the world and to the multiplicity of their divinities as the verifying projections of the human psyche's own real multiplicity.

James concludes his postscript by stating that he agrees with a statement by psychologist and parapsychologist Edmund Gurney:

For practical life at any rate, the *chance* at salvation is enough. No fact in human nature is more characteristic than its willingness to live a chance. The existence of the chance makes the difference . . . between a life of which the keynote is resignation and a life of which the keynote is *hope*. (p. 549)

### Concluding Comments
Such is the work of an IFS therapist and practitioner:

1. To bear witness to the operational world of the multidimensional multiplicity within the human being, and

2 To retrieve the exiled inner entities with the help of the befriended extreme protectors in collaboration with managing helpers for the purpose of lifting the burdensome weight from all of the overwrought parts in order to resource them with a resurrected life—body, mind, and soul—and this done in the service of hope for self, for others, for our home in the universe.

With Boston as the present epicenter of IFS, it is fitting to say that on this side of the pond, we are standing on the pioneer shoulders of William James, the one who revealed his thoughts in the Gifford Lectures on the other side.

*If you bring forth that which is within you, it will save you.*
*If you do not bring it forth, it will destroy you.*

—Gospel of Thomas, Logion 70

## PART TWO: AN IFS THERAPIST SEARCHES

### CHAPTER ONE: FREUD AND MAN'S SOUL

#### Self-Awareness and Consciousness-Making

Bruno Bettelheim's little 1982 book, *Freud & Man's Soul,* makes me smile every time I return to it; his words are filled with so much respect and reverence for the phenomenon of soul. In the following few pages, I tease out some of his thoughts that I feel are relevant to an IFS understanding of the self, Self, and SELF trinity. Bettelheim dares to voice corrections to what he determined to be inaccurate translations and subsequent erroneous interpretations of Freud's understanding. It seems to me that Bettelheim helps us greatly to grasp the heroic genius that is Freud's contribution to consciousness-making and gives us a strong, albeit unintended and late, argument in support of William James's express praise of Sigmund Freud. Some of what Bettelheim tells us about Freud, the man, his theory, and practice, fits with the fundamental approach to selfhood that James expressed and what is advanced in the practice of IFS therapy.

Freud taught that achieving greater self-awareness is an "arduous struggle . . . , a spiritual journey . . . , and that we [need] 'confidence' to know the dark, hidden and unknown forces inside us" (Bettelheim, pp. 4-6). These forces are not necessarily what we might imagine to be the raw powers of evil, but they are those energies that constitute the personal and universal content of what is not yet subject to the hospitable and healing light of consciousness. To participate in bringing all of who we are into the light is the spiritualization of our life into the physical reality that we are in during the interlude between birth and death.

This knowing of ourselves demands that we believe, with courage, in the possibility of such a quest and that we have "confidence" in the process and the outcome.

When I first became acquainted with Freudian thought and language—a foray into a forbidden area by the Vatican authorities of the 1960s—the term "sublimate" was spoken of mostly in the arena of sexuality. Here was one of Freud's beautiful concepts of the many that were misunderstood and mistranslated by countless self-proclaimed authorities in the associated world of psychology and psychiatry at that time and for decades thereafter.

In the world of spiritual and pastoral theology in which I lived at that time, we were taught that we were to overcome the sexual impulses of the ID, rise above them, and transform that energy into something nobler, more refined, more spiritual. The words sound good, but the translation, in practice, led to a demeaning suppression, a damaging repression, and a supercilious denial of our body-brain-mind reality. Back then, it all felt wrong; it is all wrong today. IFS gets it. All parts of us are welcome. Psyche and Eros are a loving pair.

Bettelheim reminds us that Freud read and studied Goethe (1749-1832) deeply and modeled his language on that of the German giant in order to evoke in his readers an emotional and intellectual response at the conscious and unconscious level; meaning, at the level of the soul. Freud had no intent to sidestep or set aside the energies of the ID, of that unknown reality. Sublimation is not an acolyte of illusion or delusion; it is a process of integration that requires uncompromising hospitality. In a parenthesis, Bettelheim writes: "It was Goethe, incidentally, who introduced the term "sublimate"—*sublimierin*—into the German language in reference to human feelings that must be worked at, improved, and elevated" (p. 9).

In IFS, we understand **working on** our feelings as inviting them into consciousness, **improving them** as promoting their authentic expression in service of the entire system, and **elevating them** as giving them

50

the full measure of respect in the relationships between all parts. All feelings are welcomed and are offered their rightful place at the table, thereby eventually eliminating the need of protective defenses. One can feel Bettelheim's passion when he insists that Freud

> chose [expressions/words] because they carried deep meaning and were vibrant with special humanistic resonances . . . often poetic. Whenever Freud thought it possible, he tried to communicate his new idea in the most common words that his readers had used since childhood. (pp. 8-9)

IFS builds upon this tradition of reverence for the soul. It is the Incarnated Psyche that Freud analyzes, up close and personal. Bettelheim puts it this way:

> Freud wished to emphasize that by isolating and examining the neglected and hidden aspects of our souls we can acquaint ourselves with those aspects and understand the roles they play in our lives. (p. 12)

This is the IFS therapist's declared goal. I quote again from Bettelheim's book:

> The purpose of Freud's lifelong struggle was to help us understand ourselves so that we would no longer be propelled, by forces unknown to us, to live lives of discontent or perhaps outright misery, and make others miserable, very much to our own detriment. . . . But to know ourselves profoundly can be extremely upsetting. It implies the obligation to change oneself—an arduous and painful task. (p. 15)

The IFS therapist does not shrink from this purpose.

In the following quote, we can hear James's motivating intention and Richard Schwartz's deepest desire in what Bettelheim considers to be Freud's greatest achievement.

> All of Freud's work to uncover the unconscious was intended to give us some degree of rational control [mindful more than logical] over it, so that when acting in line with its pressures was not appropriate,

or—most desirable—the power of the unconscious could be redirected through sublimation . . . to serve a higher and better purpose. (pp. 16-17)

I am inclined to see, in the common IFS language, the deliverance of "exiles," of weary "managers," of obsessed and compelled "firefighters" (those extreme protectors). I see them rising from their imprisonments with a resurrected energy. I see their rising, their being made sublime in and through consciousness. I see them as the ones who were always there and the ones who developed to fulfill the intent of the SELF—the birth and full evolution of the Self.

## Introspection

"Like [James], the father of American Psychology, Freud based his work mainly on **introspection** [emphasis added], his own and that of his patients" (p. 19). (See Freud, 1926, *The Question of Lay Analysis.*) In the language of IFS, we speak of direct and indirect access to those who populate our inner world. We look at them. We invite them to show themselves, and when they do, we welcome them. We ask them to reveal themselves further, and we listen to their counsel. We partner with them to share in the task of the evolution of the Self. We follow in the footsteps of fathers Freud and James. We want to avoid and to correct in our own therapeutic work what Bettelheim said of American Psychology in the early 1980s:

American Psychology came to neglect soul, psyche; to neglect to look inward toward the inner nature of things[, that which] gives true knowledge and permits understanding of what is hidden and needs to be known . . . to avoid the utterly destructive consequences of acting without knowing what one is doing. (pp. 24-25)

To allow ourselves to be so fully affected by the reality that is the other so as to understand the other ("stand under" for the purpose of holding the other) is to love the other. Furthermore, I hear Bettelheim reminding us that it is our willingness to do the hard work of knowing ourselves from the inside-out that gives evidence that we truly love ourselves and, therefore, are able to love the other. This is what is understood when we say someone is finally "rational." Here rationality is thoughtfulness, mindfulness, and not mundane logical reasonableness. Rationality is the essence of our humanity as we "struggle to discover the truth about ourselves" (p. 30).

When Bettelheim quotes Freud, he refers to two works: Freud's 1927 book, *The Future of an Illusion,* in which Freud deals with the nature of religious ideas; and Freud's *The Question of Lay Analysis.* Bettelheim writes:

> I do not know whether you have guessed the hidden link between "Lay analysis" and "Illusion." In the former I want to protect analysis from physicians, and in the latter from priests. I want to entrust it to a profession that does not yet exist, a profession of **secular ministers of the soul** [emphasis added], who do not have to be physicians, and must not be priests. (p. 35)

Victor Frankl spoke of the doctor of the soul. Schwartz teaches about the liberation of the self. James wrote about the way to holiness, sanctification. Jung woke us up to the SELF. Our ministry is to midwife the Self.

### Soul, Psyche, and Self

True to the purpose of his little book, Bettelheim tells us that the term **"soul"** was translated into English as **"psyche"** when it would have been more appropriate to translate it as **"self."** But, as we are well aware, the **self** and the **SELF** are not acceptable objects of experimental research. **So thought William James.** At the turn of the 20th century, James placed his hope in the new Freudian Analysis. James had met Freud and Jung at Clark University when he (James) attended the lectures organized by Stanley Hall in 1909, the year before Hall's death.

In the following extended quote, Bettelheim characterizes the function of the Freudian analyst in a way that an IFS therapist can call one's own:

> Someone who could greatly facilitate the emergence of a new personality, making the process of the change a safe one—Freud often used the simile of the midwife. As the midwife neither creates the child nor decides what [the child] will be but only helps the mother give birth to [her child] safely, so the psychoanalyst can neither bring the new personality into being nor determine what ought to be; only the person who is analyzing [himself] can make [himself] over. (p. 36)

Is this not what IFS therapy intends to effect? what James perceived as the emergent "new birth?"

Furthermore, Bettelheim understands Freud as teaching that Body stands for Soul, and that mental illness is soul sickness. To think of mental illness as the illness of the self and of the Self is not fantasy. Every soul must be treated as a unique system, and the approach to that soul must be individualized. With regards to a soul's individual personal life in this world, psychoanalysis and [Lay] therapy "deals with events that never occur in the same form—that can be neither replicated nor predicted" (p. 42). Both psychoanalyst and IFS therapist, lay or not, are "concerned with the discovery of events in the past life of the individual and with their consequence for [the individual], and neither the events nor the consequences can ever be exactly the same for two persons" (p. 45).

Bettelheim reminds us that "Freud was a very complex person . . . ; his self-analysis was his great achievement" (p. 47). James divulged that it was the same for him, and Jung confessed that doing so saved his life. Schwartz declares that he dared to look within to find the leadership of the SELF. To know oneself is the alpha and omega of one's existence, the royal road to the Source of Love, and the only way to give and receive true embodied love.

54

*If you want the truth,*
*I'll tell you the truth.*
*Listen to the secret sound, the real sound,*
*which is inside of you.*

—Kabir (15th Century)

## CHAPTER TWO: DAMASIO ON SPINOZA AND WILLIAM JAMES

### Secular Religiosity

In Antonio Damasio's 2003 book, *Looking for Spinoza,* he speaks at length of the difference and similarities between Spinoza and William James in regard to the religious dimension:

Intolerable as it was in his own time, Spinoza's brand of secular religiosity had been rediscovered or reinvented in the twentieth century. Einstein, for example, thought about God and religion in similar ways. He describes the God of "naïve man" as "a being from whose care one hopes to benefit and whose punishment one fears; a sublimation of a feeling similar to that of a child for its father, a being to whom one stands to some extent in a personal relationship, however deeply it may be tinged with awe." (Damazio, p. 279)

In describing his own religious feeling—the religious feeling of the "profounder sort of scientific minds"—Albert Einstein wrote that "such a feeling . . . takes the form of a rapturous amazement at the harmony of natural law, which reveals an intelligence of such superiority that, compared with it, all the systematic thinking and acting of human beings is an utterly insignificant reflection." In words of great beauty, Einstein described this feeling as "a sort of intoxicated joy and amazement at the beauty and grandeur of this world, of which man can form just a fair notion. This joy is the feeling from which true scientific research draws its spiritual sustenance, but which also seems to find expression in the song of birds." I believe this feeling, which Einstein called cosmic, is a relative of

55

Spinoza's *amor intellectualis Dei,* although the two can be distinguished. Einstein's cosmic feeling is exuberant, a mixture of heart-stopping awe and heart-beating-fast preparation for bodily communication with the world. Spinoza's *amor* is more restrained. The communication is more interior. Einstein seems to blend the two. He believed that the cosmic feeling is a hallmark of religious geniuses of all ages, but that it never forms the basis for any church. "Hence, it is precisely among the heretics of every age that we find men [and women] who were filled with the highest kind of religious feeling and were, in many cases, regarded by their contemporaries as atheists, sometimes also as saints. Looked at in the light, men like Democritus, Francis of Assisi, and Spinoza are closely akin to one another." (Damazio, p. 280)

How similar are Einstein's and James's subjective experience of the numinous? Damasio tells us that "James's thinking on these matters also revealed a kinship with Spinoza," although "not one of full acceptance." James read Spinoza while preparing a course on the psychology of religion at Harvard that "eventually formed the basis for James's [1902 book,] *The Varieties of Religious Experience.*" James did so "on the rebound from a severe bout of depression" (p. 281). Damasio reminds us that "the casting of the problem of human salvation in cognitive and affective terms showed James at his more intellectually penetrating.

### The Experience of God is Private

Damasio writes that for both Spinoza and James,

Their experience of God was private. . . . James's sweeping dismissal of organized religion are quite Spinozian. . . . James, using the budding knowledge of the late nineteenth-century psychology, which he himself helped construct, *located the source of the divine not just within us but in the unconscious within us* [emphasis added]. He spoke of the religious experience as something *"more."* (p. 282)

56

Spinoza and James are pointing us toward a fruitful adaptation in the form of a natural life of the spirit. Their God is therapeutic in the sense that it restores the homeo-dynamic balance lost as a result of anguish. But neither man expected God to listen. Both believed that the restoration of balance is an individual and internal task, something to be achieved. . . . Both acknowledged "that human beings are mere occasions of subjective individuality in a largely mysterious universe." (p. 282)

Damasio confesses that he does "not favor the attempt to neurologize religious experience, especially when the attempts take the form of identifying a brain center for God or justifying God and religion by finding their correlations in brain scans. . . . Yet spiritual experiences, religious or otherwise, are mental processes." He dares to face the issue of "locating the spiritual in the human organism." He writes,

The spiritual is a particular state of the *organism,* a delicate combination of certain body configurations and certain mental configurations. Sustaining such states depends on a wealth of thoughts about the condition of the self and the condition of the other selves, about past and future, about both concrete and abstract conceptions of our nature.

Always from the Spinozian tradition, Damasio adds the following:

By connecting spiritual experiences to the neurobiology of feelings, my purpose is not to reduce its dignity. The purpose is to suggest that the sublimity of the spiritual is embodied in the sublimity of biology and that we can begin to understand the process in biological terms. As for the results of the process, there is no need and no value to explaining them: *The experience of the spiritual amply suffices.* (p. 286)

*We were present in the primal flaring forth,*
*and in the rains that streamed down*
*on the still molten planet,*
*and in the vestigial seas.*
—Joanna Macy, 2007, *World as Lover, World as Self*

## CHAPTER THREE: A MEDITATION ON RADICAL CHANGE, RADICAL HOPE

### The Concepts of Radical Change, Radical Hope

To expand on the concepts of radical change and radical hope—the intended outcomes of IFS therapy—I am indebted to Jonathan Lear for the following thoughts based on his 2008 book, *Radical Hope: Ethics in the Face of Cultural Devastation.* I am grateful to him for the liberal use of his concepts and language, and I am indebted to my philosopher son, Joshua Duclos, for the gift of Lear's book.

Internal Family Systems therapy invites both therapist and client to a radical change. Life as they both know it will be coming to an end. Therapy is an ethical endeavor. The pressure is on all norms and values that previously guided the living of a life. They will be suspended by choice or necessity. What was previously known as one's ethical life— what defined one's meaning and purpose—will come to a halt. In the ensuing paragraphs, I freely borrow and paraphrase Lear's nuggets of wisdom.

A crossroad moment will appear. A bridge to be crossed will necessitate burning it behind us. Everything we thought to be the elements of a good life will need to be given up. If the co-travelers intend on facing the Radical Change that real life demands, then a moment of commitment that surpasses past and current understanding of what constitutes a good life is at play. The mystic, the poet, and the prophet know this by experience.

58

There is a hint in the metaphor of a radical change that roots will be pulled up. A purpose higher than the previous one supersedes and might appear antithetical to what was the past's highest good. Recall Abraham who is asked to sacrifice his son. The asking presents as an insane, monstrous edict in its literal interpretation and presents a radical change from the profoundly natural mammalian charge to care for one's offspring, a charge that is hard-wired in our affective brain. There is no facile escape into the romantic in this. I see a **Self** who is asked to sacrifice one's **self** at the behest of the **SELF.** The angel's hand reminds me that we are not to do violence to our self in the process of sanctification, of transformation, of resurrection. The same applies to the IFS therapist and client who are called to suspend their current ethical understanding and stance. They are called to tolerate, in depth, the collapse of their ethical life. That implies letting go the notions with which and though which they have previously understood themselves as ethical persons. I am reminded of having read that Jung asserted that to enter into the individuation process, one had to commit treason.

The IFS therapist and client join in an existential challenge when they have reached a covenant: to be devoid of knowing what to hope for in the end but to engage in Hope, no matter what. This is a hope that reaches beyond the limits of imagination. This unknown future cannot be encountered with the same strategies with which one faced the unknown in the past. This calls for a radical approach because this future hope offers radically different possibilities; it reaches down and drinks at the taproot.

### The Ultimate Daring

When all that is known is left behind or even lost, when the way to be in a world that no longer exists is threatened or eradicated, it is not a hope to survive that is needed, but a daring to boldly face the prospect of annihilation as the price to pay for the radical change. This, says Lear, is the honorable way to go forward. Such a radical change

59

in our lives implies discontinuity and requires the maintenance of fundamental integrity through the process of transformation. There is no passage possible in and through the abyss without a commitment to Hope. Because death is a real possible outcome, psychologically and/or physically, a grounded hope in the emergence of a good life, a goodness, must be beyond our capacity to create and comprehend—the dark night of the soul in the chaos of the here and now, some would say; a firm hope of resurrection—a new life that defies intelligibility.

Often, if not always, this resurrection demands and effects the demise of our current subjective sense of self in order to be handed an integrated sense of transcending Self beyond the power of our limited strategies. This kind of commitment is daunting for both therapist and client. How can we hope for something that transcends our capacity to reach, let alone grasp? We speak of a hope that dispels despair, for we rarely choose radical change. Radical change befalls us, and we accept its challenge without an assurance of the future unknown. This is the mark of courage—a quality of the SELF-led person. This is the commitment to radical change and radical hope that the IFS therapist dares make to the patient as an invitation to welcome the guidance of the SELF.

*The body has to be spiritualized and the spirit has to be incarnated,*
*both things must take place.*

—Von Franz, 1980, *Alchemy*

## CHAPTER FOUR: MYSTICAL JUDAISM AND IFS

### Paradigm Shift

Anyone who is familiar with Jung's thoughts has probably chanted "As above, so below; as below, so above," a refrain Rabbi David A. Cooper (1997) quotes at the beginning of his book, *God is a Verb: Kabbalah and the Practice of Mystical Judaism*. If there were ever a mystical saying, this one surely qualifies and is an apt introduction to the subsequent pages in which Cooper leads to an understanding and practice of mystical experience in the conduct of everyday life. He dares to offer an initial description, not a definition, of mystical awareness as he understands it. Such an awareness is "what we experience when the sense of past and future dissolves and we are finally present, totally, in the moment" (p. 37). This awareness and all of our competing polarities are not extinguished, they are in balance and harmony within the universal life-force that yields to no measurable definition. Body, mind, psyche, and soma are experienced at the end of the journey—for we live in time and space—no longer as an amalgamation of fragmented multiplicities but as a unity in multiplicity. The wholeness that results allows for the emergence of an awareness beyond the limits of our deductive reasoning.

Cooper takes us on a meditation to the outer reaches of mysticism and physics, often using the language of a poet while doing so. In the chapter, "The Nature of God," he offers us a paradigm, which for the purposes of this extended reflection might give us an entry into the esoteric nature of the SELF. Richard Schwartz, in his May 15, 2018, webinar "Internal Family Systems Therapy (IFS): A Revolutionary & Transformative Treatment of PTSD, Anxiety, Depression, and

61

Substance Abuse," hints, in an aside, that we might just have to live without fully understanding the nature of the *SELF* [emphasis added]. But, his aside ought not to discourage us in our pursuit. To refine what SELF is *not* will surely reward the inquiry.

In the same way that our understanding of God (and the words we use to name God fail miserably—"God" in English, "Dieu" in French, "Deus" in Latin, "Got" in German, etc.,—leads to devastating conceptual distortions to our detriment and to the detriment of others. So also does our miserable handling of the words *self, Self,* and *SELF* that we have adopted to describe that which is within us that guides us to a conversation into the never-to-be-attained wholeness our nature so deeply desires. Cooper says,

> God is not what we think IT is . . . , for God is not a thing, a being, a noun . . . , IT does not exist . . . , for IT takes up no space and is not bound by time (p. 65). So, also, is the SELF other than we imagine it to be. The Jewish mystics present us with an option born of inspiration and spiritual discipline. To the kabbalist tradition, the IT *(Ein Sof),* which means Endlessness, best states the unfathomable that should never be called any of the names we humans have tagged onto IT for our own purposes. Any and all attributes we assign to IT (what we call "God") cannot define IT. (p. 65)

I am reminded of the spiritual discipline of the *Via Negativa*, the negative way, of the early Christian Church warning that whatever we say of God, we must immediately affirm the opposite. In other words, we must equally "deny" both. The endless, the infinite, the immeasurable is always beyond our delimited, finite, and definable nature. We can hypothesize that the SELF must be dealt with similarly.

## Ein Sof

In the following extended exegesis, I intend to parallel a kabbalist's grappling with the felt experience of the Ein Sof with my own wrestling with the operational understanding of the SELF. I borrow David

Cooper's language related to the Ein Sof to discuss the mysterious nature and workings of the SELF. We must not reduce what follows to the realm of the concrete. We can arrive at little—perhaps nothing—via reason and logic, while retaining its reasonableness. Nonetheless, in the domain that falls outside of the descriptive sciences, it is possible to arrive at the guidance of practical wisdom. I might have this upside down and the wrong way around, but I find it helpful to think about the problem of the elusive IFS SELF in the symbolic language of Judaic mysticism. I am not talking of a crass substitution of terms; I am not equating Ein Sof (the IT) to the concept of the SELF, nor am I equating the SELF to the IT. My initial leaning is toward an understanding of the SELF as the "Presence of the IT" that permeates the entirety of all the parts of the mind, brain, and body phenomenon that we are.

As a first premise in this inquiry, Cooper mentions the teachings of the 12th-century kabbalist, Isaac the Blind (c. 1160-1235), who taught that IT (Ein Sof/Endlessness) "precedes thought . . . , and even precedes Nothingness . . . , out of which thought is born" (p. 67). We are unable to imagine the infinite nature of nothingness, for nothingness has no limits, and our limited minds are demonstrably finite. And IT even transcends infinity and "is inaccessible through any intellectual endeavor" (p. 67). But Cooper does not despair. He leans firmly on the level of awareness of the mystics who "develop[ed] a relationship with Endlessness, the source of creation" (p. 67). And what is astonishing and hopeful is the fact that "the secret teaching in developing this relationship with the Unknowable is hidden in the mystical foundation of the nature of relationship itself" (p. 67). This reminds me of the Christian theological teaching of God as Trinity, who by nature, is relationship.

Is not the aim of IFS therapy to effect the harmonious relationship of parts to the whole, the shining of a light, beyond our personal source, on the relationships that populate our inner world and manifest in the outer world according to the mystery of the seen and unseen, above and

63

below? Whatever name we might assign to God in all of the religions of the world, each, at best, represents an aspect of the IT and offers some insight into the nature of IT. I agree with Cooper when he says, "Whenever God is discussed in this [writing, I] am not talking about a thing in itself, but a representation of a far greater mystery" (p. 68). When we, in the IFS community, talk about what we call SELF, Self, or self, it behooves us to be able to identify which of these words refer to that "far greater mystery."

David Malan's schema of the Two Triangles (the triangle of conflict and the triangle of person) and Jung's typography of the Psyche are useful reminders of the complexity of the therapist/client relationship. (See D. H. Malan, 1979, *Individual psychotherapy and the science of psychodynamics*.) In the therapist/client therapeutic relationship, wholeness-making enterprise matters. A "me-to-me," "self-to-self," or "ego-to-ego" relationship, whichever term you prefer, might have elements of Self-energy, qualities of Self-Leadership, to the extent that a wisdom beyond our making enters the field and promotes the qualities of the SELF in the interaction. Internal Family Systems identifies these qualities of SELF as Calmness, Clarity, Curiosity, Compassion, Confidence, Courage, Connectedness, and Creativity. Notice that this describes the SELF by the observable and felt qualities that the Self (the SELF-led center of consciousness) cannot author. The self will have to cede its executive function to the Self that emerges out of the self's evolutionary return journey to the SELF.

To return to a previous point, and to make my position less ambiguous, I say here that the multiple understandings of God seen across the globe are never an understanding of the Ineffable Endlessness. The IT is not comprehensible. For that very reason, humans have projected their internal imagery onto the gods and failed to notice this as an act of idolatry. How devastating this forgetting has been for humanity. How many wars were, and are to this day, fought to protect and preserve one's own god, to defend that same god, and all because of claiming to

64

know god's will. And, in the world of psychology, how many battles continue to be fought by partisans of one school or another to assert the existence or nonexistence of a self (capitalized or not), to affirm or deny incompatible definitions of the same. To me, it seems that we are repeating similar fruitless debates as those of the scholastics who argued in the damp stone cathedrals of Europe as to the correct number of angels on the head of a pin. At least they accepted the existence of angels (as parts in the human multiplicity).

If Jung was on to something when (and this is how I understand him) he proposed that the SELF, at the Core of the Psyche, is the archetypal image of the OTHER that is undefinable and which participates in the IT's nature and is the provident source of the individual's divinity, then, he said, the person is born embedded in and identified with the SELF as a self yet to be recognized by the person, endowed with the incipient quality of the SELF. Through awareness, the self consciously transforms into a Self, existing through and by the SELF's energies. It is the person's life's task to effect a separation from the self's original unconscious identification to an eventual conscious relationship with the SELF that creates a third entity, the Self. A trinity within.

Remembering the concept of the here-and-now, familiar to the phenomenologists, which is central to the theory and practice of Fritz Perls' Gestalt Therapy, I am pleased to acknowledge the antecedents in the Kabbalah. Cooper writes that "the presence of the Divine is revealed in the fullness of each moment" and that "our hearts melt and the floodgates of our inner yearning open wide" (p. 68). He is speaking of the Self's yearning for the SELF, the divine expression of the OTHER from within, and I add, of course from without. The Endlessness is within and without because IT is everywhere and nowhere, always and never, present and absent. We have no language for IT. We have no adequate language for Mystery, nor for the mysteries that initiate the Self's return journey into the limitless SELF from out of the death of the self. We have no adequate words for what is not a word. Those who claim to know God's words (*their* God's words) are not speaking for the Ein Sof, the nameless one, the YHWH, the I Am That I AM of the Jewish tradition.

But we are language-bound beings, and as such, we struggle to approximate in words our deepest experiences. Cooper tells of Abraham Abulafia, the great 13th-century Jewish mystic, who said about one who achieved spiritual awareness, "Now we are no longer separated from our source, and behold, we *are* the source and the source is us. We are so united with IT, we cannot by any means be separated from IT, for we are IT" (pp. 68-69) and at the same time, we are other than IT, for only as separate can we be in relationship with IT.

Consider the following three translations, among many, of a passage from the New Testament in the Letter to the Galatians (chap. 2, v. 20):

1. My old self has been crucified with Christ. It is no longer I who live, but Christ who lives in me. (*The Holy Bible,* New Living Translation)
2. I no longer live, but the Messiah lives in me (*The Holy Bible,* International Standard version).
3. . . . . and I live, now not I; but Christ liveth in me (*The Holy Bible,* the Douay-Rheims version).

If we read the confession of Paul (Saul) of Tarsus, attesting to his own spiritual transformation, in light of mystical traditions of the Middle East of his time, along with the practical wisdom of the Kabbalah, the archetypal psychology of Jung, and the spiritual pragmatism of William James, we can see the possibility of the long, deeply nurtured history of the self's transformation into the Self through the energy, grace, and wisdom of the SELF. One could interchange SELF, Christ, and Ein Sof because none of these words are nouns; they are verbs.

To add to the ineffable phenomenon hinted at above, Cooper writes, "Mystics throughout time, in all traditions, have said the same thing. We do not have to search for God, because the presence of the Divine permeates all things. If there is search at all, it is God searching for

66

Itself, so to speak" (p. 69). Keep in mind that the God that is searching for Itself is our image of Itself, which we call God by any other name. An image, not of the ego's making, but one welded into the neuronal networks of the brain over the evolutionary millennia into an archetype.

## God is a Verb

Let's say, for the purpose of this inquiry into the reality of the SELF, operative in our internal families, that the image of God that roams about in our day and night hours, in our waking and sleeping hours, in our conscious and unconscious states, and in our night and day dreams, is what Jung refers to as the OTHER at the center and depth of the psyche. And, let's accept that Cooper is on to something when he renames God as "It, God-ing, rather than God . . . " (p. 69). At this point, I find myself stunned by the process of imagination that comes to the rescue of my failing cognitions. IT communicates with me, as with all that is, via the God-ing process that intends to transform my little self into a Self energized by the SELF, transforming me into not quite a god, but somewhat of divine qualities.

As each part of all that is "is in a dynamic relationship with every other part" (p. 70), so it is with the parts of our psyche (mind, brain, body). And, all of our parts are susceptible to the power/energy of the IT to *grace* our being with a transforming moment that changes us forever, that tips the scale of the ego/me self-leadership to that of Self-leadership, a spiritual transformation in time and place. James's Gifford Lectures focused on the varieties of such a religious experience. When Cooper encourages us to enter into the process-experience of breathing in the Now, of moving in the Now, he suggests that we will fall into the awe that "leads to wisdom" (p. 70).

To offer ourselves to others, as guides to their wholeness-making, demands a terrifying and consoling dedication to the awesome Nameless. Cooper invites readers to engage in the following meditation:

Take a few moments to close your eyes and allow yourself to sink into this idea. . . . The teaching of the mystery of *Ein Sof* is that the center of our being, out of which awe arises, is that about which we are awed. It is It! When we contemplate our continuous process of opening, right here, right now, we realize that God-ing is always with us. (p. 71)

The work of therapy is the God-ing, the Self-ing of client and therapist in the Now. We co-partner with the OTHER, with the IT. We cannot let heaven interfere with what is our lot to decide. "This astounding Talmudic [conviction] indicates that human reason carries precedence over heavenly mandates," over what others and our own self asserts is the will of a self-defined God (p. 74). I am comforted by Job's argument with God and with God's response. I will return to this later.

Cooper says, "When we accept each moment as a new opportunity for fulfilling our purpose, we are always present, always succeeding, always changing the world for the better, we are always 'here'" (p. 78). The mysterious simplicity of this statement confounds our compulsive desire to do, to be in charge, to be able to take credit for our climb up Jacob's ladder.

I return to the theme of the Now. Only in the Now can we find the wherewithal to fulfill our destiny—our imperfect wholeness and our ability to contribute to the imperfect wholeness of all of our relationships. Cooper makes reference to a Jewish sage who asked his listeners if they knew who is rich. Apparently, his interlocutors held their silence. Thus, he answered his own question. Reportedly, he said, *"The one who is happy with his lot."* This is the one who finds peace in the chaotic nature of daily life in the Now (p. 79).

## Attention and Awareness

Mystics know and speak of the ones who populate our inner world. In the language of the past, all the descriptions of angels and demons, of good and bad spirits, of mythological figures, are meant to help us approximate qualities we find within ourselves (Cooper, p. 141). The opposites are within the psyche and the Ein Sof. Mystics across cultures find the angels and demons quite real, as do schools of psychology that access these and other multiplicities to discover intentions and levels of awareness. Cooper says,

> It is important for us to understand that an intention behind an act does not insure its results. Intention must be balanced with awareness. The greater awareness of this internal world, the greater the probability that something good will come out. The denser the awareness, even if one's intention is good, the greater the risk that things will not turn out so well. (p. 141)

Runaway and dissociated parts (subpersonalities) might have the best of intentions to protect the burdened, exiled parts, but without the awareness of their own burdens and of their own limited or outdated strategies, the enterprise is destined to fail in the end. Cooper continues:

> If our intentions do not assume that things will turn out for the good, what do we do?" The answer is that we must attune ourselves to the constant ebb and flow of ongoing creation throughout contemplative practices and through spiritual work that builds awareness. . . . And we must make every effort to attain the highest level of consciousness so that our actions may be inspired by the ingredients of judgment and wisdom, spiced with a large dose of faith. (p. 141)

The Self's faith in the SELF, we might say.

Internal Family Systems voices the necessity of compassion and hope. Cooper tells us that the *Torah* speaks of the blessing of being "surrounded by light and loving-kindness" (p. 147). IFS calls on the SELF to infuse the Self with the energy of the IT's qualities. The "Ein Sof embraces everything, including the totality of good and bad" (p. 156). The narrow moralism of distorted traditions is far from this expansive reality. "We are neither good nor evil in our nature. We (the Me, the I, the self) are simply the product of accumulated influences in our lives, plus the most important variable: our free will" (p. 157). But, when parts that originate either in the collective or the personal unconscious (operating in, though, and by the structures and networks of our brain and body) have their partial or complete say, the ego's operation of free will suffers a humiliating blow.

Cooper stands firmly in a long tradition that upholds the interplay between good and evil—to use these easily misunderstood words that might be misinterpreted one for the other; they are not each other. "Rather . . . , each has the spark of the other, and if pushed too far, this spark can be ignited" for good or for ill (p. 159). Therefore, what is needed is a new paradigm. "Rather than destroy [evil], our task is to uplift it. . . . Mystics say that there are an infinite variety of shadings, each of which can be raised to new heights" (p. 160). IFS therapists say that our managing, protecting, and exiled parts want to be uplifted, are ready to join with the SELF-infused Self and play their chosen roles in a new, more expansive consciousness. This will be what Jewish mystics refer to as the messianic consciousness, the era of loving conscious "relationships with one another" (p. 171). This is a state of being that the ego-state, the self, has never before experienced if separated from the always available SELF. It is the reconciliation of all opposites at their apogee.

When I, as an IFS therapist, contemplate the above, I do not find it difficult to entertain the qualities of a messianic consciousness in an individual's intrapersonal and interpersonal relationships as the hoped-for aim of IFS therapy. Furthermore, when Cooper writes that "by definition, greater awareness means less self-identity, for the sense of self continuously dissolves as we merge into a vast interconnectedness of creation" (p. 180), this again can so aptly refer to the metamorphosis of the self (me/ego) into the Self via the SELF-led dedication of client and therapist to the work of witnessing, unburdening, and resourcing into an expanding wholeness.

When the multiplicities become one without losing their relational identities, the phenomenon might be understood as the divinization of the human. This is the sanctification James dared to describe. This is the result of a realistic spiritual practice, observable and measurable in the world as the fruit of contemplation and action. To repeat, perhaps this is what the Gnostics understood as the sought-after resurrection—"the heralding of a new era, a transformation into a consciousness previously unknown in which realities undergo a profound change" (p. 294). At the end of *God is a Verb,* Cooper asserts that in order "to bring about a new reality of messianic consciousness, we must find a way to make a crack in our barriers so that the light of awareness will shine through . . . one step at a time as we open ourselves to a higher consciousness. . ." (p. 301).

When the self, as a miraculous seed, consents and opens itself up to its descent into death, it allows new life to rise into the light as a new Self, energized by the generous gifts of the SELF, the messenger-image of the Ein Sof. Cooper closes his epilogue in this way:

> *Once we make a crack, the barrier can be split open quickly. Higher awareness is a huge reservoir. All we need to do is to remove our fingers from the dam of self-identity. If we have the courage to do so, we will be flooded in light* [emphasis added]. (p. 302)

And, in classic rabbinic fashion, he adds,

> *May each and every one of us be blessed to realize the messianic consciousness within us; may we gain strength and insight to open our eyes; may our lives be filled with the ongoing truth in which we are saturated with love, caring, and kindness. And may we serve the world from this level of awareness. And, let us say, "Amen."* [emphasis added]. (p. 302)

*Helping patients to remain regulated*
*while focusing their attention on things that would normally*
*dysregulate them is one of the arts of psychotherapy.*
—Daniel Hill, 2015, *Affect Regulation Theory*

## CHAPTER FIVE: AFFECT REGULATION AND INTERNAL FAMILY SYSTEMS

### The Bodymind

In the preface to his 2015 book, *Affect Regulation Theory: A Clinical Model,* Daniel Hill presents a "model that integrates psychoanalysis and its schools of thought with other approaches. . . " (p. ix). He explains that this model is a "developmentally based approach to psychobiology . . . how the mind emerges from the body into a 'bodymind'" (p. ix).

In the same way that theology is poetry, so also is psychotherapy. As the organic arises from the inorganic, so spirit arises from soma. In Christian nosology, we might see the metaphor of incarnation in the above; that is, mind in body, body infused by mind, body and mind as one bodymind. When Hill writes that he works "with the core of [his] patient from the core of [himself], we can extrapolate the concept to think of the healing nonconscious dialogue that occurs reciprocally between the SELF of one (the therapist, in this instance) to the SELF of the other (the patient) via the voluntary, humble intent of each other's Self.

In the forward of Hill's book, Allan N. Schore, author of the 1994 groundbreaking book, *Affect Regulation and the Origin of the Self: The Neurobiology of Emotional Development,* reminds us that "Hill observes that the 'unitary self' is in actuality fundamentally composed of a multiplicity of self-states" (p. xviii). We, in the IFS community, call these self-states "parts" in our use of a chosen symbolic language for therapeutic effect in conversations with each other and

72

with our patients. Nonetheless, the psychobiological terminology of affect regulation theory does help elucidate what we might be hinting at when we use the nouns self, Self, and SELF in IFS theorizing. Schore continues:

> Each of these discrete self-states represents a different mode of feeling, thinking, and acting, and thereby different ways of being in different relational contexts. In this manner, each self-state is its own personality system, what Hill calls a "context-dependent assemblage of affective and cognitive processes that assemble us into versions of us." (p. xviii)

In our internal conversations with our parts (of a collective or personal unconscious origin), the IFS therapist recognizes the functionally independent versions of our selves as real personalities—with their own myriad subpersonalities—playing contextual roles in the world. It is evident that this attempt to tease out a more lucid understanding surely does not do justice to what calls for a wider search of the literature. At best, what I continue to present for consideration is a sampling of the thinking of a selected few from among many who address the perennial question: What is this self, these selves, of whatever capitalization, upon which humans have pondered and of which so much has been expressed in the arts and sciences?

## Our Multiplicity

Hill is one of those psychoanalysts who is a learned practitioner and student of the sciences related to this subject. He addresses the focus on multiplicity when he states, "What we think of as a unitary self actually consists of a set of self-states" (p. 29), a conviction emphasized earlier by Schore. Hill further discusses what he means by saying that "we are different versions of ourselves in different relationships, in different roles, and in different contexts in general. . . . Each generates a particular sense of self and others and different ways of relating" (p. 29). How familiar this all is in the internal family that lives in us, and lives us.

73

If the center of consciousness functions in concert with, or in available contact with, other unblended self-states (parts), the activated self-states are neither involuntary nor automatic. They could be partially, but not fully, dissociated as are alters in a dissociative-identity-disordered individual (p. 30). In IFS, when speaking of blending or of the self (me/ego) being blended, I am reminded of Hill's phrase of "state-shifting," which is a healthy adaptation that can become "suboptimal in dysregulated-dissociated states in which we are automated and reduced to a single way of being" (p. 31). William James references automatism in his discussion of religious experiences and is fully aware of the unhealthy side of what Hill called "automaticity," an admittedly borrowed term.

Pertinent to the IFS explanation of the reality and nature of what we call parts; that is, those parts of ourselves that evolved from our personal developmental stories, Hill further speaks of "compartmentalization and altered states of consciousness" (p. 32). It is of importance to note that, in a healthy psycho-biologically based spiritual/religious experience, one that arises from and promotes a SELF-energized state, the individual (the Self) is not reduced to a "single way of being." Whereas "dissociated self-states are automatic in the sense that they are activated involuntarily and that we are reduced to a scripted set of behavioral and psychological responses" (p. 35). This is the opposite of a religious experience that bears the fruits of wholeness—the IFS qualities of the SELF: Calmness, Clarity, Curiosity, Compassion, Confidence, Courage, Connectedness, and Creativity. When self-states are partially to fully dissociated, the content of their being is similarly quarantined and unavailable to the center of consciousness. In such states, these parts are apt to cause devastation, some as exiles below the surface of awareness and others erupting as either extreme protectors—"firefighters," in the language of IFS. They are those parts that are apt to ignore the destructive results of their reaction, as other fear-ridden managing parts remain stuck in a rigid, repetitive role.

74

## Self-states

It is worthwhile to take note of what Hill conceives as self-states— "assemblages of a central affect regulating system and five cognitive systems: (1) attentional, (2) perceptual, (3) representational, (4) memory, and (5) reflective" (pp. 37-38). Here, we can ascertain that the entire mind-body-brain is at play.

To give attention to the fifth cognitive system, in particular, as a way of describing what I understand to be a blended state, I borrow Hill's language: A self is blended when its "reflective functioning is either severely compromised or deactivated entirely . . . , when affect is dysregulated, [and] when compromised . . . , high-level reflection is replaced by the activation of scripts using forms of mentalizing that assimilate information into primitive schemas and generate certainty" (p. 44)—assuredly, a certainty akin to delusional thinking. Therein lies the functional structures of those parts of our internal system that offer resistance to change, for change requires the ability to doubt, to face uncertainty, and to trust in the collaboration of all of the parts of the self in manifest conflict. Only the Self, fueled by the SELF, is up to the challenge.

## Metacognition

The work of IFS therapy is possible, as is the work of all effective psychotherapy models, perhaps because we humans "are capable of metacognitive processes that enable us to think about thinking and feeling" (Hill, p. 44). We can engage with and also engage our parts—our self-states—with each other. One way or another, "the organization of the self (me, ego) is affect-state dependent" (p. 49). So, also, is the Self, the more evolved self, that center of consciousness more harmoniously connected to the multiplicity, more in harmony with and through and by the SELF. This is our true Self—always in evolution, always imperfect, always in relationship in the great experiment of love.

75

We must not forget, in the collaborative endeavor, to witness, retrieve, unburden, and resource disordered parts of the personality (separate from or antagonistic to the whole) that the brain is an enormously complex "information-procession machine. . . ."

> Neurons combine to form neural networks which in turn combine to make up modules (e.g., a face-recognition module); and these modules combine to make up larger systems (e.g., the perceptual system). Systems comprise subsystems, which themselves comprise subsystems, and so on. (p. 50)

The genius of IFS therapy is that it can engage with this complex system via a dialogue with this world of possibly endless possibilities. I made contact with an early exiled part of myself that expressed itself as a lamenting Greek Chorus that filled an ancient agora. At first, I despaired at the seemingly endless task of dealing with this crowd, but I soon learned that I did not have to engage each Chorus member, I only had to make contact with the one who looked at me. Offering this early subsystem—a toddler afraid to disappoint a fragile mother—was a simple way out of its fixed relative posture, one that released the Chorus of its lamentation. Hill says,

> Complex systems self-organize into new organizations as a result of myriad small, simple changes, with each element doing its own simple thing while the whole is acquiring increasing complexity and emergent properties. At some critical point, there is a qualitative shift in the organization of the system. (p. 51)

## Integration of the Multiplicity

In IFS, we speak of the SELF leading the system to its birthright—the integration of the multiplicity into a whole. The therapist brings a SELF-to-SELF intent via the interactions of the therapist's Self with the emerging Self of the client, something that we initiate and conduct from the center of our brains—our limbic system. Just imagine how transformative it can be when, from a centered and grounded limbic system, a person eventually makes contact with another person via their limbic system and effects a resonance that invites that person into a subjective experience of affect tolerance and resilience. Imagine the quieting of disturbances.

No matter the school of psychotherapy, the fact is that techniques don't heal; relatedness does. Techniques and strategies and methods give context and style to relatedness—give criteria to evaluate the potential effectiveness of the approach. The elixir is the comingling of Self-led energy from both sides of the equation, and this is mostly a right-brain enterprise in spite of the unitary left-brain approaches that many models advance. Hill, a psychoanalyst with a scientific bent, says,

> In Western culture there is a tendency to think that our left-brain, rational processes are in control. This is the central theme of [Iain] McGichrist's [2009] book, *The Master and His Emissary.* The left brain *thinks* it is in charge, but in reality, it is unaware that it is the emissary of the right brain's emotionally based bidding. The right brain is the seat of emotional and social intelligence . . . , and psychotherapy is first and foremost a right-brain endeavor. (Hill, pp. 74-75)

Our early experiences find their imprint in the affective chain of our brain's information system. The right brain holds, in imagery, the content arising from the brain stem and limbic system; the left brain gives language to the felt imagery. Having spent many years treating personality-disordered individuals, and aware, as Hill describes, that "character traits consist of implicit memory systems developed as an adaptation to different situations and activated in specific contexts" (pp. 78-79), I remember a frequent returnee to the emergency room telling me that no one could love him because there was no one there. I later understood, as an IFS therapist, that an extreme protective subpersonality was letting me know that the "self" had been effectively hijacked, that layer upon layers of exiles suffered beneath his borderline-antisocial protecting mask. When his attachment system was activated, his implicit memory system mediated his sense of self in an attempt to co-regulate with another implicit or explicit system in a way that meets Hill's descriptive definition of transference:

Transference . . . can be understood as an activation of implicit memory systems in response to unconsciously perceived likenesses between a present relationship and a past relationship to which one has adapted. (pp. 77-78)

In that exchange, in the middle of the night, the patient was not experiencing the reality of present time but the implicitly stored realities of his early life projected onto our encounter. Mercifully, a well-intentioned protective part sought to relieve him of an unbearable hurt, although in a misguided way—suicide. There was no one there, he said, and thus, a profoundly dedicated but panicked protector desperately wanted to end the exile's pain and his own futile attempts to alleviate the host (the patient) by killing all three. Suicide is most often murder by a desperate and misguided protector in the individual's internal family.

Given that we "are overwhelmingly and most basically implicit beings" and that we have a natural propensity to co-regulate with another implicit being, it makes therapeutic sense that the therapist's Self offers to the self of the patient at least an initial knocking at the door, an invitation into the safety of the present moment. Therapy will have as its goal "alterations to implicit memory systems . . . changes of the most basic kind, changes to the way we are, changes to our implicit selves" (p. 79). I am inclined to interpret Hill's statement as referring to all of those parts of us that want to benefit from the light of awareness and consciousness shed by the SELF.

For each part, subpersonality, complex, self-state, depending on one's theoretical ground, affect is at the heart of our subjectivity, and implicit communications of affect are the fundamental means by which we convey our subjectivity and encounter the subjectivity of others. The exchange of implicit communications of affect establishes the intersubjective field. In Schore's model these are understood to be communications between "implicit selves" (Hill, p. 80). I submit that our parts are also "implicit selves."

## The Implicit Self

Again, we see the references to multiplicity and, furthermore, Hill, who brought Schore's scientific understanding of psychobiology to the world of relational psychoanalysis in the New York area, is one of those practicing theorists who have helped translate interpersonal neurobiology into "novel 'evidence-based' formulations of psychotherapeutic treatment grounded in the neurobiology of regulation theory" (p. xv). Hill expounds on Schore's concept of the implicit self in the following pivotal quote:

> The implicit self . . . refers to the psychobiological state of the self in a given moment. . . . Schore's ideas about the implicit self are, I believe, an update of Donald Winnicott's "true self" based in spontaneous experience and of Daniel N. Stern's (1984) observations of the subjective sense of self. The detached experience of dissociation can be thought of as a detachment from implicit self-experience—from bodymind. (Hill, p. 80)

(See Winnicott, 1965, *The Maturational Processes and the Facilitating Environment;* D. N. Stern, 1984, *The Present Moment in Psychotherapy and Everyday Life.*)

I propose that our parts that arise from the storage bins of our personal unconscious live on the continuum of dissociation, our most basic and creative defense against the residuals of life's traumatic experiences. (See Colin A. Ross, 1994, *The Osiris Complex,* and, 1997, *Dissociative Identity Disorder.*) Where would psychotherapy be without the manifestation of the therapist's Self-led presence and engagement, with the therapist's bodymind in the sacred, therapeutic moment with the client? Internal Family Systems joins the practitioners of other "evidence-based" therapies in this regard. Hill says,

Implicit communications are the primary means by which trust and the therapeutic alliance are established. Facial expressions, eye contact, gestures and postures, and prosody convey *unequivocally* the therapist's interest, receptivity, recognition, and acceptance of the patient's implicit expression of self-experience. . . . Therapeutic sensitivity and nurturing intentions are implied, communicated unconsciously from implicit self to implicit self.

Implicit self-states, communicated involuntarily, may be very different from the conscious, explicit self-state communicated in words via the left brain. The left brain is responsible for constructing verbal narratives of our experience and tends to put a socially acceptable, self-enhancing spin on things. [See Michael S. Gazzaniga, 1998, *The Mind's Past*.] Implicit communications, on the other hand, are involuntary, direct communications from one nervous system to another, without editing. There is a certitude that accompanies implicit communication that is unmatched in explicit communications. When explicit communication is different from a simultaneous implicit communication, we do well to trust the implicit—the implicit self cannot fake it. (Hill, p.81)

This implicit self is the authentic self, the self that is the *prima materia,* imperfect, incomplete but real substance out of which will emerge the Self through the purifying fires of the SELF in the crucible that is life.

The above extended quote from Hill merits further consideration and reflection as it pertains to my attempt to explicate what I understand when I, as an IFS therapist, use the terms "self," "Self," and "SELF."

1. The explicit verbal narratives that the self composes via the mechanisms of the left brain serve the intent of the self or the Self. For clarification, and perhaps for simplification, I use the term "self" to represent the state of the center of consciousness as vulnerable to or even affected by interjecting parts. I use the term "Self" to represent a more "SELF-led" center of consciousness that, consequently, is more able to differentiate itself from the usurping

influences of a dissociating part or parts—a center blessed, endowed, energized with the quality of the SELF, a center that is hospitably welcoming to the needs and to the gifts of all parts of the internal system.

2. The implicit messages that cross over directly from one human nervous system to another may be automatic and immediate, bypassing conscious direction. But a self partially or fully blended by a part, from a mildly annoying subpersonality to an independently operating despotic alter, would operate under the voluntary management of that part. Whereas, a Self-led individual may have, over time or in a moment of mystical insight, given itself over to the practical wisdom of the SELF, according to James's explanation of a religious experience, an experience that does not necessarily leave the domain of the ordinary. Einstein was reported to have said that everything is a miracle. Therein lies the certitude that escorts the implicit communication, both when the self has been transformed into a faithful servant of the SELF as a Self, and when the self has been captured by the content and processes of those entities arising from the personal or universal unconscious—the system that is populated by all the members of our internal family.

3. Yes, indeed, the implicit self cannot fake it. This fact applies to the ordered and disordered self. The psychobiology and neurobiology of this phenomenon is beyond my grasp to explain, but the implications for the conduct of one's life, for the conduct of psychotherapy invites an extended meditation beyond the scope of this essay. Suffice it to note, that even SELF-led Selfs such as Buddha and Jesus were neither perfect nor complete. They were, as traditions reveal, aware of their evolutionary nature. (See K. Armstrong, 1993, 2004, *A History of God.*) Buddha continued to practice breathing and smiling to ward off a slide from his implicit state; Jesus prayed, called out to his Abba in his moments of

81

crisis and despair. And, we humans, one and all, are not spared the crucible of the evolutionary development of the self. (See R. Kegan, 1982, *The Evolving Self.*) into the Self on our return home to the SELF. Science, religion, and poetry dance together in this search for the Elusive SELF.

*. . . the loneliness of extreme old age is a matter*
*not only of what is now gone but also what is now present.*
*Old age is a diaspora.*
—Luke Timothy Johnson, 2015, *The Revelatory Body*

## CHAPTER SIX: OLD AGE AND THE INTERNAL FAMILY SYSTEMS THERAPIST

### Reaching Advanced Old Age

Nearly a half century ago, when I taught Developmental Psychology to nursing students, my thinking was framed by Chapter 7, "The Eight Ages of Man," in Erik H. Erikson's (1950) book, *Childhood and Society*. Now, however, I realize that I had only superficially perused another of Erikson's books, *The Life Cycle Completed,* (1998), in which he expands on his understanding of *very old age*, having reached that stage himself. I also want to thank Theodore Lidz, M. D., for the psychoanalytical understanding he generously offers in his 1976 book, *The Person: His and Her Development Throughout the Life Cycle.*

The students received my approach with open and critical minds. However, in this chapter, I delve more into relevant key concepts found in Helen M. Luke's 1931 Jungian analysis of old age expressed in her book, *Old Age: Journey into Simplicity.* I do so with an eye to furthering my understanding of the SELF central in IFS philosophy and methodology as applicable especially to old age.

Some of us in the IFS community have reached old age and advanced old age. Eighty years of age seems to meet a basic criterion of advanced old age, even in the 21st century. In my musing about the lifelong dance I have entertained with my self, my selves, and my Self, I note how often the SELF took charge of the dance, swept me to the center of the dance floor, and held me there—mesmerized in a dervish spin—in a moment out of time. How often did this experience offer me a correction, alter the map I had plotted, close and open gates, or send me head-over-heels down a ravine or to a near-death climb up a mountain into a wilderness beyond my imagination. At other times, the contact touched me while I rested on the lee side of a hill caressed by a light breeze, or on my first sighting of a painting, or while reading a poem for the first time, or when contemplating the elegance of a locomotive, or when taking in the endearing smell of an infant.

And then there were the times when young exiled and underdeveloped parts of me screamed for rescue while extreme protective parts, often adolescent rebels, took over the helm of my ship and cast bow and stern into foaming shoals. But this is a story revealed and discussed in my earlier writing. (See C. Robillard and M. Duclos, 2003, 2005, *Common Threads: Stories of Life After Trauma,* and 2011, *Cultivating Hope with Abuse Survivors.*)

In these and in so many more universally attested experiences across cultures and the globe, countless folks realized their confrontation with the presence of Otherness. For some, that moment was at the hour of death or a moment of near-death—one of calm or one of terror. To those who experienced an unshakeable calm, we on the outside bow before the touch of an invisible hand that fated such a saving destiny manifested after much pain and suffering.

In the second half of life, especially into very old age, the journey into one's internal family with all of its members reveals itself differing from the forages attempted in one's younger years. Individuals, from childhood to advanced old age, who graced me into communion with their internal family members in the sacred time and space of therapy, attest to the difference between figures born of the client's developmental stage and those rising from the archetypal reservoir. What follows concentrates on the tasks of the second half of a life nearing its end.

When I think of polarities in IFS, I think of the conflicts of opposites and that our task in our later years, as defined by Luke, is to learn "through the bitter conflicts of the opposites to discriminate every smallest thing or image as unique and separate" (p. vii), to get to know

84

them by witnessing them, by inviting and retrieving them into the now so that, in trust, they will let our Self protect them and manage the roles we are all called to play in this world until the end. Luke writes that the goal of these last years is to glimpse the "objective cognition, which Carl Jung called the central secret [to having] begun to distinguish the ego from the Self [SELF] which is ours and not ours" (p. vii). "The choice . . . is whether [we] will let go of everything else so that a new man who is the creation of Mercy will be born, or whether [we] will hold on to the old man, to rejection of that emptiness which is the fullness of Mercy" (p. viii).

This is the paradox William James so fully grasped; that "the true journey of the soul [is] to offer in sacrifice our past strengths and triumphs" (p. ix). The archetypal journey of the great souls that Luke references confirms that the "apex of achievement [is] known in the agonies and dangers of a general letting go, through which emptiness comes, into which glory may enter" (p. x). How clear a reference this is to the dying of the ego so that the Self might arise from the ashes. And for the elderly, there is a particular obligation that can be discerned by the following criteria: "If an old person does not feel [the] need to be forgiven by the young, he or she certainly had not grown into age but merely fallen into it, and his or her 'blessing' [of the young] would be worth nothing. . . . [It] would not spring 'out of humility that knows *how* to kneel, *how* to ask forgiveness'" (p.27).

When Luke analyses the transformation of William Shakespeare's King Lear, she notes: "The exchange of blessings between one human being and another is the essence of life itself." How apt a description of the IFS therapist who, with all dedicated therapists of every school, takes on the mantle of the elder and practices the occupation of "listening to the smallest of concerns of [and] talking with . . . , never preaching to . . . , those who are still caught" in the disarray of their fracturing; always interested in and concerned with "offering a glimpse of inner freedom" to the other (pp. 28-29). And this inner freedom comes about when we can "recreate in imagination" the beings of our inner world "until [their] reality in the psyche is realized" (p. 36).

### Devotion

Devotion is what saves us. "Devotion to something beyond the ego, something that [we] love with real integrity without counting the cost. . . . This object of devotion will carry for [us], for the time being, a projection of [our] hidden and often unconscious awareness of the Self" however distorted is the projection of our devotion (Luke, pp. 37-38).

Saul of Tarsus is an example of the devotion of a zealot-executioner transformed into Saint Paul, a committed, willing victim, one who became devoted to the SELF, which is how I read Helen Luke's use of the term "Self" in the above quote. Luke quotes British poet and theologian Charles Williams as having written, in 1938, in *He Came Down from Heaven and the Forgiveness of Sins,* that "unless devotion is given to a thing that must prove false in the end, the thing that is true in the end cannot enter" (Luke, p. 38). During our early stages of devotion, what we understand SELF to be reveals itself to be quite other in the end. The God to whom the adherents of a religion devote themselves in their idealistic youth turns out to be the fiction of an earnest imagination that must yield to its negation. The teacher from Nazareth was seen to be a traitor to the fiction of a wrathful deity as he discovered the One he claimed as his Merciful Abba. Thus, we are led to bow to the all-accepting and endlessly hospitable SELF to the great benefit of our internal family.

### Co-inherence

"Co-inherence" refers to the relation between the human and the divine and alludes to the mutual in-dwelling spoken of in patristic literature. Luke reminds us that in Shakespeare's *The Tempest* Prospero finally arrives at the *temenos,* that center of the labyrinth—the safe place, the center of the soul, the self's rebirthing place, the holy pre-cinct—"where the unconscious content can be safely brought to the light of consciousness" where the ego returns to its womb, the SELF. Such is our destined goal—to reach that space-less space "in the uncon-scious where an individual, through long years of inner work, may at last find his way to the self-knowledge which is the City of God" (p. 38).

The related note at the bottom of Luke, p. 38, is worth including here: "** cf. Oxynhyinthus Papyrus, Gospel of the Hebrews, quoted by Clement of Alexandria, text restored by E. G. White. *The Apocryphal New Testament,* ed., by M. R. James, 1927: *'And ye shall know your-selves that ye are in God and God in you. And ye are the City of God.'"* Yes, we are in SELF and SELF is in us; and, if we are willing, our center of consciousness will be Self-led.

### Remembering William James

James saw the religious and psychotic experience as made of the same cloth. To illustrate this concept, Luke quotes from Shakespeare's *Midsummer's Night Dream*: "The lunatic, the lover, and the poet are of imagination all compact" (Luke, p. 40). Luke explains:

If this absolute power of the imagination overwhelms a man's rea-son, drowning his ego-consciousness so that, in Jung's words, there is nobody there to give it form, it creates the lunatic. In the lover, it is experienced first in projection and may lead either to possession by ego-centered desire, or to the ever-growing consciousness of the love and compassion that transcend emotion; but it is the poet's eye in each of us that "glances from heaven to earth, from earth to heaven." Thus, the therapist's role [is] not only as mystic and prophet but that of poet. With such a responsibility, it is no wonder that the prayer of all conscious therapists echoes their song and grateful laughter when the SELF messages the wisdom of the *Ein Sof.* (p. 41)

But that wisdom does not appear in neon lights on the billboard in the internal or external agora. Luke speaks of it as Jung's . . .

> unknown "something" in the unconscious which seems to urge every individual through dreams, through synchronistic events, wherever [it] touches the realm of the archetypes toward greater consciousness, and when the time approaches for the final "letting go" preceding the experience of death, [it] begins to urge the ego toward [death] by pressing for [its] freedom again. (Luke, p. 43)

The unknown something must be free. It will let itself be imprisoned by us until such time as we place the key that it gives us into the lock of our own making and welcome its presence. Luke says, "In the 'acausal orderedness' (Jung's phrase), the moment of full consent comes only when the individual suddenly awakens to the fundamental roots of his Shadow projections and accepts them all" (pp. 44-45). To take back, as our own, all of the brokenness we see in the world and in others, all of the psychological underdevelopment and all of the capacity for darkness and evil with an inviting embrace—the infantile adult, the enemy, the disgusting and rejected—that is the key that opens us to the experience of Otherness through the surprising energy liberating the Self.

And how does the Self know that it is being liberated into Selfhood? It is through the experience of felt relatedness. For as long as unintegrated parts of the psyche are also blended with the center of consciousness (the fragile "ego," "me," "I") there is only the illusion of freedom: "Since there is no separate identity there can be no relatedness, no exchange" (Luke, p. 69). Differentiation is the thing, and more than an "I-it" separation. Indeed, as philosopher Martin Buber (1878-1965) taught in 1923, it requires an "I and Thou" relationship; that is, a full, direct, mutual relationship between persons—a relationship that implies caring, concern, and compassion for the connection to hold firm. The IFS therapist has no intent to exile, to eradicate, to kill off any part of the psyche while walking the path of integration. An often-repeated statement—"all parts are welcomed"—translates into a commitment to love all parts, including all parts of the therapist, all parts of the client. The IFS therapist welcomes all—all that *is*. In the mental health treatment system, welcoming all parts is, sadly, anathema because of fear and misplaced social control. But this is neither the time nor the place for that conversation. So, I return to the commitment to love, a topic explored by Thomas Lewis, Fari Amini, and Richard Lannon (2000) in *A General Theory of Love*, which I discuss in Chapter Twelve.

When Luke tells us, "Even in that hell [of] refusal . . . rejection of love . . . , 'It,' 'He,' 'She,' is there in the darkness, and there is much evidence which reinforces a belief that at the moment of death itself the root of love is suddenly revealed for who knows how many" (p. 73). I dare to extrapolate that at the moment of the many deaths of the ego over a lifetime, love is what energizes and reveals the resurrection of new life. Luke adds:

> The true healer is always an "intercessor," not a remover of symptoms, which then simply go from one part of the psyche to another. Moreover, the word to "intercede" is very near to the word to "forgive" or to "pardon." To "give for," to "yield between" in their true meaning is each an expression of the love which "endures all things, bears all things" without any demand. (p. 80)

To let all parts be free to be themselves—friend or foe to the emerging Self—to let go of wanting to make self and others better, to take them as they are, to be as we are, I as I am, and you as you are, is to be like the ONE who IS, like the "I AM." This is how we make it possible for our self and for every other to be touched by the OTHER. This is how we create a hospitality that sets us all free to be fully all that we are in an ever greater harmony. We make it possible for friend and foe to find their amity in the emptiness of cohesion.

## The Mercy

Luke proclaims that the Mercy that is "emptiness" is Compassion— "compassion," say the Buddhist; "agape," say the Christians. It is what "contains all opposites." This is how Luke begins her commentary on "Little Gidding," the fourth and final poem of T. S. Eliot's (1943) *Four Quartets,* that discusses time, perspective, humanity, and salvation. I read *Four Quartets* during my early middle years, and I admit that the meaning of the poems barely sank through my shallowest understanding. Even now, despite being guided by Luke, I am still challenged to my core. The choice is mine—is ours—in late old age "to let go of everything else so that the new man, who is the creation of Mercy, will be born, or . . . hold on to the old man, to [the] rejection of that emptiness which is the fullness of the Mercy" (Luke, p. 90).

Luke continues: "In the undifferentiated unconscious every image flows into every other and *is* every other" (pp. 96-97). In the early years of moral development, after the awakening to the tree of knowledge of good and evil, we . . .

> go individually on the long journey in the dimension of time in which [we] may learn . . . through the bitter conflicts of the opposites to discriminate every smallest thing or image as unique and separate. Thus, we gradually approach the "objective cognition," which Jung called the central secret, and find at last that, having distinguished the ego from the Self [SELF] which is ours and not ours, we begin to enter the dance: and now there comes a change—it may even be felt as a complete reversal. (p. 97)

In that developmental process, we are offered the opportunity to be introduced to our parts. We are presented with the option to take the return journey to the SELF as a Self.

## The Basic Question

The basic question, "Who am I?" haunted our ancestors since the first moment of reflection. By the time of the Luxor Temple in Egypt, the question had become an instruction: "Man, know thyself, and you are going to know the gods." This profound statement found a permanent place in stone. So, did the "Know Thyself" inscribed on the *pronaos* of the Temple of Apollo. Luke says it is our task to . . .

> gain objectivity about the ego, [to] recognize to some degree our projections, [to] realize that the human brain cannot bring enlightenment, [to] glimpse that we are the other and yet not the other—one yet many [and] experience the truth that we know nothing about who we are and never shall. In Jung's 1957 book, *Memories, Dreams, Reflections,* he says: "The older I have become the less I have understood or had insight into or known about myself." (Luke, pp. 98-99)

As a theology student in New England during the early 1960s, I chanced to be at a meeting where Richard Cushing, Archbishop of Boston, was giving some remarks about the Second Vatican Council after his return from Rome where he had visited privately with Angelo Roncali (Pope John XXIII). Cushing stopped in the middle of his remarks and, in an aside, said that both he and the Pope had agreed that, in their advanced old age, they knew very little and knew themselves even less. Silence gripped his audience. As I returned to the monastery that day, I somehow knew that this was the most important thing Cushing had said, but I did not realize how important. Today, a half century later, I catch a glimmer of that brilliant and humble realization. I once thought I knew myself. That illusion has been mercifully torn away. I have been blinded and see more clearly now; my hands invisible in the darkness. *I just am, and I do not know what that is.*

### Suffering

In the last and brief section of her book, Luke reflects on the place of suffering during the quest to know one's Self during our later years. Given the tenor of her words, it is evident that she knows of what she speaks—the healing and cleansing work of suffering—something not to be avoided at the cost of the loss of Self. She insists that we must be . . .

willing to pay the price in suffering of the kind which challenges the supremacy of the ego's demand. This is the crux of the matter, (and we may pause here to recognize the exact meaning of the word "crux" [the decisive or most important point at issue]). The ego will endure the worst agonies of neurotic misery rather than one moment of consent to the death of even a small part of its demand or its sense of importance. (p. 104)

If only this suffering were dramatic, meriting the acclaim of the crowd. If only it were to be carried out up-front and center gathering in fame and glory. But, alas, such is not the case. This suffering takes place in the same hidden room as prayer. And the work? Well, it is the "tracking down some of the continual evasions of the ego by uncovering our fear of humiliation. . . . For the truly humble person [the work having been done], no humiliation exists. [It is thus, that] the way to humility lies through the pain of accepted humiliation" (p. 105).

Accepting Luke's invitation to reflect on the meaning of the word *crux*, I am brought to the moment of the archetypal figure of the SELF on the crossbeams of Golgotha, pulled apart to the four corners of the compass, as the template for our total and final emptying before the plenitude.

A long-remembered statement attributed to Thomas Aquinas comes to mind: *humility is reality with humor*. Oh, not frivolous bellyaching as a defense against absurdity, but the relaxed and smiling acceptance of our total dependence on the truly unknown that holds us in existence. How can one better describe the wisdom of the advanced elderly who chuckle at their not-knowing and are curious about the inevitable "surprise?"

The opposite of humility-bearing suffering is "hubris"—that arrogance, conceit, and haughtiness that morphs into the intentional use of violence to degrade others and which leads to one's nemesis, to one's ruination and downfall, to the destruction of the nascent Self back into the isolation of the unconscious, if not even into the non-conscious locked beneath numbed sensations. I can think of no other more terrifying hell, not even Dante's inferno. The ego, when identified with a blended hubris, cannot accept the human condition and, in Luke's words, "says unconsciously, 'I ought to be like God, free of all weakness,' forgetting what happened to God Himself on the cross" (p. 106). To suffer is to *under-stand* is to carry the burden of mankind. Such is the chosen vocation of the psychotherapist.

## The Self-led Therapist

The last nine pages of Luke's book, dedicated to the creative aspect of suffering, cascades to a final tranquility that would have made William James smile. She links the psychological and the religious into one and the same fullness blossoming out of emptiness.

We may be emotionally moved and filled with horror and pity when we hear of the tragedies of human lives at a distance, but the emotions lift no burden, they carry nothing. In contrast, the smallest consent to the fierce, sharp pain of objective suffering in the most trivial-seeming matter may have an influence, as the Chinese sage puts it, "at a distance of a thousand miles." We may be entirely certain that some burden somewhere is lightened by our effort. Close at hand the effects are immediately visible. Those around us may know nothing of what is happening, but a weight is lifted from the atmosphere, or someone is set free to be [himself], and the sufferer acquires a new clarity of vision and sensitivity to another's need. (p. 108)

Not only is it the therapist who is called to the creative suffering so fundamental in all spiritual disciplines and implied in the praxis of psychotherapy, but it is our human lot, our fate, our destiny embedded within us as SELF. To do the opposite is to be caught in the glue of self-defeating narcissism. "Nothing is as blinding as neurotic self-pity. We walk around in a fog" (p. 108).

93

Lest we forget that suffering is not the goal, Luke reminds us that "intense conscious attention" to what transforms us into greater wholeness surprisingly lifts the weight we willingly bear and find that it is extraordinarily light (p. 109). Jesus declares, "My yoke is easy, my burden light."

And then there is the joy that is nothing like what we think of as happiness, fun, pleasantness, good times. It is not of our making. It ensues. And we fight it off, for it demands that we give up our illusions. Luke is so right when she writes,

> There is in man a fear of joy as keen as the fear of suffering pain, because true joy precludes the pleasant feeling of self-importance just as suffering precludes all the comforts of self-pity. (p. 110)

How grounded in the ancient great traditions of the East is this perennial philosophy lived and taught by the well-known wandering rabbi who has shaped the psyche of the West.

The end point of a therapeutic experience is not the removal of symptoms but their transformation in the alchemical crucible into a pragmatic growth of hope and joy in the real dimensions of life. The end point of very old age is to be touched by the wholeness of the SELF and to thereby live humbly in, with, and through the SELF as a servant Self.

## Ego Integrity

When the ego has achieved integrity, it has reached an abiding Selfhood. The Self no longer fears death and accepts death as the last moment of inevitable dying. Despair, on the other hand, is the gnawing sensation that eats up every bit of realism and leaves one with the nauseating "feeling that time is now short, too short for the attempt to start another life and to try out alternate roads to integrity" (Erikson, *Childhood and Society,* p. 269). The self-disgust of such a person fills the consultation rooms with a sadness that weighs immovable on the soul as it oozes forth. It arises out of the client's despair. It "hides despair," wrote Erikson. It sucks all residual hope out of the air. The question persists: Why has Hope not emerged out of the client's first year and a half of experiences? Was the preponderance of his or her relational experiences not those of trust in the caretakers? Erikson, borrowing the words from *Webster's Dictionary,* defined Basic Trust as "assured reliance on another's integrity" (p. 269), This is what the client, whose infancy tipped the scale of experience on the side of felt mistrust, seeks in the therapist—that assurance of integrity from a Self-led other. "Healthy children will not fear life if the elders have integrity enough not to fear death" (p. 269).

In the hard work of suffering through that early developmental stage in the repeated remediation of previously uncompleted tasks, even into the substages of personality evolution in very old age (i.e., reduced energy, failing health, narrowing of concerns, preparing for death, and dying), those early exiles and their persisting outmoded contemporary protectors need relief in the arms of Hope. In IFS therapy, this is when young exiles will no longer fear leaving their imprisonment in the accumulated negative polarities that are the outcome of the infirmed evolution of the psychological development of the ego, the self. When client and therapist become more and more SELF-led Selves, when therapists accept to function as elders to their own internal children and neither fear the loss nor desire the extermination of those antiquated ego-states (self-states, subpersonalities, complexes), then there is sufficient courage (heart) in the dyad for clients to welcome all of their parts with the grounded Hope of sought-after Integrity.

The person, who in advanced old age, who has borne the burden of the human and the divine on the way to the hilltop to make one's life holy (whole) through sacrifice and the accepted suffering of crucifixion in the emptying of all judgments about good or bad, of pretense at merit, that person undergoes a religious experience beyond all understanding. As Augustine said, "If you comprehend it, it is not God." (See also Rohr, July 7, 2018, "Economy," Daily Meditations.) If we think we comprehend the SELF, surely it is not the SELF. If we think that we are the ones who solely transform the center of consciousness from its necessary illusions to incomprehensible clarity in the SELF, we have fallen into a delusion. James gave us language and courage to talk about this emergence, travel, and return of the self to the SELF via the Self in his pragmatic approach to the dance of nature and grace.

*So conscience manifests itself as the daimonion with Socrates,*
*and then it also begins to be called one's genius, one's guardian angel,*
*one's better self, one's inner, higher man [Self] or "inner voice."*
*Then it begins to be called* Vox Dei.

—C. A. Meier, 1986, Soul and Body

## CHAPTER SEVEN: INNER IMAGES HEAL

### Contacting the Self

If we sought to make imaginal contact with the SELF, or the SELF sought to make contact with us, it would not be a stretch to receive varied images of the Wise Old Man or Woman or even of a Wise Animal or of an ancient symbol—a pillar of light, for instance. Such an archetypal figure visited me in a midday dream, years ago, during a time of soul-wrenching loss and abandonment. The dream came to me after I had spiraled into a felt state of deeply familiar aloneness. Only after sinking into the poetic imagery awakened by dream symbology did I touch, for the first time, the exiled infant, begging to be loved—seen, retrieved, unburdened, and resourced—by the only one who could do that—my Self. At that time, I wrote the following poem.

### Devotion

Pillar of light
sharp blinding and bright
you draw me near
beneath that earliest
instant of despair
rooted since then
in the pit of fear
above the call to dare
a life set free
no longer caught

97

imprisoned without a key
in the cage I sought
that night in panic
she cast me out of bliss
to choke her pleasure
as I milked her breasts
threatening to open
and put dryness to an end
where no lips or kiss
in reverence and devotion
had yet unlocked the treasure.

(See C. Robillard and M. Duclos, 2003, 2005, *Common Threads: Stories of Life after Trauma.*)

## Inner Images Influence

In our daytime lives, we most often experience a connection with the SELF by living the eight qualities that Richard C. Schwartz (1997) identifies in *Evolution of the Internal Family Systems Model* in evidence under the leadership of the SELF, by being in the Self State, which Daniel Siegel (2010) describes, in part, in *The Mindful Therapist*, as "well-being [that occurs] when a system is *integrated*, [which] *involves the linkage of differentiated* parts [whose] *integrated flow* [is characterized as] *flexible, adaptive, coherent, energized, and stable*" (p. 262). And, when William James sought to verify what would validate an authentic religious experience, he referred to the virtues spoken of as the good fruits and the beatitudes in the New Testament. (See Part One, Lectures XI, XII, and XIII: The Varieties of Religious Experience.)

In the forward to Pieter Middelkoop's 1985 book, *The Wise Old Man: Healing Through Inner Images*, Robert Bosnak, author (1988) of *A Little Course in Dreams*, tells us that the Wise Old Man is "an archaic character of collective soul that lives buried deeply in everyone"

98

(Middelkoop, p. ix). We can make contact and interact with this and other figures through the process of active imagination, and Middelkoop "uses active imagination as the primary form of therapy" in his decades of practice (p. ix). The Internal Family System supports such a dialogue between clients and their parts as well as facilitates the direct contact of the therapist's Self with the client's hurting blended self. A dialogue with the entities of the inner world has a long history across ages and cultures and across spiritual and religious practices. That psychotherapeutic disciplines have appropriated this conversation is neither surprising nor esoteric. Our *selves* talk to us all of the time, and we talk to them, not only in the halls of our psychiatric institutions, but in ordinary life situations.

I remember Etienne La Rose, my French teacher during my senior year of high school. One bright spring day, I caught up to him on his daily walk through campus as he audibly talked to no one I could see— a familiar scene that fascinated the student body. I boldly approached him and asked, "To whom are you talking?" He answered with his usual wide-open smile, "To myself, of course. As long I know that I am doing the talking, no one is going to take me away in a straitjacket to the Bangor State Hospital." Surprisingly, this made a lot of sense to me, for I was aware that I, too, talked to myself, but in silence. (Ten years later, I completed a psychology practicum at that same hospital.) Over time, I learned that we are influenced and even controlled by entities other than our personal parts—entities beyond the veil. Such is the experience documented in humanity's long pre-history and history.

The purpose of all psychotherapy that respects the multiplicity of the mind and brain, which includes the body, and that wants to heal through inner images, is to "meet and understand . . . the forces that appear as persons or as animals and sometimes as wonderfully strange beings quite unlike any we have ever encountered in our ordinary life" (Middelkoop, pp. 4-5). Through his study and experience, Middelkoop has been able to state that "fairy-tale-like happenings . . . appear to have been organized from a central point," a point he calls the "core of the Self" (p. 20). This is "a person with whom we can have contact . . . , who develops initiatives with regard to us, [and who is] a guiding hand" (p. 2). It is important to state that I understand Middelkoop's *Self* as the *SELF* in my chosen vocabulary.

This "core presents itself in personified form" (p. 2). I think of a published novelist friend who tells us that she makes contact with her characters (not unlike so many other novelists), listens to them, writes what they say, and records what they do. She is the scribe of these revelations and conversations, of their collaboration. I think of the divine inspiration of sacred literatures.

Once again, in our continued discussion of the Elusive SELF, particularly in the world of IFS therapy, we seek to expand our grasp of what we mean when we speak of Self-leadership, of a way of being in this world that is inspired by a wisdom beyond our making. This all returns us to the sorting out of the roles played by the conscious and unconscious domains.

Carl Jung contrasted the ego (self), as the Center of Consciousness, from the Self (SELF) that both comprehends and is the center of the totality of the human psyche. The fundamental aim of psychotherapy is to promote an amicable relationship between the ego and the SELF. The beauty and the mystery of the SELF is that the . . .

Self [SELF] appears to know what is good and what is bad for human life and, moreover, that it is capable of executing a strong favorable influence on life. . . . I have come to think of the Core of the SELF as the *Imago Dei* and of all the other archetypal figures as "divine beings" [as *energeia*]. (Middelkoop, p. 10)

As the core of consciousness arises from the depth of the unconscious—a resurrection of sorts—the SELF, which is both the center of the psyche (visualize a sphere) and its totality, finds its core at the junction point, at the center point, at the boundary of the conscious and the unconscious realms. In this existence, "the ego strives for something

100

but so does the Self [SELF], and . . . the ego may be confronted with different tasks" (p. 11). In those early developmental months, the ego emerges out of its original merger, its oneness with the SELF, and must gain the necessary strengths to exist in the outer sphere with a sense of autonomy; that is, I am a "me" distinct from all others. I have my own will. Failure at this willfulness predicts a future lack of power (energy) to align with the SELF as the "I" negotiates the tasks of initiative, competency, and identity in order to be generative in this life and become a Self. But an excess of undifferentiated willfulness predicts a runaway power that fends off the needed guidance from the SELF and the Self of others. What the ego (me) needs is "to find a mode of life that enables it to live in constructive harmony with the Self [SELF]" (p. 11).

In an earlier definition of terms, and as a reminder here, it is worth recalling that Middelkoop uses the term "*Self*" for what I refer to as the "*SELF*" and the term "ego" for what I call the "*self.*" I use the term "**Self**" for the ego who is in functional harmony with the **SELF**. And when the *self* is under the sway of other energies, other parts of the psyche that are, or apparently are, in disharmony with the *SELF*, we refer in IFS therapy to that self (ego) as being blended with a part or parts and, therefore, negatively affecting the person's wholeness.

The IFS protocols of Witnessing, Retrieving, Unburdening, and Resourcing are forms of active imagination that initiate the discovery and the acceptance of all the parts that populate the world of psyche and that intend to balance their polarities and unify their opposites. The me, the ego, the self, is imbued with the guiding energy of the SELF when the self is open to and accepting of the SELF's practical wisdom. Notice again that there is no uniformity in the use of nomenclature when it comes to speaking of the Elusive SELF. My use of the terms SELF, Self, and self, at the risk of saying this ad nauseam, is an attempt to approach the undefinable SELF by my Self that benefits from cooperating in this effort with the SELF's leadership.

101

At this point, I want to include two personal examples of active imagination. Both events came unannounced. None of the entities spoke to me in my native tongue, Canadian French, nor in my adopted language, American English, but in the symbolic language of images and gestures. They actively engaged with me as I actively engaged with them. I received them with courage in one instance and with cowardice in the other. I heard them as delivering a message from the SELF that demanded my participation

.

**Two Examples of Active Imagination**

Fifteen years ago, I recorded in free verse, the following experience (revised) in which I was visited by a vulture and an owl. I asked questions of the visitors. Why are you here? What do you want? What are you telling me? How are you trying to help me? And I listened and responded to what came up within me.

*The Vulture and the Owl*

While resting in the Tahoe, with the Border Collie in the back seat,

I wait to see which of my books the Bookman's Shoppe
will want to buy from out of the three boxes I left behind moments
ago.

I let myself relax: muscles     breath     heart.

Living on sleepless nights and little food,

watching the anger wash out of me after
an unexpected physical assault
only to be replaced with a belly full of loss and grief
chest and throat grappling with emerging sobs

102

in the car    in the office    in the grocery aisle
while eating lunch
most everywhere—I fall into a slight state of in-between,
a fertile ground for active imagination.

It reminds me of my Quebec embossed print—
*Entre le Chien et le Loup*—
that time between day and night when one cannot tell
where the forest meets the meadow,
whether it is a dog or a wolf standing there.
Surely a time to stay alert.

Eyes wide open,
I take in the high-country light-blue sky.
Young clouds move swiftly on the west winds, then
two birds crowd the space in front of me inside the car:
one covers the driver's side window,
the other fills the windshield above the steering wheel.

First,
a dark, dusty, feathered body of a vulture,
his head pointing away from me into the distance.

Turning away from the vulture,
I see the muted round face of a large gray owl,
my gaze fixed on them for an unmeasured time
before the vision thins out and I can see the sky again,
the vulture shimmering when I blink.
I mumble thoughts of death,
of the vulture's task to pick clean the bones of the dead,
to clear up the remnants, absorb the debris,
make the landscape pure again.

103

I think of leftovers,
clueless about my own inner decay, my conscious list seems long
enough and
time is short for cleansing.
In a state of in-between, I feel the urgency when

the owl captures my attention—
a second message of looming death.

I think of the owl out at night hunting unsuspecting creatures.
Mice come to mind.

I remember a dream of long ago during analysis—
a mysterious Jungian crone living in Montpelier, Vermont—
a dream of mice walking the mop boards in a rustic parlor,
a dream I described to her in minute detail.
Her very living room in the family farmhouse outside of town,
she reports, with a rare mixture of startled surprise and awe.

But I digress. I am well aware of my many personal mice
in need of harvesting by the night owl who
comes to visit me uninvited and unannounced at high noon with a
vulture.

Yet, while the vulture appeared first, he turns away from me.
Nothing personal on his part.
He has a job to do, a job he carries out.

It becomes clear to me. I have no say in the matter.
No place for feelings here.
It's an unavoidable get-on-with-it thing.

This is how to become a man.

The owl, on the other hand, faces me full on,
her eyes locked onto mine.
I think of her inviting me to partner in her hunting,
to offer her my mice as a sacred offering.

She is here to devour and transform these shadowy creatures
who live in my walls and leave
a trail of soul-rusting urine and droppings on my painted tin ceiling.
She invites me into the time left for soul-making.

I tremble a sigh of relief when I recognize her
as a symbol of wisdom—
that unmerited prize at the end of life—
integrity instead of despair,
won at the price of bone-blanching naked truth.

### The Strawberry, the Fish, and the Bee

The second visitation occurred a week later and was without words.
Everything was visual movements. I first wrote the poem below, and
later in the day, while still fully aware of the visitors' presence, I
recorded my reflections.

A strawberry
as huge as a watermelon
startles me,
blocks my view of this world,
promises tantalizing sweetness.

A bee
golden, glowing bright,
the size of my thumb,
a queen in search of a new home
enters into one of the folds.

A fish
dull silver-gray, dead,
mouth agape,
eye sockets empty,
welcomes into its nether world
the prospect of future honey.

After reflections, a few months after the assault and betrayal, and a day after my vision of the vulture and the owl, I wrote the following:

- It is almost twelve hours since, once again, I awoke in the dark morning hours before sunrise. I am in much need of rest, if not of more sleep. Thank you, Edmund Jacobson, for your relaxation techniques of long ago.
- The open window lets in the mid-afternoon mountain air. Children are noisily playing in the neighbor's yard. Surely, I won't fall asleep during this rare afternoon rest. It makes me happy to hear them laughing. I can manage a quieter face and a slower heartbeat paired with a slightly deeper rhythmic breathing.
- Eyes closed, I begin to drift off into a state of in-between. A huge strawberry appears close at eye level. I see a single golden bee approach a deep fold in the strawberry, which immediately turns into the empty eye socket of a dead fish. Cowardly, I open my eyes to stop the imagery. I am aware of the smell of death. I shudder, but I again catch, in awe, a merciful glimpse of the golden bee.
- There is no going back. There is no going back to life as I knew it. The assault and the ensuing events have broken open a door that

106

can never be closed. I will not hide from this murderous rage and flagrant betrayal. I will not live this experience of violence in secrecy. I will let natural retribution come before forgiveness. Healing, for everyone, comes from within. My pain was birthed by how I lived my storyline. My co-dependent tolerance for countless betrayals harrowed the ground of the eventual righteous violence and self-justifying abandonment that fell upon me. My residual chains from the past have been weakened. For that, I will forever be grateful. My hope at the moment is that I might find the weakest link and finally set myself free in all of my relationships by speaking and living the harsh but authentic truth of who I am. I envision the same for all. (For deeper insight into this subject, see C. Robillard and M. Duclos, 2011, *Necessary Illusions: Musings of a Man and Woman.*)

These personal experiences are only two incidences portraying how "inner images can have great influence on us. They can cause us to be in a particular mood or cause us to have a particular feeling; similarly, our thoughts can be directed by them" (Middelkoop, pp. 140-141). This is the basic understanding that directs the work of IFS therapy and which speaks to our multiplicity and to the age-old wisdom that it serves us well to know *our selves, all part of our psyche*—those from the archetypal domain and those from our temporal life. To make beneficial contact with our inner images, Middelkoop suggests the following conditions:

1. Close yourself off from the outer world for a while, and . . . occupy yourself only with what goes on inside you. It is advisable to close your eyes. . . . [Be] curious. . . .
2. Allow the images to change spontaneously.
3. [Actively involve] the ego [by] tracking down the inner logic [of the image], taking action, [and starting] a conversation with the people you meet. . . . (pp. 141-143, p. 156)

107

The inner images might be animals who want to be your guides (p. 147). Our task is to make friends with them (p. 152). Some images present as opposing figures, who also want to offer us guidance, and act as polarities that set off inner dynamics revealing more of our inner world (p. 148). Middelkoop adds the following, which resonates with IFS: "When we look at the figures in the imaginations, we get the strong impression that there is a central organization. It is for this reason that in the introduction we spoke of the core of the Self. We are not in a position to expand further on this" (p. 149).

Furthermore, it is worth noting that in IFS we use the language of parts, a language that admits the inclusion of terms from any and all traditions and contemporary science. Of special significance is the way in which Daniel Siegel's theoretical science of the Interpersonal Neurobiology (IPNB) complements the IFS praxis. (See D. J. Siegel and R. C. Schwartz, 2015, *An Historic Moment.*)

First, notice Middelkoop's understanding of this systems structure and his avowed awe at the inexplicability of the phenomenon he calls the *core of the Self.* He even references a central figure in the active imagination of a client who revealed "himself the Eternal One and Life" (p. 149). This is not unlike the experiences of mystics, of the inspired ones of the world's religions, large and small. Their poetry speaks the language of metaphors, for, as Rohr writes in the July 29, 2018, Daily Meditations, "The One and the Many,"

Metaphor is the only possible language available to religion because it alone is honest about mystery. [But], we must never be too tied to our metaphors as the only possible way to speak the truth. Rather, we must approach all metaphors and symbols humbly and respectfully, keeping all the inner spaces of the mind, heart, and body open at the same time. I would call such respectful and non-egocentric attention, *prayer.*

For those who seek to find words to express the experience of one's interiority, as lived through a lifetime, it is the same, whether one be a mystic, a poet, a prophet, a philosopher, a theologian, a psychologist, a psychotherapist, a physician, an intellectual, a cowboy, a peasant, a tradesman, a salesclerk, a mother nursing her baby, a picker of fruits and vegetable, or myself—a traveler of life's journeys. In the end, words fail us all. We descend into the realm from whence we came hoping to see clearly the who that we always were—the self that is transformed by the SELF into the Self, who becomes one with the SELF, as it always was and will be in the infinite and eternal evolving present.

Accepting the inadequacy of language in this search for the Elusive Self, I find it reassuring that "the Self [SELF] can provide an extensive range of learning situations" in the transformative process of the self (Middelkoop, p. 157). "The Self [SELF] has at its disposal a fabulous repertoire of healing or, if you like, *therapeutic actions*" (p. 158).

The dialogue with all parts of our internal world combines with all that exists and is the business of the self from the dawn of consciousness. "However forceful the intervention of the Self [SELF] may be, nothing will be undertaken unless the ego [the self] wishes it and gives it full cooperation. The ego retains its total freedom and the Self [SELF], however impressive its manifestation may be, will modestly withdraw as soon as the ego no longer requires [welcomes] its assistance" (p. 159).

In the Golden Verses of Pythagoras (569-500 BCE), the philosopher rejoices to realize that his disciples, who have tasted of the wisdom given to them . . .

by the ONE who had burned
the Sacred Tetrad in our hearts, that pure and immense symbol,

the source of Nature, and the pattern of the Gods . . .
have penetrated the secrets [and] have found haven in port.
(Antoine F. d'Olivet's French translation from the Greek converted into English by Marcel Duclos, 2018.)

This is the person who has confidence in being in the present, in staying in the experience of the present, in living by the *Leadership of the SELF,* that Image of the "IT," that One and Only Reality by which, in which, and through which the likeness of the SELF manifests—the Mystical, Cosmic Christ in another language and understanding. (See the writings of Pierre Teilhard de Chardin, S.J., philosopher, paleontologist, geologist, mystic; especially his 1959 book, *The Phenomenon of Man.*) Middelkoop speaks of such confidence:

> By learning to have confidence we mean learning to have confidence in the Self . . . the willingness to self-surrender and active decision taking without having any clear idea where we are going or whether we will come back unscathed (p. 163). [Signs and guides may appear and take us forward.] It is not so much a case of saying that [we] are confident as of doing something that proves [we] are confident (p. 164). [Thus,] the strength of the ego is reinforced so that it can freely enter into communion with the Self [who] has a freedom of its own. (p. 164)

This is a matter of existential trust.

Furthermore, Middelkoop writes, "The relationship between the ego and the Self has to be mutual. The ego will want to know where it stands, and . . . the Self leaves it in no doubt: 'I am always near'" (p. 165). The Self, in turn, will want to know what the ego is prepared to do. A trial will take place. When events occur that seem monstrous and wicked, such confrontations "do not require much violence. The monster merely needs to be told that you are not afraid of him" (p. 170). This is the very approach taken by the IFS therapist, who, with the qualities of "presence, patience, persistence, perspective, and playfulness employs a refined but simple IFS language of the art of helping— thanking the part for letting itself be known, encountering it with the qualities of SELF, especially compassion. (See F. G. Anderson, M. Sweezy, and R. C. Schwartz, 2017, *Internal Family Systems: Skills Training Manual,* p. 3.)

Middelkoop speaks to his reader to say that "as soon as you yourself begin to employ and strengthen your own power, the use of force is no longer necessary" (Middelkoop, p. 171). The harsh ascetic measure of the past and the reactive strategies to eliminate these parts are both unnecessary and detrimental, for they further exile the desperate members of our internal family and assault our well-intentioned managing and protecting parts.

To be sure, however well-intentioned parts might be, they can be ill-informed and themselves riddled with desperate exiled parts. Thus, "imaginal figures that arise from the unconscious are often very fearsome, [and the] freedom of the ego is not so self-evident as all that. The time for fooling around has gone, and you had better not mock the figures you meet there" (p. 171).

To repeat myself, "compassion" for these figures is the IFS *sine qua non* essential to intervention and solution. By interacting with them in hospitality, the Self tips the scale on the side of the union of opposites—to the point of harmony. It is up to the willing "self" to become a Self in this drama of active dialogic imagination.

Middelkoop concludes his comments with this final paragraph, which I quote at length:

The live drama in which you become involved in imagination differs from the drama enacted on stage. Not only are you allowed to handle your role in any way you wish, but the actor is also free to alter the play. The relationship between conscious and unconscious becomes highly variable as soon as the ego enters the imaginal inner world. A strange adventure then begins, in which we can bring all our qualities to bear. You don't have to abandon your rational, analytical thought. On the contrary, it is very useful, but without intuition as well you don't get anywhere at all. (p. 174)

To close this chapter, I repeat that our intuitive grasp of our natural multiplicity and attending range of dissociation, confirmed by the science of Interpersonal Biology, makes it possible for us to bring

111

the prospect of peace, justice, and joy to our internal and external families—near and far—for today and tomorrow.

*In certain kinds of walking and talking,*
*the soul comes out of hiding and*
*shows itself with unusual intensity of emotion.*
                          —Thomas Moore, 1994, *Soul Mates*

## CHAPTER EIGHT: JUNG ANTICIPATES IFS YEARS AFTER FICINO

### Know and Love Yourself

The IFS therapist commits to the easy burden of hospitality, to the welcoming of all aspects, all dimensions, all parts of the patient. In Chapter 5, "Psychotherapists or the Clergy," in Carl Jung's 1958 book, *Psychology and Religion: West and East,* he writes,

> It is a moral achievement on the part of the doctor, who ought not to let himself be repelled by sickness and corruption. . . . We cannot change anything unless we accept it. . . . But if the doctor wishes to help a human being, he must be able to accept him as he is. And he can do this in reality only when he has already seen and accepted himself as he is. (p. 339)

Of course, this is the perennial obligation to know oneself. "In actual life it requires the greatest art to be simple, and so acceptance of oneself is the essence of the moral problem and the acid test of one's whole outlook on life" (p. 339). I have to love the other as myself, even my enemy. Jung pushes the thought even farther:

> But what if I should discover that the least among them all, the poorest of all beggars, the most impudent of all offenders, yea the very fiend himself—that these are within me, and that I myself am the enemy who must be loved—what then? (p. 339)

The "what then?" presents the challenge of challenges. Jung continues: "Modern [and postmodern] psychotherapists . . . will admit that to accept himself in all his wretchedness is the hardest of tasks, and one which is almost impossible to fulfill" (pp. 339-340). The implications

113

of this thought direct the psychotherapist to avoid deceptive idealism—that offspring of perfectionistic grandiosity. We are who and how we are. We embody all of the qualities of all the gods. To think otherwise destines us to the trash heap, even when we euphemistically call it the "transfer station." "[We] are to live our proper lives as truly [as the anointed one] lived his in its individual uniqueness . . . " (p. 340). That is to say, completely, which is nothing like perfection, to the end as fully as one is.

I will now journey with Jung into the landscape of his vast internal world to glean insights into this, the mission of the hospitable psychotherapist who admits to his neurosis—that "inner cleavage—the state of being at war with oneself—that splitting of personality" (p. 340). The possible cure for such a rendering asunder of one's self (me, ego) demands that we drop into a "state of complete abandonment and loneliness [in order to] experience the helpful powers of our own nature" (p. 341)—that conversion into a reconciliation of opposite polarities within so as to effect a conscious balance, a complete humanity.

To return to the archetypal image of the SELF, the Christ on the cross, traitor to God and Country, holding the dynamic opposites of all that is in a unified whole, it is useful to recall other scenes of the archetypal SELF's humanity in the canonical and non-canonical gospel literature that has come down to us—the adolescent who wanders off leaving his parents in panic to negotiate the Jerusalem pilgrim crowd in search of him; the same adolescent who presumes to tell the temple priests how to do their job, and who, when found insulting his elders, tells his parents that he is following a higher calling, thus bringing about social and religious shame upon them in the holiest of Jewish places; the self-declared rabbi who snubs his mother, brothers, and sisters who arrive to see him by telling his attendants that he does not have time to see his family at the moment, being engaged in teaching and healing, his self-proclaimed higher calling; the leader of an itinerant band of disturbers of the status-quo who tells his associates to fend for themselves since he has accepted a dinner invitation with other friends across the lake; the unmarried man who stands up for prostitutes against a righteous crowd, stones in hand, and who dares to ask an outcast alien woman for a drink of water at her village well; the heretic who refers to the proper religious authorities as *a race of vipers;* the Jew who hangs out with the reviled tax collectors; the country carpenter who takes on the trappings of the messiah king and taunts the anxious police with social unrest; the peace-lover who resorts to violence to make his point—toppling the temple money-changers' tables and assaulting them with a whip thereby halting the unholy commerce of the powerful temple elite; the prisoner who in the jaws of defeat, one he brought down on himself, bleeding and destined to the fate of a vile criminal, brags about his kingdom, lucky for his judges, he says, one not of this world.

This is no sweet baby Jesus. This is one crazy prophet, perhaps a criminally insane SOB in the eyes of some, who holds the ultimate polarities in real and irreverent union. He did not live according to a socially sanctioned plan. He lived a life that revealed itself to him, and he ran with it. This is how new ways of being are born and made. This is how new ways of healing come about. This is how IFS therapy (one among many) uniquely reaches the Self-led consciousness of the like-minded.

Again, my mind returns to William James when I read the following words by Jung:

[The] psychotherapist . . . must have no fixed ideas as to what is right, nor must he pretend to know what is right and what [is] not—otherwise he takes something from the richness of the experience. He must keep in view what actually happens—for only that . . . act is actual. (p. 343)

Note: "a thing is 'real' if it 'works.'" [Trans.]

This is the criterion James applied to validate authentic religious experience, what we can apply to the behaviors that reveal Self-

115

leadership, behaviors that express IFS's Eight Core Qualities and the gifts of the Holy Spirit and the right view of the Buddhist. And, it must be held in the forefront of one's mind that there is no perfectly moral person. God is not perfectly moral. God is beyond the bounds of morality.

However, one does not access the core qualities as a Self without daring the domain of the unconscious, without daring to enter the crucifying point between the ultimate opposites—the conscious and the unconscious. In an address to clergy, Jung put it this way: "The opening up of the unconscious always means the outbreak of intense spiritual suffering. . . ; how thin are the walls which separate a well-ordered world from lurking chaos" (p. 344). Remember that Jung's subjects are psychology and religion when he says that "religions are systems of healing for psychic illness" (p. 344). Thus, it is that we psychotherapists face the unavoidable choice in our profession. Jung is not hesitant to teach that we are forced into the role of medicine man and priest, that we all need supra-human truths to perform the healing rituals of our calling. (Recall that Freud wanted analysts to be neither priest nor physician.)

> We must first tread with the patient the path of his illness—the path of his mistakes that sharpens his conflicts and increases his lowliness till it becomes unbearable—hoping that from the psychic depths which casts up the powers of destruction the recurring forces will also come. (pp. 344-345)

It is our human destiny and mandate to participate in the emergence and activation of our consciousness into an operating center, which in IFS, we identify as the Self led by the SELF.

The ultimate moral question is unanswerable without first contending with two questions: "Where does consciousness come from?" and "What is the psyche?" (p. 345). I raise attention to these questions, not to answer them, but to raise our awareness of their crucial importance to the entire discussion entertained in these essays searching for at least

116

a glimpse into the reality of the Elusive SELF that operates as the center and periphery and essence of the Psyche.

When in the IFS healing ritual/protocol we witness the benevolent intent of the images/figures/parts that first manifested as apparently malevolent, we know that polar opposites have found common ground, that the stars have aligned, that forces beyond our power to unleash have resourced patient and therapist into a new sphere made in heaven, in the kingdom of the gods, in the universe of multiplicity.

Jung wrote of his understanding of the healing process in a language not so different than James's and that prefigures the language that underpins IFS, and this is not the only modality that would merit mention in a larger discussion.

It is as though, at the climax of the illness, the destructive powers were converted into healing forces. This is brought about by the archetypes awakening into independent life and taking over the guidance of the psychic personality, thus supplanting the ego with its futile willing and striving. . . . To the patient it is nothing less than a revelation when something altogether strange rises up to confront him from the hidden depths of the psyche—something that is not his ego and is therefore beyond the reach of his personal will. He has regained access to the sources of psychic life, and this marks the beginning of the cure. (pp. 345-346)

I recall the middle-aged woman, who as a child of five, had been locked in a chicken-wire cage by a family member and then kept in the dirt cellar of the apartment house in which she lived. For her, who still felt as if she were in that cage, the "something altogether strange" that rose up in the inner scene in the Witnessing phase of an IFS session was the Christ figure who extended a hand. The SELF came to the aid of the Self. As the session evolved, the exiled child asked both the therapist and the Christ to take her out of her dungeon, confident that her jailor would have no power over the three of them. When retrieved (during the Retrieval Phase) from the horrors of the unending past and safely in

117

the present with not only the Christ and the therapist but, especially, with her adult Self, the little girl participated in the healing ritual of the Unburdening Phase. She sent all of her emotional and cognitive burdens into the deepest part of the ocean and welcomed, in the Resourcing Phase, the quality she most admired in the Christ figure that came from her recollection of a picture in a children's book of Jesus opening his arms to the little children. This was the beginning of not only the "cure" of her re-traumatizing dissociations, but the unfolding of her beauteous Self-led life—an epiphany of the qualities of the SELF.

I also recall a long-term patient in a psychiatric hospital where, some 40 years ago, I was doing a Clinical Pastoral Education internship. The patient's official diagnosis was chronic schizophrenia. The six 3-inch binders that held her recorded diagnoses and treatments were an extended study in psychiatric nosology. To this day, I am grateful to this woman who allowed me, a stranger on the unit, to approach her slowly and incrementally over several weeks, first nonverbally at a distance, then within arms-reach, walking up and down the interminable hallways alongside her, a half-step in front of her so that she could keep an eye on me. (She spent most of her daytime hours walking.) Eventually, I told her that I had been noticing how she walked swaying from side to side and wondered if there was something that she wanted us to know by her movements. She had been nonverbal for more than a decade. She did not, at first, respond to my query. Some days later, I told her that I wanted to walk like she did so that I might feel what it was like (hoping to learn something from her). I asked her to let me know, in some fashion or another, if she did not want me to companion her in this way. When she did not object, I began a weeklong experiment. I walked up and down the hall with her for twenty minutes at a time every chance I had during the course of the day. One day, the image of a huge bell in a church tower overtook me. I stopped and she stopped alongside of me. This was the first time that she had followed my lead or responded to my behavior. I told her that I felt like a bell in a church tower; and

118

she softly said, "Yes." Her first word in years, since even before her hospitalization.

This well-educated woman regained access to the source of her psychic life that had never abandoned her—her SELF. From the first joining in with her symbolic somatic language to the nonintrusive presence over time came the eventual story of her sexual trauma by a church official back in the old country. As the price of a cover-up, her father had sacrificed her in order to keep his prestigious clerical position. This woman had been walking across a bridge away from the church at the sound of the church bells at Vespers for these many years, hoping to be seen and heard and relieved of a past not of her making. When I left at the end of my internship, she was talking and no longer silently screaming her story up and down the ward. The senior psychiatrist took over her therapy, which he had been supervising. He was a European and had the touch she needed. To this day, I am grateful for the synchronicity of our meeting. I have often thought of the unknown elements of an IFS treatment that were imbedded in the somatic and Jungian approach that guided me without my knowing it. Schwartz was in the discovery phase of his method during that decade. Ideas arise in the world soul beyond time and space and find their blossoming in a willing one. We are, each and every one, all in the One.

I freely admit that these two patients live in my storehouse of heroes and heroines who have been my best teachers and guides into the catacombs and honeycombs of the psyche living in the flesh. I am ever so grateful to Jung for his daring to confront what lies below the surface of the water and for the analysts he trained who went on to teach ensuing generations. I was taught by the second generation.

Jung ends his essay with the following powerful assertions:
This spontaneous activity of the psyche becomes so intense that visionary pictures are seen or inner voices heard—a true, primordial experience of the spirit. . . . Such experiences reward the sufferer for the pains of the labyrinthine ways. From now on, a light shines

119

through the confusion; more, he can accept the conflict within him and so come to resolve the morbid split in his nature on a higher level. (p. 346)

This is what these two, and many other patients, allowed me to witness. This is the experience of depth psychotherapists—the certainty that as much as *theoria* and *praxix* are essential and necessary; it is "the attitude of the psychotherapist [that] is infinitely more important." It is when I did not have the proper attitude, did not live out of the SELF in the sacred moment and place of healing, that I failed to be of service to the other. A while back, I wrote a minimalist poem in atonement, using alliteration to drill down to deafening depths, in direct rescuing contact with these burdened exiled, protective, and managerial parts of myself to offer them the healing light of day.

**for too many patients, i**
suffer sun-stroked sorrow
alone     altogether abandoned
when withered wishes
caste cancerous caution
aside    away    along
long lingering lonesome
trails    trouble thoughts
because bitter burdens
thrash    try    trigger
mutinous memories    maim
poor professional protection
when windy wallowing
is inept    insufficient
at atonement again
for failures forgiven

**Ficino's Psychology**

I am also grateful to the Jungian analyst Thomas Moore whose books nourished me over the years. Having travelled some similar roads, I benefitted from the personal and professional subtexts of his writings. Moore completes his little 1983 book, *Rituals of Imagination,* in a surprising way. He provides his reader with a 10-page essay on the Psychology of 15th-century Renaissance Florence scholar Marsilio Ficino, who was better known as a theologian and philosopher than as a psychotherapist, but psychotherapist he was. Again, Moore never fails to surprise with the breadth of his knowledge as a true humanist.

I reference Moore's book because he gifts us post-moderns with a 500-year-old esoteric understanding of the importance of the soul, an understanding that is germane to our discussion—necessary, Moore implies. Quoting from Chapter One, Volume Three, of Ficino's *Three Books of Life,* Moore writes:

> If there were only intellect and body in the world, but no soul, the intellect would not be drawn to the body (for it is altogether immobile, and lacks the effect of motion, as if it were the furthest possible distance from the body), nor would the body be drawn to the intellect, since it is ineffective and inept in itself for such motion, and very remote from the intellect. So, if a soul, conforming to each, is placed between them, each one is easily attracted to the other. (Moore, p. 62)

We can substitute "mind" for Ficino's choice of the term "intellect." And soul, in his system, reaches out to the polarities of mind and body, and I would add, informs them into a whole. The role of the psychotherapist then, according to our Renaissance scholar, is to be the *"physician of the soul"*—Ficino's own words quoted by Moore and anticipating Frankl's 1989 book, *The Doctor of the Soul,* "the healer who finds in this world that which nourishes the soul" (Moore, p. 63).

Ficino invites the disquieted one to act in ways that the actions have a ritual quality to them that "speaks to the soul and nourishes the soul by attracting different kinds of spirits" (p. 64). Letting this symbolic language wash over me, I think of the IFS rituals inviting the spirits (parts) alive in our mind-body-brain to feed our soul.

Moore acknowledges that the root metaphor for Ficino's psychology is astrology [and music], more specifically, the planets" (Moore, p. 65). When I substitute the IFS concepts and language of parts, I see an apt metaphor for the multiplicity we so value today. Moore writes:

A person with all of the planets at play in his psychological life would be an individual of good temperament. These planets, like the notes in a musical scale, have to be "tempered." They have to be "tuned in" so they sound clearly in the life and character of the person. The psyche for Ficino, then, is polycentric, at least when it is in good condition. As Ficino says, if you are ever faced with a choice among the planets, choose all of them. (p. 65)

I see the individual of "good temperament" as one who is balanced and alive in the dynamics of the opposites with a "polycentric" psyche with all elements playing their role in the life of the whole. This is the natural inner sphere of multiplicity.

In the world of IFS, we choose all of our parts, we welcome all of our parts. The fully human person experiences and lives all parts with the responsibility to hold them in dynamic tension within the centerpoint of one's being. It is noteworthy to see how the above symbolic vision offers support and, centuries ago, validated the hospitable views of Interpersonal Biology and Internal Family Systems. Doctoring the soul implies mind and body, implies staying in and with the experience, suffering it through to the end "to feel as deeply as possible the tension created by this onslaught of the unfamiliar and unwanted spirit" (p. 66).

The psychotherapist is thereby called to stay with the patient—body, mind, and soul—witnessing the patient's experiences; retrieving the client's internal planets that are out of alignment; and orchestrating the multiplicity into a non-colliding orbit; unburdening the patient's planets (parts) from the attracted debris, and resourcing the whole with new harmonious orbits. Of course, this analogy can be stretched to the absurd, but it is more than surprising to encounter a renaissance perspective that is consonant with a contemporary approach requiring that "the psychotherapist . . . read a person's life and environment for images and the varieties of spirits it contains (pp. 66-67). This is what the IFS therapist and patient commit themselves to in the psychotherapeutic alliance—to engage in soul-making in a Self-to-Self connection.

## We are Transformed by Symbols

I return to a recurrent theme, that of the imaginal world in which the symbols of transformation operate. In the visual arts, humans have discovered and given expression to images that have symbolized some of our most profound felt experiences. In Chapter Six, "Old Age," and Chapter Seven, "Inner Images," we encountered the symbol of the cross, the *crux*. In *Symbols of Transformation*, Jung (1976) writes that each of us must bear the cross as a chosen burden in the heroic transformation of our own self. He expanded on his understanding of the phenomenon of the hero, a topic that relates to the beautiful complexity that is the journey to Selfhood, to Self-leadership through the carrying of one's individual cross. In everyday life, the heroic transformation most often appears ordinary and commonplace, making it nearly impossible to detect, at first glance, in our lives, and in the lives of others. The great myths of human existence are not found in the Disney World versions of the hero's and heroine's exploits. It is not sugar-coated in self-defense into banalities instead of the sacrificial nature of real living as an incarnated spirit with all of its burdens, the most central one being the shouldering of the self, or selves, we discover ourselves to be.

Jung says this when he comes to the point and identifies what constitutes the cross the hero carries. Before any other "tension of opposites" that arises at any moment in an individual's life, it is the destiny to bear the weight of the divine and the animal that sets the ground, that is the living symbol informing the anointed Self's unavoidable task to return the separated self to the One.

The cross, or whatever other heavy burden the hero carries, is "himself," or rather "the self," his wholeness [self, Self, and SELF], which is both God and animal—not merely the empirical man, but the totality of his being, which is rooted in his animal nature and reaches beyond the merely human toward the divine. His wholeness implies a tremendous tension of opposites paradoxically at one with themselves, as in the cross, their most perfect symbol. (Jung, p. 303)

This self that we discover ourselves to be is the creation of an "other than our self." Thinking of the myths of a virgin impregnated by the divine opens us to see the self as divine from its source: "The idea of supranatural conception, can, of course, be taken as a metaphysical fact, but psychologically it tells us that a content of the unconscious ('child') has come into existence without the natural help of a human father; i.e., consciousness" (p. 323). Instead, the self (ego) arises out of the "archetype of Transcendent wholeness—the self" [SELF] (p. 303).

When an IFS therapist readies to face the patient's burdens, the therapist must be ready to continue that excruciating confrontation of his or her own self hanging on the cross as the quintessential burden, as the transformational and recreative symbol that aims to bring to an end the ultimate opposite of one's being that is manifested in the polarities living at all levels of the psyche-soma-mind-body paradox. This is a paradox to the self (ego) who comes into being out of the compressed light in the dense darkness of the SELF. The self does not know from whence it comes. It must discover that it is not its own creation, and what a volcanic surprise this is. When life furnishes the necessary eruptions and disruptions at crucial developmental stages, moments of unavoidable initiatives, of identity crises, of the pain of differentiation and connection, when the self faces self-collapse into alienation and even extinction, it all makes sense. The self came to exist out of the SELF,

124

came to be, in time and place, a son or daughter of God. This is what Jung referenced when he spoke of "supranatural conception."

In staying with the theme of the hero's journey, of the self's (ego) necessary travails in its return to its origin, the SELF, the myth of the Anointed One is enlightening.

> Christ, as a hero and god-man, signifies psychologically the self [SELF]. That is, he represents the projection of this most important and most central of archetypes. The archetype of the self [SELF] has, functionally, the significance of a ruler of the river world; i.e., of the collective unconscious. The self [SELF], as a symbol of wholeness, is a *coincidentia oppositorum* [union of opposites], and therefore contains light and darkness simultaneously. (p. 368)

This merits repeating. The goal of human life is to ultimately realize in time and space, through the harmonizing of the human and divine in oneself after having let go of the illusion of our self-originating self-hood, a return to the wisdom of the SELF.

When the aforementioned mythical virgin, the Anima, opens herself up to the descent of the fertilizing breath of the divine, she willingly allows herself to be immolated on her cross and be SELF-led. Her Self, the center of her consciousness, yields to the divine core of her being. She becomes the heroine who bakes the Holy Bread of Life to nourish the multitudes. She becomes the mediating *anima, her Self, joining the self* in creative union with the SELF. She becomes the archetypal symbol of our soul that holds us in the dynamics of emerging wholeness, that confirms our self as participating in the numinous as a child of God, as having some share in divine nature. (See Jung, 1958, *Psychology and Religion,* pp. 391-392.)

I advance that the self is of the same nature as the SELF, and becomes more in the image and likeness of the SELF—that image of the OTHER—as it allows itself to be SELF-led, to become a Self in imitation of the One who took on the mantle of his calling. Jung says, "For psychology, the self [SELF] is an *Imago Dei* and cannot be distinguished from it empirically... (p. 392)." There is no way to deny that the Western psyche has been formed, for the past two millennia, by the Christian myth. Even those who deny its theological content do so because of its influence on the formation of the religious symbol system in the Western psyche.

During the mid-1980s, I attended a seminar having the proletarian title, "The Psychological Use of the Gospels," offered by the Jungian analyst Paul Huss as part of the doctoral program in Psychology and Clinical Studies at Andover Newton Theological School just outside of Boston. We learned how to discern, in the imagery and stories of that literature, the archetypes (imprints, templates, living images) of our Western psyche with longer roots in the human psyche reaching back to the great religions and spiritual systems of the past around the world.

The IFS world welcomes all of the living images and entities that populate the human psyche across cultures. That is why the client, and the therapist, who enters into the mystery and system of the internal family, is *ipso facto* embarking on a hero's journey, a journey into the darkest of nights and the brightest of daybreaks, for "the hero is the protagonist of God's transformation in man" (Moore, 1983, p. 86). As the SELF gives birth to the self, the self enters the crucible of transformation and becomes the Self who incarnates the SELF into the post-paradisiacal world, thus giving the ALL, the IT, God, an opportunity to heal the broken and burdened by experiencing the cost of healing the ITs OWN CREATION.

There is a saint and sinner in all of us, a murderer and a life-giver, and every light and dark color in the spectrum as there is in the Source of all that is. We think ourselves to be one or more of these as well as being the many polarized parts of our psyche. In the case of the hero function, "the ego [the self] [can] all too easily succumb to the temptation to identify with the hero, thus bringing on a psychic inflation with all of its consequences" (Moore,1983, p. 86). And the most devastating of the consequences is for the ego (self) to begin to worship itself—the

126

ultimate idolatry—and to ignore and then forget how intimately close God is permeating every cell. We are, and we are not, God. We are, and we are not, SELF. In the world, each of us manifests the SELF that we are when we live SELF-led as a self willingly transformed into a Self in love with all that is.

We have a clue as to whether or not we have such a love when we have our being in and by and through the qualities that transcend the artificial boundaries of calcified religions and spiritualties. In the end, were the self to commit to being transformed into a Self, according to an archetypal image of the divine SELF as multiply manifested in human history, such a person would be committing to a humble hero's dedication to combat fear to the end of the last moment of the last hour of life—the ultimate task at any age and certainly in advanced old age. Jung does not spare his words:

> For the hero, fear is a challenge and a task, because only boldness can deliver from fear. And if the risk is not taken, the meaning of life is somehow violated, and the whole future is condemned to hopeless staleness, to a drab grey lit only by will-o-the wisps. (Jung, 1958, p. 354)

This brings to mind the *velleities,* the vague desires, which James dismissed as unworthy of the religious state, as antithetical to the hero's journey, to the Self's dedication to the return.

*. . . as I strolled round looking at your sacred monuments,*
*I noticed among other things an altar inscribed: To an Unknown God.*
—Acts 17:23

## CHAPTER NINE: SELF AND *DEUS ABSCONITUS*

### Psyche as Sacrament

John P. Dourley, Catholic priest and Jungian analyst, is only one of many who, in the latter part of the 20th century, contemplated the relationship between the psyche and the religious concepts of Christianity. In his 1981 book, *The Psyche as Sacrament: A Comparative Study of C. G. Jung and Paul Tillich,* Dourley compares the psychology of Jung and the theology of Tillich and speaks of the hidden God in our unconscious—the *Deus Absconditus.* Within this context, he reminds us that Jung defines the Self [SELF] as the archetype of wholeness that regulates the center of personality and, further still, that Self [SELF] is the divine reality within that preserves us from self-destruction, a task we can accomplish by uniting, in a working harmony, the opposites that make up our humanity. In so doing, we are participating in the work of the ultimate *coniunctio.*

Jung and Tillich see the Self [SELF] as the power center that holds each of us together. When I read that the Self [SELF] is neither the ego nor the unconscious but a product of their marriage, I am led to conclude that from their union a third is born—a functional core, the center of consciousness—the *soul,* in the language of the Western ancients, or the Self, the SELF-led person, the one led by the qualities of the SELF through the energy of the Holy Spirit in the Trinitarian model.

When Dourley says that the Self [SELF] exists at both the beginning and end of life, it seems he is referring to an understanding of the oneness of the Self [SELF]. In this original oneness of the SELF, the I that is, the center of consciousness—the one who can say, *I am aware of my Self*—can, through the developmental experiences of separation and differentiation, return to the SELF, not in an unconscious state but in full consciousness. Our wholeness depends on the mystical union of our *ground of being* and of our ground of Self. Dourley supports this view when he blends Jung's and Tillich's insights into the marriage analogy.

The psalmist voiced the law of God as in and of the heart. One might say, then, that Dourley alludes to the fact that divine law is the depth of our being—psyche and *soma* as one. The collection of universal myths offers us a glimmer of understanding into the mystery of human identity, and we must not take the myths, including Christian myths, literally, for fear of missing their true meaning.

According to Dourley, Tillich says that it is only when the mind is in a state of ecstasy that it is able to perceive reality as a miracle. To repeat Einstein's conjecture: *Everything is a miracle,* which sounds and feels so right.

**Symbolic Thinking**

In the Jungian tradition, the aim of therapy is to enable us to think symbolically, a skill that has been lost across much of the modern and post-modern world. We must harken back to the best of religious traditions, based on experience and not on a priori theory, dogma, or doctrine. By using the term *experience,* I am asserting the inclusion of the totality of experiences that involve all dimensions of the human organism—all structures and functions of the brain, not just those that provide the mechanisms for the translation of experience into rational and verbal expression. We are referencing *felt* truths, à la Eugene Gendlin, that guide a person's existential behaviors.

In Dourley's fourth chapter, "The Search for the Historical Jesus," he compresses a discussion of the image of God in the psyche within the Christian myth. We are born whole but unconscious, and a lifetime is accorded us to enable us to return to our wholeness in a conscious state. Edinger presents a compelling analysis of this phenomenon in *Ego and Archetype.* The journey is not a joy-ride; it entails the hard work of suffering, which opens onto joy, the unmerited gift of radical hope. (See Lear, 2008, *Radical Hope.*) Dourley writes, "Jung contends that the restoration of [the person] to the fullness of [his] nature is a process of suffering comparable to Christ's descent into hell" (p. 60). By this, Dourley suggests that it is our mission to integrate our collective unconscious; that is, those archetypes on which our complexes (or, in IFS language, parts of our inner family) are grafted—a task in need of a conscious dedication to rise after every humiliating fall. (See H. M. Luke, 1987, *Old Age.*) This is the individuation process, the return of the self to the SELF as a Self, a mystery that is a miracle, a miracle that is a mystery.

Dourley is undaunted by his profound and humble realization of the relative position of the ego, the me, the I, toward the SELF:

The ego [self], Jung believes, is a product of the unconscious and in this respect is constantly transcended by it.

The ego [self] must cooperate with the intent of the unconscious. From this side of the dialectic, the newly emerging self [Self] is the product of the ego's [self's] effort to integrate the unconscious and so bring the self [Self] into existence as its child, the *filius philosophorum.*

The ego [self] is sacrificed to the demands of the emerging greater self [Self], it is or can be a willing victim to the self [SELF], which acts as priest in the act of sacrifice.

The symbol of the suffering Christ is therefore a symbol of what occurs in everyday life in which the individuation process takes place. It is the suffering of the ego [self] before the demands of the self [SELF] toward balanced growth. (pp. 65-66)

This is the dynamic in which we find the wisdom in the following statement: "The ego must continually die and be reborn to greater consciousness through the integration of the unconscious" (p. 66). One could stop here and ponder "the realization that the centre of the individual is also the *center of the universe"* [emphasis added] (p. 66). How comforting it is to find the antecedents of our present understanding in the hard-earned thoughts of our mentors from previous generations.

With regard to the evident polarities of our parts, as expressed in IFS, Dourley reminds us that Jung gave psychological language and understanding to Tillich's descriptions of the experience of faith, and I would add, to James's professed understanding of what we might call the courageous abandonment to the reality that is life with radical hope, so expressed by Lear. Jung taught that man "cannot conquer the tremendous polarity of his nature on his own resources; he can only do so through the terrifying experience of a psychic process that is independent of him, that works *him* rather than he *it"* [emphasis added] (p. 68). The unification and harmonizing of all the polarities of our psyche is best effected by the practical loving kindness described by IFS as Self-Leadership, a loving that is hospitable to all of our fragments.

Ever the Jungian analyst, Dourley states that James's discussion of spiritual conversion ensues from a psychic integration, or, to use spiritual terminology, ensues from *grace.* Absent this integration, consciousness is fragmented. "The fragments [or complexes] take over the personality. . . " (p. 69).

In Ronald Siegel and Schwartz's 2015 article, "The Fiction of the Self: The Paradox of Mindfulness in Clinical Practice," Schwartz speaks of *parts* of the mind; Ronald Siegel speaks of the *aspects* of the mind. These committed thinkers and practitioners have the same end in sight—the "at-one-ment" of all of our entities living in psyche and *soma*—the complete embodiment of psyche and the spiritualization of soma. One can speak of the "resurrection of the body," to use the symbolic language of the Paschal Mystery, or one could say that the individual's life journey is the revelation of the Hidden God, of the SELF through the Self. This is a metaphorical way to express the mission of Internal Family Systems Therapy.

*Individuation is a spiritual process by which*
*the personality is built up.*
—Josef Goldbrunner, 1964, *Individuation*

## CHAPTER TEN: INDIVIDUATION—THE PATH TO SELF

### A Developmental Process

I read Josef Goldbrunner's little 1964 book, *Individuation: A Study of the Depth Psychology of Carl Gustave Jung,* during my fourth year of graduate studies in theology, and I recognized myself as a gnostic, a heretic. Goldbrunner, a respected scholar of philosophy and theology, studied the relationship between psychology and religion. In his work, which I have returned to time and again until the book has become frayed, I found a template with which to validate my thinking about the said revealed truths, about the stone-cold dogma, not in their orthodox, literal interpretation, but in the symbolic language of real myth. Goldbrunner's words are still meaningful to me, especially after I sought William James's advice on the topic of the Self that I found in his Gifford Lectures. The following thoughts, gleaned from Goldbrunner, are worthy of further contemplation, and I render my comments without ponderous explanations.

First, there is this statement: "The archetypes are the 'psychic' aspects of the brain" (Goldbrunner, p. 106). "They correspond to the truths of life" that by far exceed what we can conjure up on our own by sensation alone (p. 108). When the ego "goes its own way," it is in conflict with the truths of the collective unconscious and is false. "Neurosis is a contradiction and antithesis of the archetypes; analysis must help to activate them; therapy leads to a reconciliation with them" (p. 112). In the hands of an IFS therapist who caresses every part, every aspect of the multiplicity that is the brain-body-soma-soul-spirit in all of its content and processes, the hope for peace and harmony in the inner world enhances the prospect of the same in the outer world between members

132

of the human family. Unburdening our psychotic, neurotic, and personality-disordered parts offers hope for the emergence of the Self.

The fertile and gracious waters of the collective unconscious, however treacherous and malevolent they might manifest in the many faces depicted in the myths revealed in our dreams and in all spiritual/religious traditions, are archetypes—"complexes of experiences which enter, as though by fate, and [whose] influences begin early in our personal life" (p. 112). Our inner parts build on the templates, floating up out of the wellspring of our psyche, translating into sensations, emotions, imaginations, feelings, cognitions, and actions to form social roles throughout our lifetime. When we think that we author all of the dimensions of our conscious endeavors, we reveal our foolishness. At best, we are followers or co-leaders as the moment demands. At worst, we are pushed along and usurped. Ours is the task to negotiate the trip on the map laid out for us and to return home after, we hope, doing more good than harm in this world—the ego resurrected into a Self in the arms of the SELF—the image and likeness of the OTHER. It is to IFS's great credit that it honors this slow, delicate process, as do the wise therapeutic traditions of old.

What Goldbrunner wrote, years before the arrival of IFS as a therapeutic modality, speaks to the long tradition that girths the foundations of IFS philosophy and practice:

The best thing that the analytical process can give to a man is his own discovery of his nature and the elements of his nature. The vital truths of life which he has found will become immediately clear and give the personality a *center of gravity* [emphasis added]. The helper must not upset the slow maturing of the patient by passing a hasty judgment. The helper must merely act as a careful companion of the spiritual process in which the unconscious has a lead.

It should be noted that the unconscious will retain the upper hand only if consciousness has gone its own way too long, away from and contrary to the laws of the inner world. The unconscious appears as

133

a corrective and attempts to bend the path of life back into the right direction. Man [the individual person] then has to undergo the fateful experience of being conscious of the dark part of the soul. This is the positive quality in neurosis, that it can lead man to knowledge of his nature. Both halves of the soul, the light of consciousness and the darkness of the unconscious, belong together and need each other; they are a "self-regulating system." They act like two poles between which life oscillates to and fro. The concept "Soul" embraces them both. (pp. 113-114)

This long tradition enjoins the practitioner to put off "hasty judgment" demeaning the other's persona, mask. With a plea for forgiveness for those moments early in my professional life, I own that I "smartly" intervened to crumble the other's "persona," to rip off the other's protective mask, simply to maintain my own.

After World War II, when I was ten years old, my father gave me an official job; he assigned me as the "weeder" of his expanded Victory Garden. He had planted the customary three rows of carrots, each 20 feet long. One morning that summer, after the carrots had pushed out of the soft earth and spread their first two sprouts to an inch or so tall, I decided to exercise my official duty by pulling all of the new-sprung weeds that companioned the carrots. I was certain I would gain my father's praise when he returned home for supper. Headlong I went, up and down those three rows, never looking back, being in a hurry to join my friends in the neighborhood schoolyard for our daily baseball game. Later, after washing my hands and face for supper, I waited by the back door for my father's arrival. I beamed when he stepped out of his Ford coup. He walked with me to the garden, a warm smile on his moon-shaped face. I was beaming, proud of my diligent work. At the garden's edge, I froze and swallowed a horrified screech. During the blistering summer day, the carrot shoots had wilted to their deaths. I had killed the carrot crop. My father placed his arm on my shoulders and then taught me a life-long lesson: "The carrots were too young and not strong

134

enough to stand up on their own," he said calmly. "They still needed the help of the weeds to hold them up. You did a perfect job. You did not leave one weed standing in the patch. We'll plant a new crop tomorrow." Nothing more was said as we went in for supper, his hand rubbing my crew cut, his familiar gesture of affection.

My father spoke with a French accent, but I can summon up the above few words with reliable accuracy. Later I heard his words when I was too quick to correct my children, when I failed to be patient with my students and supervisees, when I pulled and pushed a patient (the one suffering before me) ahead of the individual's natural healing rhythm, when I metaphorically scorched the weeds in their gardens to the detriment of the tender plants. I had not yet learned to welcome, appreciate, and love all that grows in my own garden, all of my parts. Tradition wants us to learn from the unconscious and "bend the path of life back into the right direction" and not yank it in that "right," opposite direction—a lesson my mother taught me. I do not recall her exact words, but I still see an image that has been with me since my troubled grade-school years. The image is of a young birch tree, bent by the wet, heavy snow of a late Northern New England winter storm, tied to a stake, being coaxed back to upright to avoid breaking it. My mother is telling me that a bad habit can only be corrected a little at a time, and very gently, otherwise it will either break or return to its bent state once the stake is removed.

Today, I recognize a "self-regulating system" operating in all of this. In IFS therapy, a therapist speaking directly to a member of the internal family requires the same scrupulous honesty that Jung taught as a prerequisite to engaging directly with the archetypes and complexes in Active Imagination. (See R. A. Johnson, 1986, *Inner Work*; P. Middelkoop, 1985, *The Wise Old Man*.) The figures of our inner world tolerate our human frailties but not our deliberate deceptions.

135

## The Soul

There can be no discussion about the individuation process without considering the Soul—"the object of psychology" (Goldbrunner, p. 133). I again quote Goldbrunner in the following lengthy excerpt from a paragraph that embraces the height and depth and breadth of "soul."

> The soul is like a large country. The struggle with the archetypes . . . is a voyage of discovery into the unknown territory with all the dangers, troubles, and fears bound up with such an enterprise. Will the "ego" be able to take it on and withstand it all? It can shield its eye to it, escape or put up immoveable boundary posts. Then a swamp bereft of all conscious cultures will develop in the unconscious. A vital problem will have failed to have been solved. But the ego can also take the risk of marching in, entrusting itself to the unknown and—losing itself. . . . For this happens when a man succumbs to the first onslaught of the feelings and puts them into action. The only way that is worthy of a human being is exploration and spiritual appropriation, that is, cultivation and control. Admittedly, the ego returns changed; inwardly broader, better informed and sustained by an inner feeling that is expressed in a premonitory knowledge of the breadth and depth of the soul, of its brightness and darkness. From now on this "knowledge" influences every deliberate decision: it is a *conscience*. It says to the ego: You must now take this new province into account and incorporate it into your behavior; its voice is like that of a secret, invisible adviser. Jung describes this feeling as the new and slowly developing *center of consciousness*. Its center is no longer in the ego, as the sum of the contents of consciousness, but in a *point between* consciousness and the unconscious. Jung calls it the *Self*. . . . Individuation aims at the formation of the *Self*, which is why it can also be called the *"development of the Self"* [emphasis added throughout]. (p. 131)

136

This addresses what intrigued James and led him to explore the psychological dimension of the religious experience of the ego's descent into an emptying and subsequent assent into a fullness not of its own making.

### The Problem of God

Goldbrunner, in solid Jungian tradition, is addressing the problem of God, a problem not without a life-or-death struggle when he says,

A struggle to discern the meaning of the Whole, to discover whether it is immanent in the world or whether it can only be discovered when man surrenders by a curious decision to a transcendent "unknown" power, of which he is the creature. That is the problem of God. (p. 133)

Again, this is a discussion for another time. One can say that the "Higher Power" of Alcoholics Anonymous and the revelations of the world's mystics that reference the "unknown power" of an identified or unidentified source is what generates the energy for one's individuation, one's unburdening into a functional wholeness.

"The process of personality-formation lasts throughout life. Life itself analyzes" (p. 134). In this statement about the process of personality formation, Goldbrunner is not talking about the construction of the mask but of the building of our Self-led wholeness as a system composed of all parts of our whole that originate in our personal and universal unconscious. Any attempt to steady the march of the self to wholeness by ignoring the depth of the psyche lends itself to a doomed effort, as it violates the laws of the *soul* and assures a downward slide into imbalance. The problem of God is the problem of soul; it is the problem of the internal system that is deprived of the conscious awareness of the existence and activity of the entities that are the substrata of our inner and outer life. "As above, so below; as below, so above," said the ancients.

137

Jung was painfully made aware of the immeasurable depth of the psyche in his confrontation with the archetypal beings in the collective unconscious when his ego descended below the line and when these living images broke through into his night and day dreams, living images with which he interacted in what he called "active imagination." In IFS, through indirect and direct contact, client and therapist offer hospitality to all archetypes that manifest as themselves or as complexes (parts) in order to effect the balance of polarities in every human dimension—to effect individuation.

In the Western world, the reality-based "biographies of saints are a rich source of psychological information on the collective unconscious," as are the writings of mystics (Goldbrunner, p. 138). Goldbrunner recognizes that "poets are able to provide a further insight into the secret depths of the collective unconscious and its contents" (p. 139). The great poets provide us with information about the depth of the soul itself.

In Chapter 11, "Soul in Action," of Edward Hirsch's classic 1999 book, *How to Read a Poem: And Fall in Love with Poetry,* he weaves a meditation on the role poets and poetry play in the understanding of our individual relationship with what we claim to be our soul. Hirsch speaks from an experienced personal authority when he tells us that we need a "silent space" to listen to our poet's voice, to "listen to the words and [to] daydream [our] way back into the house of being. . . . Poetry is like prayer in that it is most effective in solitude and in the time of solitude as, for example, in the earliest morning" (p. 244). This prayer contains no self-directed words. Rather, it is the soul's opening to the wisdom of the Morning Star. It is the empty moment full of what Ralph Waldo Emerson's sighing expressed in his 1841 essay, "The Over-Soul," "when we suddenly intuit something of the soul's elusive, defining epiphanic power" (Hirsch, pp. 244-245):

The soul is not an organ, but animates and exercises all the organs[,] is not a function[,] is not a faculty, is not the intellect or the will, but

138

the master [thereof]; is the background of our being . . . an immensity not possessed and that cannot be possessed. (p. 245)

Hirsch also unearths thoughts on the subject as he contemplates Walt Whitman's poem, "A Clear Midnight," but he first explains that, as in Gaston Bachelard's book, *The Poetics of Space,* "the word *soul* [emphasis added] is an immortal word" (Hirsch, p. 246). It is the word that names "in the self what is essential and irreducible, permanent and beyond human limitations" (p. 246). Then, commenting on Whitman's poem, he says that Whitman employs the word *thou* when addressing the Soul "as something almost independent and sacred dwelling within himself" (p. 247). At this point, Hirsch's prose brings us to the brink of unknowing. He interprets Whitman's words, "*free flight into the wordless*" [emphasis added], as the "soul's soaring into the mystic realm beyond language" (p. 247).

From time immemorial, poets who are experienced philosophers, psychologists, and prophets have attempted to define Soul and have failed to fully comprehend the Self. Self eludes the power of words, confounds the apparatus of science, surpasses the reaches of the mind. The Soul—the Self—is not measurable. We can only observe its effects in the world of behavior. That is how James identified its presence via the process of "sanctification." Hirsh tells us that, in Emily Dickinson's terms, "the withdrawal from the occasional world is a necessary prelude to spiritual disclosure" (p. 253). "It is characteristic of her," he says, "to sever the soul from the power of the collective [the popular opinion] and scandalously reclaim it for the autonomous self" (p. 254). In the language of IFS, this self is the SELF-energized Self. As in lyric poetry, "We cannot live what we cannot feel" (p. 258). I submit that it is the same in the domain of the psyche. No understanding can exist without the body's companionship. Sensation is a prerequisite to reality-based cognition.

After this brief excursion into the kingdom of poetry, we return to Goldbrunner where we find that the process of individuation effects a center that does not lie in the ego; it effects an ulterior consciousness. Gradually, "the ego feels itself as one complex among others; that is, it only knows that it is that and takes its bearings accordingly. . . . Consciousness and unconsciousness confront one another" (Goldbrunner, p. 143). They do so, not as adversaries, but as two territories of one kingdom. They and their populations find their appropriate roles as leaders and followers, opposers and supporters. They aim at the end of divisions. They gather parts into a whole. A central leader emerges, one that holds the two territories as one kingdom. In the world of the body-mind, "the new center is the center of the total personality"; that is, a Self-led personality (p. 143). "The process of individuation advances slowly but steadfastly. The tensions and opposites fade and alternate, and the Self is born, the goal of individuation" (p. 144). This is the goal of IFS therapy. Truly a working "peaceable kingdom."

*We play at paste,*
*Till qualified for pearl,*
*Then drop the paste,*
*and deem our self a fool.*
                    —Emily Dickinson (1830-1886)

## CHAPTER ELEVEN: ALCHEMY AND THE SELF

### A Side Trip

In this meandering and encircling search for the Elusive SELF, a side trip into the world of alchemy presented itself when I spotted on a far shelf in my study Carl Jung's 1951 book, *Aion: Researches into the Phenomenology of the Self.* As has so often happened in my life, a book selected itself for me, blanketing all others and leaving itself as the only choice. So, I accepted the invitation as a gift, which brought me to return to earlier readings and to see how William James felt at home in the inner world of SELF, how archetypal religious symbols informed the study of the psyche.

To think of the SELF and the Trinity in the same breath, if you allow me a mixed metaphor, is not a reach beyond our grasp. No detached personal way exists to allow some understanding of the phenomenon we call SELF. For SELF, like Trinity, only allows itself to be experienced in a loving relationship. In Richard Rohr's September 11, 2018, Daily Meditation, "Trinity," he says that Scottish theologian Richard of St. Victor (1110-1173) "taught at great length that for God to be truth, God had to be one; for God to be love, God had to be two; and for God to be joy, God had to be three!" (See Augustine, *On the Trinity,* Book III, note 2.) How dynamically elusive is this quotation.

In the same meditation, when commenting on the non-dualistic experience of the Trinity as expressed by the 4th-century Cappadocian Fathers, Rohr says, "Paraphrasing physicist Niels Bohr (1885-1962),

141

the Doctrine of the Trinity is saying that God is not only stranger than we think, but stranger than we *can* think."

Our metaphoric grasp of the Elusive SELF is surely totally other than we can possibly think, but our task is to approach it with a humble daring. Again, Jung leads the way into the humble daring of the alchemist-philosopher Gerardus Dorn (1530-1584) whose thoughts Jung describes and analyzes in *Aion*.

### *Aion*

*Aion,* one of the major works of Jung's later years, is a further discussion of "the symbolic representation of the psychic totality through the concept of the Self [SELF], whose traditional equivalent [in Western culture] is the figure of Christ" (Jung, 1951, back cover).

Delving into the thick of things, Jung tells us that the ego is not the SELF. The ego is the "complex factor to which all conscious contents are related. It forms, as it were, the center of the field of consciousness; and in so far as this comprises the empirical personality, the ego is the subject of all personal acts of consciousness" (p. 3). I (ego) am the one who acts in this world. This I that I am "on the one hand, rests on the *total field* of consciousness, and on the other, on the *sum total of unconscious content"* (p. 4). Does this not admonish us to never forget that the knowledge of the SELF is beyond our comprehension, as is God? But we can trick ourselves with words, succumb to the deceiver part of us. Thus, we must be reminded, as Jung prudently does, that "personality as a total phenomenon does not coincide with the ego, that is, with the conscious personality, but forms an entity that has to be distinguished from the ego" (p. 5). This leads me to think that I, when I distinguish the ego (self) from the Self, that this Self is the self that is birthed by the SELF and energized by the SELF's own spirit. Jung reminds us that he has "suggested calling the total personality, which though present cannot be fully known, the self [SELF] . . . [given that]

142

the ego is by definition subordinate to the self [SELF] and is related to it like a part to a whole" (p. 5).

All analogies fail at some point, and so does my allusion to the Trinity, but I consider this analogy to be of some merit. As the individual person can do nothing against God, by any definition, but can be overtaken by God, "the ego not only can do nothing against the self [SELF] but is sometimes actually assimilated by unconscious components of personality that are in the process of development and is greatly altered by them" (p. 6). This assimilation can be the result of a psychotic or neurotic process. In IFS, we speak of the self (ego) being taken over or blended by parts (or, in Interpersonal Neurobiology, by traits) of the psyche living in the collective or personal unconscious that are committed to transformation, to the process of individuation, but which are not immune to disruptions and potential disintegration. John Weir Perry discusses this at length in his classic 1953 book, *The Self in Psychotic Process.*

James was fully aware that mystical experiences were of the same material as a psychotic experience. The difference between the two was in the outcomes for the personality's integration into a functional wholeness over a dysfunctional fragmentation. The saint, as referenced by James, is the exemplar of what IFS calls a SELF-led person—a Self who participates in the gifted quality of the SELF and participates in its nature.

In footnote 3 of his September 12, 2018, Daily Meditation, "Theorsis," Rohr quotes Maximus the Confessor (508-662 CE): "The saints become that which can never belong to the power of nature alone, since nature alone possesses no faculty capable of perceiving what surpasses it."

The ego [self] does not have the power to transform itself into a Self since it does not have the ability to perceive its source and its end—the SELF. The self [ego] can only actively yield to the creative leadership of the SELF and willingly participate in its *energia* for the purpose of individuating into a Self.

## Symbols and Evolution of Growth

Perry helps elucidate what Dorn was expressing through his symbolic alchemical language. Perry explains that the internal world of the psyche is a galaxy of symbols and functions that come into play in the evolution of growth [which Jung] terms the "individuation process" (Perry, p. 45). Perry further expands his thought in the following quote:

> The drive toward individuation is apparently a spontaneous urge, not under the leadership of the ego, but of the archetypal movement in the unconscious, the non-ego, toward the fulfillment of the specific basic patterns of the individual, striving toward wholeness, totality, and the differentiation of the specific potentialities that are innately destined to form the particular personality in question. (p. 45)

To become truly who one is; that is, to become one's True Self, the self must not self-define from the outside but must give expression, enact, by incarnating itself, the innate specific potentialities that are the individual's destiny *verbalized* in and by and through the Self. This drive is . . .

> a dynamic urge emanating from the core of one's being, laden with affect and presenting itself to consciousness in terms of archetypal symbols. . . . The term "self" [SELF] designates this pattern of wholeness that thus represents itself in archetypal form. . . . [It is] not only a center of the psyche but also a circumference that encloses it; it is the center and delimitation of the totality of conscious and unconscious. It governs and structures the total psyche as the ego does its conscious contents. (pp. 45-46)

This internal drive belongs to and is the fate and calling of the ego [self] to become strong enough to undergo the transformation crisis that the SELF lays on the self's road to divinization, the becoming of a Self, via the stumbling journey to final crucifixion before being able to sustain

144

the necessary humiliation prior to the ensuing glory in fragile humility. That glory is to be simply and imperfectly one's True Self, guided by the SELF.

When Perry affirms that "since the self [Self] is constellated only under conditions of stress, this consolidation phenomenon is apt to evade study under 'normal' or experimental conditions" (p. 46). All that researchers can do is to observe and describe the resulting behaviors and establish a correlation between reported subjective experiences and consequent indicators of wholeness and health. No cause-and-effect conclusions are possible in this domain. The SELF is an elusive entity and concept but an undeniable experience of its own origin and expression. As the center of the psyche, it is untouchable because it is in the collective or, yet better said, in the universal unconscious (the World Soul), in which everyone exists under its sway. In *Aion,* Jung writes:

> To the extent that the integrated content [of the unconscious] are *parts* of the *self* [SELF], we can expect [their] influence to be considerable. . . . The more numerous and the more significant the unconscious contents which are assimilated into the ego, the closer the approximation of the ego [Self] to the self [SELF], even though this approximation must be a never-ending process. (p. 23)

The Self lives in a state of ongoing incompletion, doing so wisely because *parts* can and do possess the ego.

Heeding Jung's admonition that the ego must never identify with the figures of the collective unconscious is imperative. "It must be reckoned a psychic catastrophe when the *ego* [self] *is assimilated by the self [SELF]* (p. 24). This assimilation of the ego by the SELF, or aspects of the SELF (archetypes and or complexes in Jung's language) is the definition of inflation (a pseudo Self, in IFS understanding), a grandiosity that is, in the extreme, a psychotic delusion of grandeur or of persecution. We should remember that the godhead is both light and darkness and not ignore the polarities of good and evil that demand of

145

the godhead a heroic struggle to adapt, organize, and regulate these aspects of the SELF into a generative harmony.

## Alchemy

Within alchemy lies the metaphorical discipline of the alchemist who exteriorizes the mythical and mystical divine urgency to know oneself. In the Book of Job, we witness the transitional moment of YHWH's evolution, that moment of His coming to consciousness, His integration of His dark side previously projected onto the Evil One, causing havoc, running amok in the world.

The Book of Job is the story of an honest man, not a perfect man, who dares to confront the creator and master of all that is. Job can do so because he has confronted his own dark side, owns it, and thereby, against all reasonable arguments advanced by his righteous and con-ventionality prudent friends, provides YHWH the momentous opportunity to know all of Himself, to see emerge out of His integration, the Wisdom that He can embrace as His bride. Out of that union (love) will emerge their son—the Word—the expression of His wholeness making possible the Quaternity through the Spirit of Love that binds them as One. But at this point, I am far ahead of the story.

YHWH, who did not understand Himself, gets to know Himself as He truly is in and by and through His interactions with a human who accepts His polarized nature. In the Book of Job, YHWH's burden of grandiosity is broken because He has to face His arbitrary, destructive impulses and, yes, repent. (See J. Miles, 1995, *God, a Biography;* see also, J. B. Russell, 1984, *Lucifer, the Devil in the Middle Ages,* and E. Dhorme, 1984, *A Commentary on the Book of Job.*)

The mythological story of Job's confrontation with YHWH speaks of the ego, which is born out of the SELF, evolves, and develops out of the SELF's love for the Wisdom that informs the ego into a Self so that it can eventually return to the SELF in full and *mutual* consciousness.

146

Jung writes that Dorn teaches us the age-old importance of self-knowledge. He does so in the language and rituals of alchemy that operate in our inner and outer worlds.

> The alchemical procedure takes place within and without. He who does not understand how to free the "truth" in his own soul from the fetters will never make a success of the physical opus, and he who knows how to make the stone can only do so on the basis of right doctrine, through which he himself is transformed, or which he creates through his own transformation. (Jung, p. 162)

In Jung's text, I understand the Stone to be the Self, from an IFS perspective. We do not create the SELF; it transcends the fire's power to cook the lead in the vessel. To know one's self is not so easy a thing to do. To become conscious of our consciousness is the ultimate in time and space, after all. Jung discusses Dorn's understanding of the matter:

> Man's greatest treasure is to be found within. . . . The secret is first and foremost *in man;* it is his true self [Self] which he does not know but learns to know by experience of outward things. (Jung, p. 163)

My true self is not the SELF but the third—the Self that is the transformed true lead cooked in the blazing love of the SELF. This objective knowledge of the Self requires that we know what we are, on what we depend, to whom we belong, and for what end we exist. (On page 164, footnote 44, of *Aion,* Jung quotes Dorn's Latin text relating to this same concept: *"Nemo vero potest cognoscere se, nisi sciat quid, et non quis ipse sit, a quo dependeat, vel cuius sit . . . et in quam finem factus sit.")*

Dorn speaks of that objective knowledge—not what I think I am, but who I really am; not my ego (self), but the objective part of my totality, the totality of my incarnated psyche, a never-completed task. When Dorn addresses the one who wants to become an adept, Jung writes that the alchemist advises the novice to seek to know the objective psyche:

> The self [SELF that] he must seek to know is a part of that nature which was bodied forth by God's original oneness with the world. It is manifestly not a knowledge of the nature of the ego [self] though

147

this is far more convenient and fondly confused with self-knowledge. For this reason, anyone who seriously tries to know himself as an object is accused of selfishness and eccentricity. But such knowledge has nothing to do with the ego's subjective knowledge of itself. (Jung, pp. 163-164)

To know this inner universe that is common to us all is to become one with everyone—an understanding that generates an objective love of all. The theological religious phenomenon of the Mystical Body of Christ is a living experiential symbol of a reality that evokes the *Mercy* humans so need for their Self-acceptance—a prerequisite for Self-understanding.

This inner universe is the collective unconscious with its archetypes and manifest complexes—some blending with the ego [self] as runaway parts, misguided in their attempt to help, and others energizing the self into a Self ever more attuned to the SELF, that alpha and omega filling the bodied Self with the spirit of the wisdom of the SELF. The ego arises out of this universe as a subjective consciousness whose raison d'etre is to know; that is, to love the SELF (p. 164).

Jung writes that the collective unconscious is "'objective' because it is identical in all individuals and is therefore *one*. Out of the universal One there is produced in every individual a *subjective* consciousness; i.e., the ego" (p. 164).

James is not the only one who references priest and theologian Ignatius. In *Aion,* page 165, footnote 45, Jung quotes, in the original Spanish and Latin, the first sentence of "Principle and Foundation" in Ignatius's *Spiritual Exercises:* "Man was created to praise Our Lord God, to show him reverence, to serve him, and thereby save his soul. "

Jung writes the following long sentence as his psychological understanding of Ignatius's fundamental principle, which, as a five-year-old, I encountered in a French translation when it appeared as the sixth question (Why did God make you?) in the Baltimore Catechism taught to all Catholic children before their First Communion. If we divest the

148

opening sentence of "Principle and Foundation" of its theological terminology, it would run as follows:

Man's consciousness was created to the end that it may (1) recognize (*laudet*) its descent from a higher unity *(Deum)*; (2) pay due and careful regard to this source (*reverentiam exhibeat*); (3) execute its commands intelligently and responsibly (*serviat*); and (4) thereby afford the psyche as a whole the optimum degree of life and development (*salvet animam suam*). (Jung, p. 165)

Jung further states, "Only an infantile person can pretend that evil is not at work everywhere, and the more unconscious he is, the more the devil drives him" (p. 166). As an IFS therapist, I have, as other practitioners have, encountered complexes, subpersonalities, traits, and parts that, however much I allow for their good intentions to be of some help to the individual, have caused or cause harm—even deadly harm. The effects of the behavior of these parts have resulted or result in evil consequences. These are the parts that most need the therapist's and the patient's compassion. No one is exempt from offering ultimate love to one's own universal or personal parts, perceived as enemies, who do not know what they are doing, parts that require, to use religious language, the Mercy of the Self crucified. This is the true imitation of the Christ, of the SELF.

In Rohr's Daily Meditation, "The Soul's Objective Union with God," of September 19, 2018, he, the contemplative, defines sin as "a state of separation—when the part poses as the whole." We can interpret his statement as describing a pseudo-self, a false self. When he refers to "possessions by devils," he also makes the analogy to the phenomenon of addiction—that of a person "possessed, in some sense trapped by a larger force and . . . powerless to do anything about it." Such possession could range from a blending that only mildly and temporarily taints the self to a full-out capturing of the self's functioning (mind, brain, and body) in a complete dissociative state. The road back to selfhood is through the self's (ego's) reconnection to the infinite and undefinable

149

limits of one's source—and awakening—a consciousness of consciousness. In Rohr's September 20, 2018, Daily Meditation, "Healing Addiction," he aptly mentions that "we are addicted . . . to our preferred self-image and to the usually unworkable programs for happiness we developed in childhood."

I add that few mental processes and brain structures were fully and freely chosen in our early years. Behavioral patterns evolved and devolved from experiences originating in the outside world of family and community. Happy the person whose growth and development were supported by Self-led individuals and communities. How much more was that person's ego (self) able to emerge open to the qualities of SELF, and how deeply sad it is to encounter the brokenness and the weight of burdens resulting from developmental trauma.

The IFS therapist joins all committed healers in the remediation of consequential damages sustained first in the development years and then in the ensuing years. As with the Self-led alchemists of old, depth psychotherapists and present-day doctors of the soul, all healers who bring their competence and dedication to the mission of Hope, are equally qualified to help the *patient* find the *Philosopher's Stone.* Jung emphasizes that like every archetype, the self [SELF] cannot be localized in an individual's ego-consciousness, but acts like a circumambient atmosphere to which no definite limits can be set either in space or in time (hence the synchronistic phenomena so often associated with activated archetypes.) But then Jung reports that according to Dorn,

The stone is implanted in man . . . and that through his knowledge of the stone, man remains inseparably bound to the self [SELF]. [And] through this knowledge the self [SELF], as a content of the unconscious, is made conscious and "fixed" in the mind. For without the existence of conscious concepts apperception is, as we know, impossible. (Jung, pp. 168-169)

Herein lies the imperative usefulness of fairy tales, legends, myths, and dogmas as "instrumental symbols with whose help unconscious

150

contents [universal and personal] can be canalized into consciousness, interpreted and integrated" (p. 169). This provides the foundation for the imaginal work in IFS therapy.

Our search for the Elusive SELF is replete with affirmations and negations and is like the *via negativa* James referenced in the Gifford Lectures. Whatever we affirm of God, we must deny. Whatever we affirm of SELF, we similarly must deny, but the alchemist would not recoil in the face of such necessity. From the compressed language in *Aion,* Chapter XI, "The Alchemical Interpretation of the Fish," Jung says,

> For the alchemist, it is clear that the "center" or what we would call the self [SELF], does not lie in the ego but outside it, "in us" yet not "in our mind," being located rather in that which we unconsciously are, the "quid" [the what] which we still have to recognize. Today [1956] we would call it the unconscious, and we distinguish between a personal unconscious which enables us to recognize the shadow and an impersonal unconscious which enables us to recognize the archetypal symbol of the self [SELF]. (p. 169)

Jung continues to remind us that the alchemist exteriorized his archetype in matter while feeling that it was "paradoxically in man and yet at the same time outside him" (p. 169). The alchemist's gnostic understanding prefigured modern, postmodern, and contemporary psychology.

Perhaps this following commentary might add further clarification to the trinity (SELF, Self, self) that I have been proposing throughout these essays:

> The union of opposites in the stone is possible only when the adept has become One himself. The unity of the stone is the equivalent of individuation, by which man is made one; we would say that the stone is a projection of the unified self [SELF]. This formulation is psychologically correct. It does not, however, take sufficient account of the fact that the stone is a *transcendent* unity. We must therefore emphasize that though the self [SELF] can become a symbolic

151

content of consciousness, it is a supra-ordinate totality, necessarily transcendental as well. Dorn recognized the identity of the stone with the transformed man when he exclaimed: "Transmute yourselves from dead stones into living philosophical stones." (Jung, pp. 170-172)

In *Aion,* Chapter XI, note 59, p. 267), Jung includes the Latin text and a reference to the New Testament: *"Transmutemini de lapidis mortuis in vivos lapides philosophicos?"* This is an allusion to 1 Peter 2:4f, "Come to him, to the living stone, rejected by men but in God's sight chosen and precious; and like living stones be yourself built [up]. . ." (*The Holy Bible,* RSV). This is the philosopher's call, the invitation of the one who loves Wisdom, and it is also the affirmation that "this truth 'shines' in us, but it is not of us: it is sought not in us, but in the image of God which is in us'" (p. 171). In footnote 60, Jung gives the original Latin: *"Non in nobis quaerenda [veritas], sed in imagine Dei, quae in nobis est"* (p. 268). We do not find the truth in the self nor in the Self, but in the SELF that informs and energizes the Self out of a boundless generosity, that "transcendental self [SELF], which is identical with God" (p. 171), the *"IT"* of the Kabala, and the One of all religious traditions.

*. . . my spiritual practice is to look within for the places that are blocking my ability to experience the flow of an immense tenderness that is endlessly giving itself to me in all situations.*
—James Finley, 2018, Searching for Love

## CHAPTER TWELVE: SOMATIC PSYCHOTHERAPY AND THE SELF

### IFS in the Somatic Tradition

The following reflections are meant to provide some context to the argument that Internal Family Systems (IFS) therapy belongs to the psychotherapeutic traditions that take the full organismic dimensions into account in its philosophy, theory, methods, and practice. I have selected a limited sampling of thinkers and practitioners of body psychotherapy from among the many who have influenced me. Although I do not explore their ideas in depth, I want to express my gratitude to those whose insights have guided me while seeking the Elusive SELF: to Peter Levine for Somatic Experiencing, to Pat Ogden et al. for Sensorimotor Psychotherapy, to Babette Rothschild for Somatic Trauma Therapy, to Eugene Gendlin for Focusing, and to Francine Shapiro for Eye Movement Desensitization and Reprocessing. For the titles of their works, see the Reference section.

In this book, I offer my interpretation of the meaning of the term *self,* as used by these authors, by bracketing the words "self," "Self," or "SELF," as I seek to clarify and differentiate the terms. Reflecting on our use of language gives us the opportunity to refresh our understanding. Repeating terms without submitting them to our evolving understanding of the reality to which they point dooms us to a defeating nominalism, and when we add the phenomenon of translation, as well as historical and cultural contexts to the mix, the need for review and reflection is moving along with the subtle, nuanced changes that our human experience generates around the world. The following discussion offers a limited number of sources on which to reflect.

153

## Core Energetics and Hakomi

John W. Pierrakos, while not a prolific writer, was an intuitive, experiential learner, a visionary, a man graced with uplifting joys and crushing sorrows. He was fully human. In his 1997 book, *Eros, Love & Sexuality: The Forces that Unify Man & Woman,* published four years before his death, he admitted in a biographical aside, that he had come, as a psychiatrist, to . . .

> shift the emphasis of my work from the defenses to the creative, the spiritual self. Now, because I have a deep respect and love for people, my interventions can cut through their defenses quickly and clearly. I know in my heart what I am doing and why. My ego is not in the work the way it was before. And I continue to work on my own issues about authority, freeing myself to be more daring. (pp. 120-121)

Pierrakos's book was a farewell to the CE community and an invitation to its members to move beyond the limits of his understanding:

> I yearn to see Core Energetics blossom in many more ways in order to help unify the split between psychology, religion, science, and personal life. My work is to reach the depths of a person's entity. To help that person open up, transform—move! (p. 21)

As a depth psychotherapist who is both a Certified CE and IFS therapist, I am pleased to see how Somatic IFS and Body Psychotherapy have an amicable, creative relationship. There is history in this relationship.

In the early stages of the formation of Hakomi Therapy—a mindfulness-centered somatic psychotherapy—founder Ron Kurtz collaborated closely with Pierrakos, as he did with Greg Johanson, a man I grew to respect during the early years of the 21st century as a fellow Board of Directors member of the U. S. Association for Body Psychology (USABP). And, more to the purport of this book, Schwartz tapped into the psychological and spiritual Hakomi tradition in his associations with Kurtz and from his early association with Susan McConnell.

I will not discuss the Reichian and Bioenergetic roots of Core Energetics here. Pierrakos envisioned a therapy that seeks to free the physical body from the impositions of an armored self that lives out of its masks, personae, parts, and other assaulting pain—the results of inauthentic living. Pierrakos provides a stunning and potentially disorienting clarity when he says that "*consciousness* [emphasis added] shapes and directs the energy that flows within us . . . , that the body has its own consciousness, its own wisdom" (pp.17-18). He adds that "our spiritual self [Self] possesses the greatest consciousness of all, is expressed in all of the manifestations of love, [and] spirituality is the expansion of consciousness without limits" (p. 18). He referred to the traumatized center of our consciousness (the ego, the self) as disintegrating into the Mask—the Persona, in Jungian language. For Pierrakos, a wounded and burdened self [ego] is unable to see and accept with clarity and compassion its "Lower Self"—the network of personal conscious and unconscious states; that is, the energy that is captive, in bondage, and burdened needing to be transformed into the creative self, one that lives from the *Core*.

As with all who attempt to speak of the "self," we often fail to bring the necessary clarity to the discussion. The object of our discourse is in fact the subject of our discourse being carried out by an observer who is unable to be only the observed. Pierrakos's language often fails in this way. Internal Family Systems therapy attempts to use ordinary words to facilitate a practical understanding for psychotherapeutic effect, but it also admits that it suffers from a similar handicap. To that end, there is compromise in the language.

Each of us has a center, a core of divine wisdom and energy. Here energy and consciousness are wholly pure, luminous, and unfettered. Energy radiates from the core as it does from the heart of a star, moving through our entire being, enlivening every molecule. The task of Core Energetics is to help the individual contact the boundless resources of the core and release them in order to create a life of

155

pleasure, dignity, and freedom. . . . Through the core, we are connected to all things, all the energy of the cosmos. The core is the source of our being; it is our divine connection with the universal forces. We know it by many names: Christ consciousness, Buddha nature, God. The core embraces love, wisdom, compassion, and pleasure. (pp. 21-22)

Pierrakos then affirms that when we let ourselves be moved by our core energies we no longer need to rely on anything else. "As we activate the qualities of our core, we bring out the higher self. . . . The core is the center of love" (pp. 22-23). When we act from the center of love, there is no more need for rules.

In Pierrakos's language, our spiritual Self lies in wholeness (the union of opposites, according to Jung). Pierrakos says,

[The] result of this unification is love: love of one self, for another and for life in all its magnificent forms. From this spiritual place which we call our *higher self* [emphasis added] comes our creative power. This power gives meaning to our lives; it opens to a path beyond material concerns, beyond the confines of personal reality. A path of unification with the great mystery, the universal spirit— God. (pp. 28-29)

Another way of saying this is "with SELF."

## A Pause to Reflect on Love

In the first sentence of the preface of *A General Theory of Love,* Lewis, Amini, and Lannon (2000) ask, *"What is love and why are some people unable to find it?* [emphasis added]" (p. vii). In asking this, the authors place, front and center, the ultimate aim of honest psychotherapy, spirituality, and religion. In the last paragraph of the preface, they dedicate themselves to the exploration of an answer to the question and tell us how they see the mission of their book: "Every book, if it is anything at all, is an argument: an articulate arrow of words, fledged and notched and newly anointed with sharpened stone, speeding through paragraphs to its shimmering target" (p. viii). These psychiatrists pour out their personal and professional convictions for readers to consider. As an IFS therapist, I again follow the method of selectivity by quoting the authors and then briefly commenting on their "arrows of words."

When authors are modest in their assertions; that is, not overreaching, it augurs well for the integrity of their argument. For example, Lewis et al. earn my respect when they say that "only a few things about love can be proven, and just a few things amenable to proof are worth knowing at all" (p. 11). What an assuring statement by learned professionals and respected practitioners. The same could be said of the SELF. I find myself agreeing with them when they write that "although this book traffics in scientific discoveries, we cannot endorse the myopic assumptions that academic papers hold the key to the mysteries of love. Human lives form the richest repository of that information" (p. 12). This certainly applies to what I assert in this book.

Lewis et al. tell us what questions they have found worth asking when it concerns the lives of fellow humans:

What are feelings, and why do we have them? What are relationships and why do they exist? What causes emotional pain and how can it be mended—with medications, with psychotherapy, with both? What is therapy, and how does it heal? How should we configure society to further human health? How should we raise our children, and what should we teach them? (p. 13)

In this quote, the IFS therapist recognizes the allusion to the parts operative in the human multiplicity manifest in the trinity of the Brain, Body, and Mind. The IFS therapist also rejoices when he learns of a physician such as Frank G. Anderson who connects neuroscience, psychopharmacology, IFS, and other modalities in the treatment of traumatized patients by attending to the multiplicity in his choice of pharmaceuticals in his therapeutic protocols. (See Anderson, 2013, "Who's Taking What?") Without doubt, the IFS therapist grasps the

157

social-justice dimensions and the child-development implications of love so emphasized by the source references in this book. Daniel Siegel, M. D., comes immediately to mind as one of these sources. He so eloquently weaves brain, mind, and relationship into the construct of the human evolution,

Lewis et al. are emphatic when they write that "those who do not grasp the principles of love waste their lives and break their hearts" (p. 13). I reference and quote from their book because, with the IFS focus and emphasis on the centrality of the SELF and its energetic qualities, some folks in the helping professions advance that nothing can be asserted if not based on the results of scientific methodologies. Internal Family Systems is recognized as an evidence-based therapy, but that does not mean that its theoretical and philosophical underpinnings are of necessity available to scientific validation. The definition of our humanity is beyond the limits of scientific inquiry and its outcomes. Science ascertains facts; it does not define truth.

The science of our day hints at structures but cannot define them. The castle of the emotional mind is not yet grounded in fact, and there is ample room left within its domain for conjecture, invention, and poetry. . . . As neuroscience unlocks the secrets of the brain, startling insights into the nature of love becomes possible. That is what this book is about—and if that is not the secret of life, then we don't know what is. (p. 15)

Notwithstanding the advances in the neurosciences since the turn of the century, the above statement stands.

By analogy, the same can be said of The Elusive SELF. It defies definition. It has no describable boundaries. It is not unreasonable to fathom it as the source of life and of love. It yields to no measurable effort. It can only be experienced. When Lewis et al. quote Einstein as saying, "We should take care not to make the intellect our god; it has of course powerful muscles but no personality. It cannot lead; it can only serve" (p. 32), we must take notice of this wisdom. We have forgotten

158

that to be rational did not first mean to be logical, it meant to be spiritual, and to be intellectual does not assure wisdom. The qualities of the Self, as expressed by IFS's eight Cs (Calmness, Clarity, Curiosity, Compassion, Confidence, Courage, Connectedness, and Creativity) do come from a supra-ordinate source, the SELF. Mystics offer us other living symbols of delight, joy, fearlessness, justice, paradise, fullness, emptiness, grandeur, and more. As good scientists who respect the physical world as it is and not as we would fancifully want it to be, Lewis et al. remind us that "the brain's Byzantine confirmation determines everything about human nature—including the nature of love, [that] the brain is not unitary nor is it harmonious" (pp. 20-21). We know that we are "asocial carnivores" as well as conceptualizers and caretakers of our young. And more than that, "words, good ideas, and logic [products of the cortex] mean nothing to at least two brains out of three" [our affective and reptilian brains] (p. 33). Our "emotional brain, although inarticulate and unreasoning, can be expressive and intuitive. . . . [It] can move us in ways beyond logic. . . . Poet Robert Frost wrote that 'a poem begins as a lump in the throat, a sense of wrong, a home sickness, a love sickness'" (Lewis et al., p. 34). It is never a thought to begin with. Love moves us. "Emotion is the messenger of love; it is the vehicle that carries every signal from one brimming heart to another. For human beings feeling deeply is synonymous with being alive" (p. 37). Emotion is synonymous with being fully present with another in the moment. That is the experience of being in Self, of being touched by the embracing SELF.

Later in their insightful book, Lewis et al., psychiatrists all, address the use of medications "to alter the emotional mind" as "tinkering with the stuff the self is made of. In the right hands, that alchemy can rescue lost lives" (p. 173). When the center of consciousness—the I—is troubled, burdened by disordered emotions and thoughts, it cannot of itself access or receive the healing, balancing energy of the SELF. The SELF must then break through—slip in of its own accord or collaborate with the welcoming invitation of an open door prompted by the compassionate presence of a caring other—a family member, a friend, or a professional helper. Lewis et al. affirm this clearly when they address the role of psychotherapy: "All therapies are not equal. Some are compatible with the human heart and work within its architecture to maximize health" (pp. 189-190). Internal Family Systems is one of those models of psychotherapy that is compatible with the human heart.

As a graduate practicum student at a state hospital, I recall the supervising psychologist telling us that relationship with our patients was not only unnecessary but a waste of time; that interns and staff were there only to *modify the patient's behaviors.* This was the policy of a ward that housed persons who had been committed to the hospital for some 10, 20, and 30 or more years. This was a place of hopelessness. We were attempting to modify the patients' behaviors for whom? That question was not welcomed. We were instructed to ignore any possible, even probable, meaning expressed by the patient's behaviors. There was no welcoming of the person of the patient whose way of being in their world necessitated hopeful hospitality. I withdrew from that placement after a semester.

Years later, I heard that nothing had changed for the residents of that ward for chronically psychotic and violent women. Instead, as a result of the food-based token economy (Cheerios and M&Ms), an additional dentist had been hired to restore the significant deterioration of the dental health of that particular population. The desperate extreme protective parts of those persons screamed their need to be heard, to have a heart-to-heart response, but instead, those abandoned and lost selves were herded into the corral of the dayroom during waking hours and then back into the locked stalls of their cells in the evening. We were trained to respond, not from an open heart, but from a self-protecting stance. How could this environment, devoid of relationship, be anything other than a desolate war zone? That was in the late1960s. Some of us rebelled.

When Lewis et al. write, "Because our minds seek one another through limbic resonance, because our physiologic rhythms answer to the call of limbic regulation, because we change one another's brains through limbic revision—what we do inside relationship matters more than any other aspect of human life" (pp. 191-192), it is impossible not to apply this statement to the work of psychotherapy, to the therapeutic relationship, when the therapist welcomes every part, every aspect, every dimension of the other—the sacred patient.

When IFS speaks of connectedness as a quality of the SELF-led Self, it is a reminder that we humans are mammals; that we have evolved to the point of being able to be in need of relatedness. "Because mammals need relatedness for their physiology to coalesce correctly, most of what make a socially functioning human comes from connection—the shaping physiological force of love" (p. 218). We are emotional (feeling) beings more than cognitive (thinking) beings. It is good to remember—a sobering fact—that "Emotions reach back 100 million years, while cognition is a few hundred thousand years old at best" (p. 228).

Lewis et al., not only as psychiatrists, but also as practicing scientists, quote Blaise Pascal **to make their point**: *"Reason's last step is recognizing that an infinity of things surpasses it* [emphasis added]" (p. 229). And among the things that surpass it is The Elusive SELF. Our understanding of the SELF is woefully inadequate. We cannot put boundaries on the *IT* of Mystical Judaism and on the *IT's* influence on the internal and external worlds in which the human swims.

No matter what humanity's future holds, we will never shed our heritage as neural organisms, mammals, primates. Because we are emotional beings, pain is inevitable and grief will come; because the world is neither equitable nor fair, the suffering will not be distributed evenly. A person who intuits the ways of the heart stands a better chance of living well. (pp. 229-230)

161

In this, patient and therapists are equals. The psychotherapies that are "compatible with the human heart," "intuit the ways of the heart," and promote a heartfelt connectedness find a co-naturality with IFS's way of being with the other.

On the last page of their modest book, Lewis et al. remind us that the search for a theory of love is beyond our ability to finalize. Science can only offer us a glancing look at what will always be fully out of clear sight. As we saw earlier, William James did not ask his Pragmatism to define religious experience, and the authors are humble enough to state that . . .

> we demand too much if we expect single-handed empiricism to define and lay bare the human soul. Only in concert with art does science become so precise. . . . Both can illuminate inner and outer landscapes with a flash that inspires but whose impermanence necessitates unending rediscovery. (p. 230)

The poets and mystics are the ones who, with the scientists, catch a glimpse of Love operating in the universe to offer Hope that suffering might lead to Joy. James referenced some of these thinkers in his Gifford Lectures. The writings of Matthew Fox, Thomas Merton, and Rohr are seasoned with quotes from the mystics of the world.

## Embodying the Self—The Somatic IFS of Susan McConnell

The terms *incarnation, enfleshed spirit,* and *embodiment of the self* are terms associated with the language of psychology, religion, and spirituality. Since no one has ever seen "God" and lived, so also no one has ever seen the SELF, other than in a symbolic manifestation, and lived. That is the calling of the Self—to manifest in and through the body-behavior dimension the active integrating presence of the SELF in this human world. When Pierrakos enjoined us *to move* in group and individual training sessions, he was talking about being alive from the Core (the SELF). In Martha Sweezy and Ellen Ziskind's 2013 book, *Internal Family Systems Therapy: New Dimensions,* McConnell, senior

162

IFS trainer, speaks about experiencing Self-energy in the language of "fluidity": "This is the fluid, fluctuating state I call embodied Self" (p. 91).

The Somatic IFS Therapist has no power at all over the SELF but can more fully embody the integrating Self as a manifestation of the SELF in a singular imperfect incarnation that is the human person. Through her years of experience and extensive training, McConnell is convinced that the IFS therapist can, through the use of the somatic tools of IFS, "help the client embody Self and bring Self-energy [SELF-energy] to the healing process" (p. 91). She identifies these tools as . . .

> somatic awareness, conscious breathing, somatic resonance, mind-ful-movement, and attuned touch [emphasis added]. Each one is de-signed to address the impact of attachment injuries on the body and each can be applied to any point in the IFS model: accessing parts, facilitating the relationship with parts, witnessing, unburdening, and integration. (p. 91)

How reminiscent of the great spiritual traditions of world religions.

(Susan McConnel's new book, *Somatic Internal Family systems Therapy: Awareness, Breath, Resonance, Movement and Touch in Practice*, is forthcoming from North At-lantic Books, Berkley, CA, in 2020.)

### Another Aspect of Body Psychotherapy

In *The Psychology of the Body*, Elliot Greene and Barbara Goodrich-Dunn (2004) put forth a description of Body Psychotherapy that they have adapted from the language of the European Association for Body Psychotherapy:

> Body psychotherapy integrates the recognition and utilization of the body into the theory and practice of psychotherapy. [The] body psy-chotherapist supports the client's internal self-regulative processes and accurate perception of external reality based on a belief that an essential embodiment of mental, emotional, social, and spiritual life exists within the client. [Body Psychotherapy] makes it possible for

163

alienated *aspects* of the client to become *conscious,* acknowledged, and *integrated parts* [emphasis added] of the self [Self]. (p. 100)

How welcoming and hospitable is this gentle approach that honors the mystery of the SELF's incarnation. How compatible with the heart-felt approach, philosophy, and methods of IFS.

### Formative Psychology

In his 1975 book, *Your Body Speaks Its Mind: Expanding Our Selves,* Stanley Keleman,* chiropractor, therapist, writer, and founder of Formative Psychology, posits that life shapes itself somatically according to subjective experience. He also makes many enigmatic statements, such as the following:

- The person who is the core of *his* life is the core of *all* life. (p. 166)
- When I began to challenge my assumptions, ideals, and beliefs, both cognitively and muscularly, I began to experience an expanded dimension to my life. I started to understand that my experience and my expression were my truth, that my way of forming my self [Self] was my life. Self-expanding is exciting and grows more exciting as it thrusts me toward individuation. . . . We spend our lifetime becoming somebody instead of maintaining an image. (p. 167)
- To love is to drop one's roles, to be present extendedly. (p. 170)
- What greater mystery is there than the mystery of being incarnated, the mystery of being in the flesh? Our bodily lives bound and unbound, embody and disembody, form us-the-mystery as we experience the collage of living layers called us. (p. 171)
- We're all in the same sea of creation. . . . This ocean of continuity shapes my inner and outer space, my bounded [self] and unbounded self [Self]. There is inner space when I close my I, and there is outer space when I open my I. (p. 172)
- Love which runs deep begins with the streamings of one's body. One's streamings fill one's self [Self] with so much feeling that

164

the feeling transcends one's boundaries and expands one's *connectedness* [emphasis added] with other persons. (p. 173)

- I understand spirituality as a heightening of the excitatory process of the human animal. The religious experience, divorced of its hokum, is the vivid experience. It is our vivid experiencing, and it is the vividness of what we experience. Its depth and its intensity correspond with how deep and intense our streamings are. . . . Our streamings are our biological field, the field of our embodied life. To experience our streamings is the spiritual experience. To live our streamings, to participate in the forming of our lives, is the great mystery and joy of existence. (p. 174)

To address Keleman's statements, I offer the following commentary:

- In the world of psychotherapy, theorists and practitioners share a common vocabulary but not necessarily a common nosology. Keleman uses the terms **"the person"** and **"the core,"** plus the expressions **"his life"** and **"all life."** These terms leave me to wonder about their meaning in his toolbox of concepts. Is it that we must be fully at the center of our somatic experience in order to be fully engaged in all of the dimensions of life? Is he insisting on the fullest consciousness we can muster as the essential condition for the forming—shaping, constructing—of a life fully lived? This enigmatic statement is discernable only through a lived experience.

- Authenticity is the thing. The dying to old concepts, old perceptions, outdated introjects, restricting and myopic values, is the arduous path to new and wider vistas. This is the process of the self as it evolves into a Self, an identity that is authentic, related to the SELF. This is the individuation process—the becoming who we are, in Jung's sense of the term—the shedding of a worn-out persona, the casting aside of no longer needed masks after expressing our gratitude for their transitory assistance. This is the journey to integrity at the end of our long years, a journey coming to rest in

165

blessed hope. Developmental psychologist Erik Erikson's work comes to mind.

- Keleman invites us to let go of all play-acting in the real game of love, which is so easy to say, but challenging in reality. A blinding beauty and shocking tremors rock the ground of our being in the exercise of a love that exacts a focused attention and an expansive presence that generates the incarnation of spirit and the *sanctification* of the Self—all so reminiscent of James.

- In this exaltation, Keleman recognizes the ineffable experience that we are *beings in the flesh*. How marvelously anti-dualistic is his understanding of our human nature. When he proclaims that it is through our bodily lives that we form (structure, make, construct, shape, develop, evolve) *us-the-mystery* that we are, the *us* that *we experience* in a *collage of living layers called us*. Reading this, I harken to the marvelous multiplicity that we are—each and every one of us.

- Keleman visualizes the vastness of the going forth and of the returning in the movement of the sea—breathing and pulsing—and visualizes the same for the spacious psyche. How the mystics rejoice.

- Jung once said that physics provided us with the most illuminating metaphors to understand the psyche, and Keleman does not hesitate to reveal his conviction that the *Love* that runs deep (Eros, Amor, and Caritas, I say) begins with the body's energetic streamings. That conviction turns any and all philosophical and religious vilification of the somatic rightly on its arrogant skull or arse. In physics, a wave can be thought of as a disturbance or an "oscillation that travels through space-time, accompanied by a transfer of energy . . . from one point to another, often with no displacement of the particles of the medium—that is, with little or no associated mass transport." (See http://courses.lumenlearning,com/boundlessphysics.chapter. waves.) This could also be true when

166

considering the streamings of the body and is a poetic way to express the connecting love oscillating between persons—near and far—between all pulsating entities.

• In nonreligious language, Keleman expresses the quintessential religious experience that James endeavored to portray in his lectures as integral to our common human experience and that IFS holds as a hoped-for outcome for both patient and therapist.

---

*Keleman died at the age of 85 in 2018. The Fall/Winter 2018 issue of the *International Body Psychotherapy Journal* is dedicated to Keleman's contributions to the field of Body Psychotherapy.

### Recovery and the Client-Therapist Relationship in Bioenergetic Analysis

Robert Hilton, a courageously honest man, was transparent in his desperate need for help. In 1972, after completing a four-year course of Bioenergetic Analysis and Training, he said,

I needed someone who worked with the body and recognized it as the energetic core of self-expression and the source of the true self [Self], but more than that, I needed a person who wanted to connect to *me,* not just a body, not just a problem, not just a character, not just an energetic system, but *me,* with all my weaknesses and needs. (See Michael Sieck, 2007, *Relational Somatic Psychotherapy: Collected Essays of Robert Hilton,* p. 89.)

What he needed most in the course of his therapeutic experience was an "illusion of control" left intact for as long as he required its protection while he learned how "to feel important somewhere with someone" (p. 89). He needed someone who would respect and welcome all of his parts, all aspects of himself, all of his subpersonalities. He also needed to be confirmed; that is, he "needed a witness and a mirroring response to confirm [his] reality" (p. 91). The IFS therapist takes the time to

167

linger attentively with a manifest part of the client to give witness to its reality, to confirm the living multiplicity that is the person of the client.

Hilton was not ashamed to confess that he also needed compassion. By reaching back into his study of ancient languages, he explains what he means. I paraphrase: The Greek word for compassion is *Esplagnia.* It comes from *splanga,* which is the word for one's inner organs—heart, lungs, liver, etc. The Latin derivative is the word *viscera.* Add an epsilon onto *splanga* and you have compassion (coming out of one's inner being). Compassion results from how a response to another affects one's inner organs (p. 91). Hilton writes, "I needed to know that I made an impact on my therapist and that she was moved within herself in regard to my life-and-death struggle" (p. 91). Hilton was stating that the client is in need of a "bodily resonance" on the part of the therapist. Compassion is not a thing of a disembodied mind; it requires a suffering with, a vibrational empathy, a visceral presence.

Along with the above needs, Hilton needed contact, by which he means physical contact. He was fortunate to have had the language and methods of Bioenergetics—a body psychotherapy modality—that understood the essential need and ethics of non-erotic mutual touch to cross the bridge of shame and to enliven a weakened self [the me] (pp. 92-93). But his need for contact, as it is for everyone, is insufficiently satisfied without the completion of the need for containment. In the therapeutic relationship he describes, he expresses the need for safety, respect, and an intimacy built on clearly declared and understood mutual boundaries. "I needed a relationship that could contain all of me, both the negativity and the rage. I had never risked this depth of expression within a relationship before" (p. 93). In his case, his therapist offered a heartfelt altruistic therapeutic love, a SELF-led love.

Satisfying these legitimate human needs on the part of a patient would indeed fail if it were not crowned with the therapist's commitment. Hilton was not afraid to reveal the extent of his need for his therapist's commitment.

168

I needed someone who was committed to our relationship; someone who could weather the storm of my rage and disappointment; someone who never once thought that whatever happened in the therapy could not be worked out; someone who was committed regardless of the outcome. I needed someone who would fight for me. (p. 94)

Internal Family Systems is committed to fighting for the *us* in each one of us, dedicated to the mission of liberating all captives within the *us* that we are, all who are burdened, all who are duty-bound to manage the internal system, all who seek to protect, even attempt to rescue the most desperate ones of *us* living and acting in and by and through the mystery of our incarnation.

I was pleasantly surprised to find a quote from Eliot's poem, "Little Gidding," at the close of one of Hilton's essays.

> We shall not cease from exploration,
> And the end of all our exploring
> Will be to arrive where we started
> And know the place for the first time.

Luke commented on this poem in her own way in *Old Age: Journey into Simplicity,* which I mention in Chapter Six: "Old Age and the IFS Therapist."

This reminds me of the self's return journey to the SELF via the cooperative travails of the Self energized by the SELF who first thrust the self into the here and now to become ever more fully conscious and thereby expand the SELF's being in this incarnate world. This is an archetypal Job experience; that is, it is not unlike Job's stand, which increased YHWH's awareness of his Shadow, and healed both divinity's and humanity's dualistic mind. "What is," is of YHWH's doing and sustaining. Good and evil is of being's nature, each two sides of the same coin—a realization we object to and reject to preserve our protective illusion.

## Roots and Development of the Chiron Approach

In the introduction to *Contemporary Body Psychotherapy,* Editor Linda Hartley (2009) quotes from Janet Adler's 2002 book, *Offering from the Conscious Body: The Discipline of Authentic Movement:*

The body is our sensation, our felt emotion. The body is our experience of ourselves, our temple in which the light of spirit burns. Unconscious worlds, numinous worlds, worlds with high order, and worlds with no apparent order can become known within the body, because of the body. (p. 6)

Hartley also quotes Lewis et al. (2000), who let us know that "psychotherapy alters the living brain [and that] the mind body clash has disguised the truth that psychotherapy *is* physiology [emphasis added]" (Hartley, p. 168).

In Chapter 1 of Hartley's book, she says that Bernd Eiden mentions that, relevant to a wider discussion of the place of IFS in the treatment of trauma, Pierre Janet also deserves to be honored as a body psychotherapy pioneer (pp. 14-15). In 1885, well before Reich advanced his Vegetotherapy theory, Janet recognized the correlation between muscular contraction and the formation of the neurotic structure, and Janet used massage and touch in his work. (See David Boadella, 1997, *Wilhelm Reich: The Evolution of His Work.*) Damasio is also "prominent amongst those who have given neurobiological evidence that thought and reflection arise out of and follow feeling and sensation" (Hartley, p. 15). When, during an IFS therapy session, the therapist asks, Where do you feel that part in your body? and, How do you feel toward that part? the therapist is firmly within the holistic tradition that honors the trinity of mind, brain, and body.

When the IFS therapist acts with the confidence that the SELF knows how to lead the Self, such a practitioner celebrates the Reichian roots of this approach. Hartley says, "Reich trusted the organism's capacity for self-regulation and inner well-being. His therapy process

170

aimed to reach the *core* [emphasis added], the deeper primacy level, which was by nature positive, spontaneous and motivated to make contact" (p. 16). Internal Family Systems therapy sees all parts of the person as acting with positive intent in spite of related negative effects. All aspects of life and death are elements of wholeness-making. The IFS mantra that all parts are welcome applies to everything pertaining to human existence and experience. Nothing is left out, which is why IFS therapy is experiential to the extent that it is somatic. To promote a Self-led life, IFS therapy is "phenomenological and explorative" with the goal "to help the client's awareness to grow and facilitate self-regulation and self-actualization" (p. 17).

### Integrating Body-Self and Psychological-Self

David W. Krueger, physician and psychoanalyst, begins his 2002 book, *Integrating Body Self and Psychological Self,* by reminding the reader that "Freud called the ego first a body ego [and that] the body self and somatic experience-representation have perhaps been left behind. . . " (p. xi). Krueger gives us a language to speak of the person's incarnation in time and space: "The body self is an idea, like the ego; the body is a fact. The body self and image [are] created by, and live within the imagination, the map within the actual territory of the body" (p. xi). In the world of IFS, McConnell is the one who joined body psychotherapy to the wedding of the concept of self with the experiential fact of the physical body. When we image the "I" that we are, we face the tangible and the intangible, the concrete and the abstract, the permanent and the impermanent. In this last pairing, we confront our consciousness as a person, aware that there was a moment when we had no awareness of our existence, and that after death, the end of our physical form, we have no evidence to contradict Jung's position that our individual personhood will persist at some level of evolved consciousness.

171

Krueger warns us that he is "attempting to mingle the language of the body and the language of the mind [and that] *body* and *body image* [emphasis added] are the intersubjective mutual creation of meaning and flesh, revealed and constructed intersubjectively, thus relationally. . . . All actions necessarily involve the body [and] every interaction with others is mediated by the body. . . . We are always embodied. . . " (p. xiii). There was that moment when self (ego) came to the realization that self was not the other, that it was separate from all that existed beyond self's skin—Freud's understanding that the ego is coextensive with the skin—that self had being in this sphere of existence only in and through and by the body. Embodiment, incarnation to borrow another image, is the ground zero of all body psychotherapy modalities.

Lest we forget, Krueger reminds us that "the self that seeks embodiment (incarnation), and the body that yearns for residence in the mind, integrate throughout development" (p. xiii). If psychotherapy is to enhance this development, it must heed the1790 epigram by William Blake that heads Part I of Krueger's book: "*But first the notion that man has a body distinct from his soul is to be expunged* [emphasis added]."

It is worth repeating that "Freud said that 'the ego is first and foremost a bodily ego' " (Krueger, p. 27). And that "since Freud used the term *ego* interchangeably with *self,* his indication was that one's sense of self, later evolving to a psychological self, [which] first begins with a body self [and evolves into] a developmental hierarchy of experience and intellectual mechanism . . . that regulate the entire self-experience" (Krueger, p. 7). Krueger also said that the "body and its evolving mental representation are the foundation of a sense of self" (p. 7). I imagine Buddha breathing and smiling, emptying his mind of concerns and trivia, settling into the sensations of being grounded, and realizing the spiritualization of his bodily form.

At the beginning of Chapter 2, Krueger quotes Diana Ackerman, the author of the exquisite 1990 book, *A Natural History of the Senses,* to set us straight about the brain: "The mind doesn't really dwell in the brain but travels the whole body. . . " (p. 29). Krueger quotes Ackerman again before Chapter 4: "The brain is a dark, silent world filled with lifesaving illusions" (p. 51).

Heller speaks of necessary illusions in his monumental 2012 tome, *Body Psychotherapy: History, Concepts and Methods:*

Necessary illusions are forms of perception that are generated by the laws that rule mental dynamics. They are *illusions* because they include more than the information provided by the senses; and they are *necessary* because without them mental dynamics would cease to function adequately. (Glossary, pp. 743-744)

When the above-mentioned authors refer to "lifesaving illusions" (Ackerman) and "necessary illusions" (Heller) they are referring, I submit, to the ineffable mystery of our human nature. On the first page of Part II of *Integrating Body Self and Psychological Self,* Krueger quotes Jung: "The body is merely the visibility of the soul, the psyche; and the soul is the psychological experience of the body. So, it is one and the same thing" (p. 77). In these two bold sentences, Krueger shouts the great revelation that body and soul are one, and I would dare add, give us our conscious personhood, a relational trinity that argues for continued existence in some unknown fashion. When Rohr writes that "God is Relationship," (May 10, 2019, Daily Meditation), is the triune flow, so is it with our own conscious triune flow when in relationship with each other and all that is.

In Chapter 9, "Dissociation, Trauma, and Development," Krueger tells us of Janet's findings of the "existence of unconscious personalities in hysterical patients constructed in response to traumatic events" (p. 126). Krueger makes mention of "multiple selves," with reference to Self-Psychology, writing that psychoanalyst Heinz Kohut "noted the existence of simultaneous and even contradictory selves in the same person with varying degrees of importance and compatibility" (p. 126). Schwartz developed IFS therapy as a way to help those parts, those multiple subselves heal, integrate, and not be eliminated.

Krueger references Daniel Siegel, who offers us another way to look at and describe the multiple selves or personalities, which in IFS we call parts—a vague, undetermined word closer to everyday experience and language—presents the phrase "a state of mind," defining it as "the total pattern of activation in the brain at a particular moment in time. . . . A state of mind determines perception and processing, emotional tone and regulation, access to memory, mental models, and behavioral response patterns" (Krueger, p. 127). All states of minds resonate in and through and by a parallel integrated state of the body. How would it not be so?

In the following paragraphs, Krueger further presents us with complimentary definitions of the term **"state"** that not only imply the role of the body but underscore its necessity:

- From Daniel N. Stern of the Boston Process of Change Study Group (1998): "The semi-stable organization of the organism as a whole at a given moment" (Krueger, 2002, p. 28).
- From Frank W. Putnam (1992): "The psychological and physiological variables that occur together and repeat themselves, often in highly predictable sequences that are relatively stable and enduring over time. Each state of mind has its own ABCS—affect, behavior, cognition, sensation. Each discreet and distinct state includes affect, arousal/energy level, motor activity, posture, mannerisms, speech, cognitive processing, access to knowledge, autobiographical memory, as well as sense of self" (Krueger, p. 128).

All of the above is what we refer to when we welcome a part into a colloquy with our Self-led center of consciousness. When the IFS therapist makes contact with a *part,* this *partial self* functions out of the structures and systems that Putnam elucidates. In the extreme, when the part has evolved into a separate self, an *alter,* Putnam's descriptive definition comes to life as an engulfing runaway, one that can possess the self into a life-defeating captivity.

It is worthwhile to linger with Krueger, who references Putnam and Philip Bromberg in the section titled "States of Mind" in Chapter 9 that

174

details the integrating elements of the body self and the psychological self. Krueger makes reference to Putnam when he writes that the phrase *states of consciousness* is synonymous with the terms *ego state, state of mind,* and *self-state*; he acknowledges Bromberg when he notes that they involve "a systematic alteration of affect . . . , behavior . . . , cognition, and sensation," plus "fundamental somatopsychic responses"; that "each self-state, if a discontinuous state of consciousness for some individuals, has its own perception, processing, memory, and style of relatedness to self and others"; that these "states are coherent and distinct, though often camouflaged from awareness, yet hiding in the open" (Krueger, pp. 128-129). This is the stuff *parts* are made of; this is the *material* of the Freudian *ego*, of the IFS *self*. The parts, the subselves, all have the same structure and system as their whole, of the self. And when the self, ego, as the center of consciousness is led by the SELF into its evolution into a Self, the Self functions and is structured to a greater harmony and balance with the inner and outer world.

Krueger describes quite well the world of the traumatized self and its fragmentation into subsets. The following paragraphs have their rightful place in their entirety at this point of my discussion.

When someone cannot escape a trauma outside, they can escape inside, partitioning off the trauma like the body walls off an abscess to prevent contamination of the whole: a state change. Dissociation is perhaps the only proactive defense mechanism; that is, when danger is anticipated, all the information pertaining to it goes down one tract, rather than throughout the entire mind. One dissociates not *post hoc* [emphasis added], as with repression and all other defenses, but as the event is actually happening. In the event of severe abuse, there is a complete corruption of the developmental milieu. . . . (p. 129)

The evolving ego/self, in the extreme, ceases its life's developmental journey and return to its source, the SELF. Instead, it stagnates while a cohort of subselves, parts, takes over. Some hide as exiles, some as fierce protectors, some as rigid managers, all in need of contact, under-standing, and appreciation.

Krueger continues to expound on the creative complexity of the em-bodied person. "The mind, as a linear model with linear dynamics of unconscious conflicts expands to a complex system of multiple states of consciousness that only appear continuous, seamless, and unshifting. Each state of consciousness is relived or enacted in its own relational context" (pp. 129-130). Krueger then quotes Bromberg: "If an analyst [the same for the IFS therapist] thinks of a person as speaking from different self-states rather than from a single center of self, then the an-alyst will inevitably listen that way." (See Bromberg, 1994, "Speak! That I May See You.")

In everyday, healthy, helping relationships, and in psychotherapy, the goal is to effect a differentiation between a part or parts and the operative central self-state of consciousness. This is at the heart of Cou-ple Therapy in IFS as described by both Schwartz, in *You Are the One You've Been Waiting For,* and IFIO founder Toni Herbine-Blank with Donna A. Kerpelman, and Martha Sweezy (2016), in *Intimacy from the Inside Out.*

The search for the states of consciousness that manifest in a session requires the intent to seek them out—not to hunt them down like prey but to search for them as a good shepherd would seek out the lost sheep or as a caring herdsman would look for a stray calf or rogue steer. The intent is always to return the lost to the flock, to the herd—the part to the whole—to value their contributions to the love of the whole. Krueger explains:

Tracking how someone gets into and out of self-states [parts] is both linear (dynamically understanding the specific feelings, coupled with meaning of trauma-danger, and triggering a dissociative re-sponse) and, at the same time, systemic (within a structure of states of mind, a psychophysiological alteration of a self-state [that] occurs

176

as a unique defense in which the individual is enabled to reflect on experience, rather than an unconscious avoidance of it). (p. 130) Again, the aim is always to bring what is hidden into the open by and for compassionate understanding. This is the crux of self-knowledge.

## Descriptive Definitions and Epigrams

To offer some clarification to further view the phenomena that concern us, I repeat the following descriptive definitions and epigrams that Krueger provides:

- A state of mind is a physiological state, not a specific feeling. (p. 130)
- A state of mind has its own developmental history, its own set of experiences, determines what is perceived and subsequently how it is processed. (p. 130)
- A state originates in the body, is basically rooted, as it is a psycho-physiological experience. (p. 130)
- A state is regulated from the beginning in an intersubjective context. . . . (p. 130)
- A self-state is mutually regulated between two people, and mutual regulation of a state is the central activity of mother and infant. (Edward Tronick in Krueger, p. 130)
- A state of mind provides an organizing context and determines perception and processing. (Frank Wills and Diana Sanders in Krueger, p. 130)
- Each ego state has a representational system that includes a self-representation and an object-representation, a predominate affective tone, a particular somatic body experience, and a cognitive organization paralleling the internalized self-other dyad. (Davies, 1996, "Reasons and Causes," in Krueger, p. 130)

---

*The mind seems to embrace a confederation of psychic entities.* (William James in Krueger, Chapter 10, p. 155)

- *All experience, thought, and feelings are embodied. . . . Feelings are first and foremost about the body; they offer us the cognition of our visceral and musculo-skeletal states[;] feelings let us mind the body.* (Damasio, *Descartes' Error,* in Krueger, Chapter 11, p. 177)

## The Body in Recovery

I end this chapter with thoughts from John P. Conger, Jungian Analyst and Body Psychotherapist, whose 1994 book, *The Body in Recovery: Somatic Psychotherapy and the Self,* helped me bridge the psychosomatic world in my personal and professional life while in Core Energetics training. With the epigram at the beginning of his Chapter 20, "Emotional Expression," Conger offers us the wisdom of William James:

A purely disembodied human emotion is a nonentity. I do not say that it is a contradiction in the nature of things, or that pure spirits are necessarily condemned to cold intellectual lives; but I say that for us, emotion dissociated from all bodily feeling is inconceivable. (James, 1890, *The Principles of Psychology,* in Conger, p. 47)

James reminds us that without the capacity to feel our sensations, our emotions, our imaginings, our perceptions, our cognitions, and our actions, it is our very human felt experience that escapes us and threatens to render us inert. Our capacity and willingness to feel is what opens the door to the creative therapeutic hour. I recall how well students of Counseling Psychology received philosopher Gendlin's thoughts on focusing that I incorporated into my students' training during the early 1980s. (See E. Gendlin, 1978, *Focusing.*) Doing so provided the interns a grounding experiential presence, philosophically congruent with any model of Counseling, and this enhanced their ability to make contact with the client. Conger puts it this way:

To meet the client in his or her uniqueness, we must let go of rigidly held assumptions or risk reducing the client to a shadowy player in

178

our theoretical system. Insofar as we leave room for a sincere encounter, we have interpersonal therapy. (p. 3)

In Part Three, "Gatherings of a Panentheist," I venture into the world of Personalism, intimating that the person-to-person relationship is the glue of all healing and that this glue implies embodiment. Conger reveals his operational understanding of embodiment thus: "Embodiment is not perfect health but rather a consciousness of wholeness and relatedness, a standing in the center of many polarities as an inventive curious presence in a state of spontaneous play" (p. 10). This reminds me of a crucial conviction in the world of IFS and Jungian analyst June Singer's pivotal 1974 book, *Boundaries of the Soul.* During my early years as a practitioner, I devoured her thoughts. She spoke emphatically of the need to enter the psychotherapeutic encounter in a non-knowing state, but one still open to learning who the client is and not what is wrong with the client—a quite Jungian approach akin to the best of the world's spirituality and, during the last decade, validated as being most therapeutic by the research that brought us the understanding and implications of Adverse Childhood Experiences (ACEs) in treating all dimensions of the human organism.

In his concern for the person who has suffered the onslaught of interpersonal trauma, Conger writes, "At the heart of psychic injury is a crushed rebellion, a voice of protest reduced to silence" (p. 141). Thus, the work of the somatic psychotherapist is to foster the client's "embodiment, [that] capacity to bring diverse internal and external elements into an organization called the Self" (p. 199).

How congruent is this perspective with the Somatic IFS views McConnell expresses? How congruent also with the world of subpersonalities that is the result of "splitting" in which a "client regresses to a childhood personality losing touch with its adult aspect of . . . Self" (Conger, p. 200)? The return of the parts to their healthy place and role in the whole evolving Self is the mission and goal of the therapeutic embodiment process.

Witnessing the marriage of the alchemical and the somatic is always a pleasure. Conger does not disappoint. As a well-grounded Jungian, he experiences the psyche as more than just a healthy functioning self (ego):

> A durable sense of self [Self] extends to the philosopher's stone, that goal of alchemy which is imperishable, that which lasts, an observing, neutral self [Self] that does not seem man-made[—]a durable self [Self] that exists past passions and dramas of the moment, sometimes revealing itself through dreams and visions. (p. 203)

This is the intersection, the meeting place of philosophy, theology, religion, spirituality, psychology, physics, science, poetry, and more.

Always a pragmatist and a man accepting of the incomplete and imperfect state of human existence and experience in this incarnational sphere, Conger states:

> The goals of a more modest psychology aim at developing a sense of self [Self] that can be trusted no matter how difficult the present moment. The enduring self [Self] knows that it can outlast every darkness, every suffering, no longer avoiding pain or fear of pain. A self [Self] that endures knows that the self [SELF] is related to others, to life itself and to nature that goes on. *Even in death, we are letting go to a nature that goes on.* [emphasis added]. The sense of ourselves as a part of nature puts to rest the ego's struggle to be exempt and special. The surrender to life's processes is the mastery of the durable self [Self]. . . . The durable self [Self] affirms an object constancy, a sense of trust from one moment to the next, a pleasure in the unexpected nature of life. *And the durable self [Self] may go to experience mystical states, [a] state of identification with nature and with the imperishable forms of God* [emphasis added]. (p. 203)

Conger's beautiful blend of Jungian and Bioenergetic Analysis is revealed when he writes, "A durable sense of self [Self] extends to the Philosopher's Stone, that goal of alchemy which is imperishable, [that] reveals itself through dreams and visions" (p. 203). What a delight to hear the strains of Jamesian music, Jung's symphonic elegance, the Jazz of body-psychotherapy modalities, the IFS sonatas, and among the treasures of human song and music, the penetrating Gregorian Chant evoking the splendor and emergence of the SELF in the company of the sounds of pipes and strings in forests and meadows, in deserts and on mountainsides, from villages across the globe.

I remind myself that the IT—the Ein Sof of mystical Judaism—is the Elusive SELF that the I is reaching for with the limited grasp afforded the self. To me it seems that the self that is elusive is The SELF that always is and is always welcoming the self into its Self-transformation on its return to the ultimate surprise—the return to the SELF in enduring consciousness. Conger speaks to us of the "durable self," which can be understood as the Self who has a sense of the abiding presence of the ultimately durable SELF, source and end of the self's developmental journey. Saul [Paul] of Tarsus, whose mystical experience on the road to Damascus, reduced him to an abject state upon the dust of the road, and who had his false self (his persona, mask, shield, armor, façade) blinded by the light of the SELF, was able to say after his recovery that it was no longer he who lived but that it was *The Christus,* the anointed one, who lived in him. I interpret this as the transformed self into the Self. The SELF was always Saul's archetypal center.

Earlier in his book, Conger stated the modest and humble nature of body-focused psychotherapy: "Our work needs to address . . . early injuries, to define them and seek ways to build a functional and durable self [Self]" (p. 31). The person who has neither been provided the materials nor the skills, or who has ignored the task of the first half of life to build an earthly foundation before crafting the spire or cupula or dome or totem of one's chosen spiritual path, will soon find that his castles in the sky now lie in ruin at his feet with only limited options remaining—resigning himself to his fate; shoring up this faltering

181

structure; clearing out the debris, recycling as much as is possible; and building a new foundation for the emerging future.

Conger speaks in the language of pediatrician and psychoanalyst Donald Winnicott about what to do when such a person presents for therapy:

> The first task is to help a client identify the false self that he or she has developed to accommodate as a child. . . . This mask of accommodation . . . compensates for failures in development. The false self blocks healing. It hides a weariness and prevents our core nature from dealing with fear, pain, anger, excitement, desire, and loss. (p. 31)

The work of this transformational healing (wholeness-making) combines courage with crisis. The Book of Job does not tell us about Job's earlier developmental experiences. Nonetheless, Job might have settled into a false assumption that his opulent life was the result of his "specialness"—that he had earned his earthly blessing because of his righteousness. He was to be challenged in his self-assessment and identity.

Conger offers the following commentary on the spiritual journey that can bless us—client and therapist:

> In the spiritual history of mankind, a debate has existed between those who feel that higher spiritual development and God's favor excludes the devotee from painful injury in this world and those who feel that God's favor may in fact lead us into devastating crisis for the sake of spiritual growth. In Job, a good man is brought down to the most humiliating circumstances. His neighbors, who think that God protects those whom He favors, assume that Job has done something to "deserve" his pain. Instead one might argue that by utilizing an exquisite alchemy of this world God refines us. Because of God's presence, we awaken to our separation which becomes intolerable. The greatest of us may be the one struck down. Job through his painful stripping down became tested in the fire of being. He stood up to

182

God and demonstrated a nature that was irreducible, the enduring self [Self]. (p. 197)

When the self, by a synergy not fully of its own making, discovers that the source of its "dis-ease"—above and beyond and beside the illness, disaster, reversal, and or the loss of everything and everyone—is its illusory separation from the SELF, then it can realize what its intolerable burden is and can begin its transformation into a Self on its return to the SELF, on its path of evolving integration into a Self in and by and through the trinity of mind, brain, and body.

As a Jungian, Conger reminds us that when speaking of the "enduring self [Self]" he is alluding strongly to the "philosopher's stone." He is of the opinion that we are not born with an "enduring self [Self]" but that its enduring nature is ours to develop through "trials of fire"; in other words, through the crucifixion of all our opposites into an integrated whole. He ends these thoughts with a striking metaphor by stating that the "enduring self [Self], our identification with the soul, is a blade that cannot be sheathed in the world" (p. 197). Soul-making is a fully active-receptive process. It is the mutual loving dialogue of SELF and self that creates the third, the Self. It is the nature of these three to be in relationship, to be one.

When alchemists toiled to find the emerging "stone"—the gold—out of the lead fired in the vessel, it seems to me that they were metaphorically expressing, in ritual, the body-inclusive incarnational and spiritual psychotherapy of the ancients and of the future. In a thundering statement, Conger nails his conviction to the door of a comprehensive IFS therapy. "So when I talk of embodiment, I do not suggest that the embodied self is free of pain or conflict. The embodied self works to be free of the past, to be fully present, to avoid nothing, to be honest and direct" (p. 198).

In the introduction of his book, Conger describes what he means by "embodiment"—"giving up illusion, grandiosity, specialness for the sake of an honest grounded reality, genuine contact and relatedness and

183

pleasure in the basic experience of life" (p. xvi). Conger, as a body-inclusive Jungian analyst, saw himself as one dedicated to helping clients live in a "three-dimensional world," which of necessity demanded living in and by and through the body in order to experience life fully. One could say he revealed his life's mission as a psychotherapist in the title of his Chapter 31, "Healing the Psyche-Soma Split." This five-page chapter merits reading for its brilliance.

## Healing the Psyche-Soma Split

The Somatic IFS Therapist can hear the words of a like-minded colleague when Conger tells us that the work of embodiment, of incarnation, is the work of "bring[ing] diverse internal and external elements into an organization called the self [Self]" (p. 199); that it is the work of healing the splitting effected by dissociation, that of losing touch with aspects of the self, and the managing of repressed elements. The original research on Adverse Childhood Experiences, which was going on in the middle to late 1990s, shows how behavior (how we are embodied, how we have being) has roots in early life experience and manifests in the body over the years either in health or in disease, in order or in disorder. Conger quotes Kohut, who speaks of the "degree of autonomy we call the self [Self]. It becomes a center of independent initiative that points to a future and has a destiny. It also has its own natural, unfeared decline and end" (Conger, p. 202). The Self is the one who discovers, and knows, and welcomes the return to the SELF—a theme Luke explores in *Old Age: Journey into Simplicity,* which I discuss in Chapter Six, "Old Age and the IFS Therapist."

Again, Conger's employment of the thought and language of the likes of Sigmund Freud, Sandor Ferenczi, Melanie Klein, and Donald Winnicott, requires a sorting out of what Conger understands them to mean in their use of the term "self." As a sound developmentalist, Conger's first use of the term "self" refers to the Freudian "ego," the "me," the center of consciousness that is in the process of evolving into a

184

"personalized being and body"—the rudiments of a Self that necessitates a sufficiently harmonious psyche-soma interplay with realistically caring caretakers. When Conger writes that in "both ego and self-psychology, embodiment reorganizes toward a functional ego and durable self," he is speaking of the "arming of our failed strategies for the new ego strategies that are appropriate to each particular life engagement, a capacity to assess each situation for what it is" (p. 203). The ego, the self, becomes a Self. We now have a functional body-self. We are healing our splits, integrating our formerly dissociated parts— organizing "our way of being," to paraphrase Conger.

I am in debt to Conger for his practical wisdom. Again, I bracketed my understanding and interpretation of his use of the term "self," as I did when consulting other sources in companion chapters of this book.

*We have language for what is within reach*
*but not the mutable form behind it.*
*Or else, why write.*

—Jenny Xie, 2018, *Eye Level*

## CHAPTER THIRTEEN: COMBING THE *IFS SKILLS TRAINING MANUAL* FOR CLUES

### Attempts at Distinctions

In this chapter, I quote and paraphrase the thoughts and language of Frank G. Anderson, Martha Sweezy, and Richard C. Schwartz (2017) found in the *Internal Family Systems Skills Training Manual*. My express aim is to attempt to clarify the distinctions I find useful and even essential between the terms **"self," "Self,"** and **"SELF."** This is neither a summary of IFS practices nor a further explanation of the fundamental theory and practice of IFS therapy. The IFS literature listed in the references does that admirably. My purpose is to tease from the manual some descriptive statements in order to identify which member of the *self/Self/SELF trinity* is at play in the particular context that I discuss throughout. I fully expect to have to guess, hypothesize, assume, hold off certainty, and to flat-out not know. This trinity is elusive and, in the end, eludes our communal best efforts at irrefutable clarity. But what is so grounding in IFS is the proof of experience; eventually the Self knows when it is SELF-led, which is the goal of IFS therapy— "to embody the Self" in order to have a felt sense of one's being.

When a person experiences a "critical mass of clarity" and "balance"; when there is "no internal chatter" clogging awareness and presence; when the inner world is "calm and spacious"; when the "mind, heart, [and] soul [are] expanded and bright"; when a person lives a "joyful connection with others" absent of "distrust [and] boredom" then that person has the confidence of being in Self, of being SELF-led (Anderson et al., p. 1). This is the presence that the therapist brings to the

186

encounter with the intention to call forth the same in the patient. The SELF of one calls out to the SELF in the other, depth-to-depth, to the benefit of the Self in both parties. Healing the fragmentation and polarization of the conflicted self (and selves/parts) happens when a sufficient presence of the above qualities conjoins the pair in a mutual healing.

In section 1, page, 1, paragraph 2, of the *Skills Training Manual* is this sentence: "Schwartz observed that healing just happens when therapist and client achieve a critical mass of this phenomenon, which is dubbed the *Self.*" I understand this *Self* to refer to the SELF, the Core, the Center of the totality of the Psyche, the Source of the healing energy, as well as to the Self, the outcome of which is the ego's (the self's and all of its parts) voluntary collaboration under the leadership of the SELF. I use and reserve the term Self to speak of the resulting third entity emanating from the I-Thou relationship between the SELF and the self. The differentiation is the distinction I am pursuing, aware that, in the end, I will either have advanced the discussion or muddied the waters in my search for the Elusive Self. In either case, I am grateful for the journey.

On the first page of the manual is the avowed link between psychotherapy and spirituality—a major theme of William James's Gifford Lectures:

> Psychotherapy and spirituality alike describe the *essence* that we call the Self [SELF] with the terms like souls, the divine, Buddha nature, or the core seat of our consciousness. In his [Schwartz's] experience, once parts make space, we can all have access to this core of who we really are.

When the self, with its parts, is transformed into a SELF-led Self, the "who we really are" that remains is always imperfect, always incomplete, always in process, always in a state of re-creation, of resurrection, then IFS therapy has fulfilled its mission as a partner to the process.

Anderson et al. further affirm that "the Self" is not a part, but is our "core resource." I understand this Self to be the SELF (p. 3). For the SELF is not vulnerable to the vagaries of the psyche's multiple parts, or components, or elements; but its energy and light can be thwarted and obscured to the detriment of the self and of the Self. "While parts can blend with (overwhelm and therefore obscure) the Self, the Self nevertheless continues to exist and is accessible as soon as parts separate (that is, unblend)" (p. 5).

On the surface, this statement might appear simple, direct, and sufficiently clear, but I offer, from my understanding, this exegesis to enhance its clarity: *While parts can blend with the Self,* we should note that a Self who is mostly led by the energy of the SELF can be temporarily or partially *overwhelmed* by parts and thereby have its view obscured and its access to the ever-present light of the SELF impeded. Nevertheless, the SELF continues to exist untouched, as does the Self continue to exist behind an opaque veil or a complete blank-out, return *as soon as parts separate* (that is, unblend), and regain its ability to bask, always in a relative manner, in the qualities (energies) of the SELF; that is, to be SELF-led.

Here is a straightforward experiential description of a Self-led [SELF-led] person. One that "has the capacity to hear, understand, and be present with parts, acknowledging and appreciating the importance of their roles in the internal family system and with other people" (p. 5). I bracket "SELF-led" to remind myself, in my Jungian understanding, that when the ego (self) as the center of consciousness is in a mutual relationship with the center of the unconscious (personal and universal), the SELF, that a third emerges—the Self who lives in both domains of the whole Psyche whose center is the SELF.

## Deviating from the Orthodox View

I might possibly be deviating from a more orthodox IFS view, but I do so in the spirit of a dedicated heretic who struggles with the inadequacy of language to express the depth and breadth of the Psyche immanent in the entire organism that is the manifest physical and psychological person. When Anderson et al. say that "the overarching goal of IFS is access to the Self" and that "the Self is the core of psychic balance, the seat of consciousness and inner source of love," I agree that "the Self is the core of psychic balance" in that it is the pivotal point between the SELF and the self, and that it is "the seat of consciousness" as the evolved self (p. 9). However, I see the SELF and not the Self as the source of love.

When I read that "the Self is neither created nor cultivated and cannot be destroyed but is, rather, intrinsic and present from birth" (p. 10), I find my Jungian soul celebrating the presence of the SELF who contains the self from the beginning and who energizes the self into a Self through mutual exchanges that evolve into a Self increasingly manifesting the qualities of the SELF in an individual incarnation.

The marvelous world of the neurosciences has brought the world of psychotherapy into compliance with the demonstrable world of brain structures and functions. In IFS, Anderson et al. declare that the Self "which is a state of being, is located within the mind just like protective parts—but [with] a difference" (p. 61). I take this referenced Self to be the "I" of which I am aware, the "I" who is the executive conducting the business of my living under the creative influence of the SELF. The Self is different than the self—the healthy ego on the way to selfhood— and in the extreme, the fragmented "me" under the usurping tyranny of alters and their parts. The statement, "The Self is a *state of being* located in the mind like protective parts [emphasis added]," opens up a much larger conversation about the co-extensive relationship of the mind and brain.

Therein lies the unresolved explanation to the question, How does the psychotherapy of a mind-body organism change the neural networks of the brain? And, if the mind is inoperative without the brain and body in our spatial and temporal existence, this does not imply that

189

the mind and brain are one. I again think back to James and to his insights into personalism within the context of universal spirituality. I am on Jung's side. When the brain sheds its responsibilities after its death, I find it absurd not to anticipate that its product, the mind's center of consciousness, the Self, exists onward. I opt to join the view of poets and mystics; the *how* remains the surprise.

Specifically addressing the phenomena of trauma, Anderson et al. write:

> Protectors, who develop in response to either small or capital T trauma and show up as symptoms, **use** [emphasis added] unintegrated networks of the brain. In contrast, **the Self accesses neural networks and connects to the external world spontaneously. From our perspective, the experience of "being in Self" (as we say in IFS) is internally and externally connected and maximally integrative** [emphasis in bold in original]. In short, the Self possesses inherent wisdom and the capacity for healing. In our view, once liberated from extreme roles, protectors revert to using integrated neural networks as well. (p. 61)

Again, I read this as being that, for *the Self who possesses inherent wisdom, healing is the SELF*, and that the Self is the one who can participate in that wisdom and in the healing of the system.

As a final offering in this commentary, I present the following poem.

### Incarnation
In this destined evolution
of the Self out of the SELF
through the travails of self-development
as a personal organism
the Self
faithful to the generative prompting of the SELF
takes onto itself
all parts and subparts of the psyche—

190

conscious     unconscious and    non-conscious—
in a soma-psychic dance
of the ever-more integrated neural networks
emanating from coordinated brain structures
and
gives presence to the SELF
in time and place     and
reasonably beyond—
the conscious intent of IFS Therapy
in Hope

*It takes courage for a man to listen*
*to his own goodness and act on it.*
—Pablo Casals (1876-1973)

## CHAPTER FOURTEEN: OF MANY MINDS AND ONE SELF

### A Few Antecedents

The following is an honest attempt to represent and interpret the concepts of SELF, Self, and self against the background of *Many Minds: One Self,* by Richard C. Schwartz and Robert R. Falconer (2017). The trinity of SELF, Self, and self is the summation of my search for the Elusive SELF. If readers are seeking a complete, referenced, and scholarly summary of Schwartz and Falconer's study, they will be sorely disappointed. If, on the other hand, readers accept the usefulness of a close-to-text spiral walk through the book in order to grasp some of the underpinnings of the internal world that we IFS therapists and practitioners navigate on our way to the Elusive SELF, then it is my hope that readers will not be disappointed.

My methodology, old and selective in its process, is how I have written all of the previous chapters, and it imitates an exegesis—a reading of the text, a sampling of the text, a commentary on the text. Mine is not a straight-line approach, other than as a sequential treatment of selected parts of Schwartz and Falconer's book. The choice of passages and quotes are solely my own; others might well have selected differently. What concepts I fail to harvest, I count on others to gather as neglected fruits left behind on the tree and to display them in the agora of community discourse. Know that a scanning of *Many Minds, One Self* does not substitute for reading the book in its entirety. It is a must read.

We are reminded in the text that in the late 19th century "Nietzsche viewed the psyche as polycentric . . . , [that] the multiple individuals

192

within [us] are organized like a political system as in Plato's *polis model* (Schwartz and Falconer, p. 31), and that Jung was greatly influenced by Nietzsche in how he understood the population of the inner world. The authors refer to Paul Federn (1871-1950) in his use of the term *"sub-personalities,"* instead of the terms *"complexes"* and *"archetypes,"* the standard terms in Analytical Psychology.

John G. (1917-2012) and Helen H. Watkins (1921-2002), of Ego State Theory International (ESTI), who treated veterans suffering from combat trauma, used the language of *ego states,* which they understood as the result of development and not as innate entities. They write, "Ego states are an organized system of behavior and experience whose elements are bound together by some common principle, and which [are] separated from other such states by a boundary that is more or less permeable" (Watkins and Watkins, 1997, p. 25). These authors understood that ego states could take hold of a person and control consciousness and behavior. They "treated the ego states as inner personalities [and] tried to foster improved communication among a person's ego states in order to bring harmony to the "family of self," a phrase they used repeatedly when teaching" (Schwartz and Falconer, pp. 58-59).

### Concerning Artificial Intelligence and Complexity

Many scientists, practitioners, and therapists support an understanding of the multiplicity that we are. They tell us that James "famously said that we have as many selves as we have social contacts" (Schwartz and Falconer, p 127). We might say that our social roles create related parts or that our parts inform our roles. They tell us that "the concepts of an ego or "me" running the show is not needed to explain the operation of amazingly complex systems (p. 129). This is a position that merits further exploration.

Schwartz and Falconer remind us that Daniel Siegel sees the human mind as having independent parts that are linked. The authors are encouraged by those who explore artificial intelligence. They reference Ben Goertzel, who wrote about "subself dynamics," saying that these subselves "are not aspects of the same person; they are fundamentally different people [and that] a healthy mind, as a rule, consists of a population of subselves carrying out I-You relationships with each other. . . (Schwartz and Falconer, p. 134)." (See also B. Goertzel, 1997, *From Complexity to Creativity,* Sections 12.2 and 12.3.) Goertzel opens up a conversation beyond the scope of my endeavor to resolve. How are we to understand the phenomenon of the person, the phenomena of different people, the "who" who is the one in the position to direct the multiplicity not as a runaway part but as the unifying center? This is what the SELF, Self, and self trinity offers as a potentially clarifying paradigm.

We also read that "IFS is a theory of holons [and that the] health of the larger system depends on the health of the smaller ones within it and vice versa" (Schwartz and Falconer, p. 141). Unburden the parts and the entire system becomes healthier, reaches a greater harmony, becomes more balanced. Resource the parts, and the system is enriched. This is what therapists witness in an IFS session. What follows is an extended quote that enriches our discussion:

Whether or not parts, in an ontological sense, are full of personalities, they respond best when therapist and client treat them that way. It's much harder to have compassion for or embrace your inner module than it is to have compassion for your hurting inner children [their managers and protectors]. Then, of course, the question arises as to who it is that is having compassion for or embracing whom. Is the Self in IFS an emergent property of the complex system of parts, or a separate seat of consciousness, or something else? Schwartz has played with that question for thirty years. . . . (pp. 145-146)

And, this has been the very question that has motivated my inquiry and the proposal that we distinguish between SELF, Self, and self in our

194

discussion and understanding of who is this Elusive SELF referenced in the title of my book.

The radical paradigm shift that IFS proposes, and which was anticipated by our predecessors, is aptly expressed by the following words of John and Helen Watkins (who influenced so many of my generation of therapists), as quoted by John O. Beahrs and included by Schwartz and Falconer for our consideration:

> *The concept that one might be a "multiplicity" rather than a "unity" is frightening. That there might lie within our self entities which we do not experience as "me," and over whose actions we may not have control strikes at the very heart of our self-concept. . . . The same fear of the uncontrollable which in the past caused people to reject a Copernican concept of the universe, an evolutionary view of human development, and the existence of the unconscious processes, impels us to deny the suggestion that each of us may be a multiplicity—not a single, unified self* [emphasis in original]. (Beahrs, 1982, *Unity and Multiplicity,* p. xii; Schwartz and Falconer, p. 147)

It is this challenge that obliges us to struggle with a near unresolvable understanding of not only the multiplicity of the SELF, Self, and self but of the multiplicity of each *one*. This is the psychic world that the mystics and poets welcome and navigate.

## Self-leadership

Part III of Schwartz and Falconer's book invites the reader and the entire IFS community to confront what is meant by Self-leadership in the inner and outer world of psychotherapy and spirituality as well as to contemplation and action. Because I have given time and space elsewhere in my book to many of these topics, I will allow those previous discussions to serve as parallel commentary and inquiry, but I do want to highlight a few of Schwartz and Falconer's choice insights that guide my thinking and lead me to suggest to which member of the trinity the statement refers.

195

- "We each have an undamaged Self" [SELF] (p. 155). The self [the ego] is born undamaged, but is subject to damage once it emerges from the SELF into time and place. The self suffers the tarnish, the distortions, and the fragmentation due to the vagaries of human existence. The self is burdened by vulnerable separate subselves serving other entities that provide self-states with adaptive and/or maladaptive skills to carry out survival roles in the environment; and the self is protected by other emergent agents that use whatever measures are needed to encapsulate one or many underdeveloped and/or wounded split-offs from consciousness. The Self is the self on its way back to a more balanced state, energized by the qualities of the SELF, not lost to the influence of more reptilian energy. It is the SELF that is undamaged, that is whole. It is the SELF that exists in a state of Harmony, in which there is a Union of Opposites. Light and Shadow are in unity. Good and Evil are in unity. In the Self, harmony is in the making, is imperfect, is in process, never assured that it is immune from the influences of its conscious and unconscious (personal and universal) agents.
- When the self consciously accepts the influence of the SELF that expands the center of consciousness over all internal and external functions (in brief, sensation, emotion, awareness, feeling, perception, cognition, and action), the self (the me, the ego) becomes an emerging Self. This Self manifests an increasing integrity that allows for the qualities of the SELF to lead the multiplicities into an internal kingdom of greater peace and joy in an evolutionary way. This describes a Self-led person.
- There is much compatibility between IFS and Mindfulness with the practice of meditation taught by Thich Nhat Hanh. As it is in IFS, the goal is to help the patient develop a personal and freely chosen collaborative relationship with one's parts from the Self (Schwartz and Falconer, p, 164). So, is it also the goal of the meditator to offer hospitality to all internal and external experiences

196

from every aspect of the total Psyche? It is the mystery of becoming one with all in compassion. (See Thich Nhat Hanh, 1975, *The Miracle of Mindfulness.*)

## The SELF and Concluding Remarks

In Chapter 17, "The Self," Schwartz and Falconer cast forth a handful of diamond "seeds" hoping for fertile ground. I have reflected on the phenomenon of the SELF over the length of this inquiry, and so will not repeat myself here. In Chapter 18, "Carl Jung," they land a knockout punch in a brief eight-page excursion that anticipates what they write in Chapter 31, "Judaism," making reference to the Kabbalah, that the "Self [SELF] was a piece of God within people that longed to connect to the Self [SELF] in others and to God" (p. 250).

That we humans dread becoming conscious makes so much sense. We must be willing to be touched by a center larger than our little "me." To smile and breathe and to accept the presence of our inner manifestations as our own requires a courage that is able to suffer the individuation process, the transformative *crux,* the death of the immature ego [self]. Integrating our unconscious parts into a conscious whole is the work of a humble return to the SELF in and through and by the energy of our divine center. (See Schwartz and Falconer, pp. 165-166.)

When Schwartz and Falconer write that "The Self [SELF] of IFS is seen as an innate, undamaged essence that will arise fully developed when parts open space for it" (p. 173), they take their place in the rich tradition of those who bow to the reality of the SELF and see life's journey as the self's return to its source, the SELF, as a Self.

*The more intimately the opposites are united,*
*the more they are differentiated,*
*I call this a coincidence of mutually affirming complementarity.*
—St. Bonaventure, *The Journey of the Mind to God*

## PART THREE: GATHERINGS OF A PANENTHEIST

### Early Influences in My Search for the SELF

The French language of my Canadian ancestors informed my early thinking. The pronouns *moi* (me) and *je* (I), *moi-meme* (myself), and *soi-meme* (oneself); the nouns *soi* (self) and *la personne* (the person); and the phrases *le moi* (the self) and *ma personne* (myself) were the words I first ingested with the traditional prayers and classic "pea soup" of my childhood. I also must not omit the puzzlement that gripped me early on when I was told about this Being everyone called God who lived in my soul. Yes, over the years this has colored my search for the Elusive SELF and led me to becoming an Internal Family Systems (IFS) therapist.

This God was complicated. He (of course, in those days, He was a he) was one God in three Persons, and one of the three Persons was the Son (of the one who was the Father), and he, the son, had two natures: one divine, one human. And here I was, this little *moi* being regularly walked to the local French Catholic church to face this assortment of *Vous* (the polite second person plural) that also included the third person of that Sacred Trinity, the Holy Spirit. Now, if this was not enough for a child who was at least three years away from the age of reason (that being seven years old when, in those olden days, he would be held fully responsible for all of his sins), I was obliged to believe in something I did not understand.

Pythagoras would have supported my unbelief in the following: The first person of this Trinity was The Father. He was an old man with a long white beard wearing a white robe who sat on a throne on a dais facing a large hall filled with people (who merited to be there). Above The Father were winged angels hanging suspended near the ceiling. Some of the suspended beings were archangels, some cherubim, and some seraphim.

The second person was The Son. His beard was brown. He had a visible wound in his chest and nail wounds in his hands and feet caused by being crucified by the Jews of his day. He sat to the right of The Father, but a bit lower. He was the one who was both man and God. He had died for our sins and was sent by the Father to pay ransom (to whom I did not know) for our debt (of which I knew nothing) and who had come to life again after three days in Hell.

The third person was the Holy Spirit, *Le Saint Esprit,* (The Holy Ghost). He was a stationary sort of golden-white dove hovering over The Father and sending his (male again) rays of bright light over The Father, The Son, and the woman seated at the left of The Father. The woman was the Virgin Mother of The Son. She had immaculately conceived her son by the action of the Holy Spirit (who had descended upon her, whatever that meant). She had been taken up to her place in heaven, body and soul, just like her son, after both of them died. The Son got there by Ascension; she got there by Assumption. Of course, the four-year-old boy understood these distinctions? There was something mysteriously enticing about it all, but where did that leave the boy? It left him staring at a lithograph right smack in the middle of a 14- x 20-inch gold-leaf-inlaid book (an heirloom in his mother's family) titled *Le Catechisme en Images.* (The Catechism Through Images [out of print]. For a reprint, see M. B. Couissiner, 2010, *The Catechism Through Images.* Whitefish, MT: Kessinger Publishing.)

There I was, this little *moi* in front of all of that, and there were some sins that if I committed and did not have perfect contrition for having committed them, my soul (was that the me that I am, *le moi que je suis,* some invisible part of me?) would not be allowed into that hall called Heaven. Instead, I would go to the fiery Hell and burn for all eternity, a sight that all those in heaven could see, including those on the dais. Did those people in Hell have bodies? Had they, like the people in Heaven, ascended or had they been assumed? I did not know. What I did know, then and there, even before the age of reason, was that I did not want to be with those in Heaven who would spend forever watching people burn endlessly somehow without dying.

My early experiences eventually led me to study philosophy, theology, and then depth psychology in order to sort out this all-too-widely-accepted delusion in the French Jansenism that had leached into the cultural soil in which I was planted, an unwilling sprout in my family's francophone New England. If this were God, I thought, I would have nothing to do with him. I concluded then, in my child's mind, that he could not be the one who made everything and kept everything going—sun and moon, wind and rain, people and animals, everything. I would keep this secret to myself. I had heard that those who do not believe what they are told by the Church (the Roman Catholic Church, the One and Only True Church, of course) are excommunicated and go straight to Hell. None of this made sense to me, but as an unknowing pragmatist, I did not want to take the chance. But my questioning remained and fueled my search for answers.

### Later Influences
Well into the later part of my professional life, IFS therapy capped my study and search for an all-inclusive method to heal the multiplicity that has been projected onto the heavens across the globe. My search to make sense of the multiplicity that is ours as humans led me to the world of archetypal psychology, the world of philosophy—Aristotelianism, Thomism, Personalism, and Existentialism—and the findings of the neurosciences, which provide the tools to treat the wounds of dissociative identity that burdens too many who have suffered developmental and incidental trauma. In my attempt to understand the *qui je suis* (the who that I am), I have delved into Freudian Analysis, Object Relations

Theory, Psychosynthesis, Self-Psychology, Developmental Psychology, Focusing, Somatic Psychology, and other such models. I have also examined the writings of Western mystics such as Teresa of Avila, John of the Cross, Meister Eckhart, and many other mystics, poets, and prophets.

As a certified IFS therapist, I have returned to the writings of some of the sources that have informed my life as a professor of psychology and philosophy and as a psychotherapist to find answers to questions that might offer a useful approach to identifying what so many have called "the self." My childhood inner struggle with trying to understand myself, my years as an undergraduate student of philosophy, and my continuing search has led me to conclude that when reading the texts of the learned, making a distinction between the terms "self," "Self," and "SELF" offers a greater chance to more accurately intuit what is understood by each term. This is what I have addressed in previous chapters.

Thus, the text of this book is interrupted by parentheses or brackets following the words "self," "Self," and "SELF" in the many quotes that populate the book. The parentheses contain either the term "self," when referring to the *me,* the *ego,* the *I*; the term "Self" when referring to the self that functions through the wisdom-qualities of the SELF, and the term "SELF," when referring to the archetypal *Imago Dei, the Other, the Source,* that transcends the multiplicity manifest in the trinity of mind, brain, and body. I append no conclusion at the end of this incomplete inquiry. The SELF will remain Elusive, not because of its evasive nature but because of its transcendence. Yet, the SELF makes itself felt. We can know the difference when we are SELF-led and when we are lost in a self that is blended in underdeveloped aspects/parts of ourselves or taken over by a mind-brain-body-networked entity as in a full Dissociative Identity Disorder that obliterates the original self that we are, the one birthed unconscious from the SELF at a moment not of our knowing. Eventually, we sense a gifted authenticity when we are present to what, in a manner, nears a state that the wise of old have labeled holiness (wholeness, sanctity) and not an illusory perfection.

## Personalism

During the 1960s, I experienced most of my study of philosophy and theology primarily in French. Because of that, I was exposed to European French thinkers. From 1958 to 1965, I lived and studied in a Roman Catholic monastery outside of Boston where many of the faculty had pursued advanced degrees at European universities and had been influenced by the intellectual ferment of the first half of the 20th century in the fields of philosophy, theology, biblical studies, history, and phenomenology. At that time, I supplemented the study of psychology on my own. I also found Existentialism and Personalism, followed immediately by Jung's Archetypal Psychology, which for me was pivotal.

I was especially strongly impressed by the insights of Emanuel Mournier (1905-1950) and French philosopher Jacques Maritain (1882-1973), who espoused the concept of the centrality of the person in philosophical inquiry; that is, that personhood holds an inviolable dignity demanding that every person be granted unconditional respect. I also found the writings of Carl R. Rogers (1902-1987) and his philosophy of unconditional positive regard. (See References for related works.) During the late 1960s, I trained in Client-Centered Therapy and studied Existential Analysis. In everything I studied, I attempted to understand it as related to and from the perspective of the human person. To me, personhood was the highest value, the ultimate criterion in all human affairs. I also must not forget to mention Abraham Maslow (1908-1970), the founder of Humanistic Psychology. (See A. Maslow, 1970, *Motivation and Personality,* and A. Maslow, 1954, 1964, *Religion, Values, and Peak Experiences.*)

I owe a debt of gratitude to the Reverend Professor Maurice Savard, OMI (1919-2015), who taught Canon Law and Moral Theology. He

202

was a man of encyclopedic scholarship across countless disciplines and sciences. He confirmed my conviction that in all matters of life and love, of law, of morality, the canon, *Tamquam incommodo,* held the highest priority in Canon Law, even in the Pre-Second Vatican Council era. Whatever law, whatever moral code, in any way, hampers one's spiritual life, individual conscience primes. The *person* is the highest value. Internal Family Systems therapy stands for this absolute and revolutionary value.

### Some Historical Perspectives on the Evolving Concept of Person

In the history of philosophy, the concept of the person was filled with dead-ends, cul-de-sacs, and misunderstandings. (See S. Moyn, "Personalism: Community, and the Origins of Human Rights," in *Human Rights in the Twentieth Century.*)

In Greek, *person* could mean "mask" as related to a "role" in drama *(dramatis persona)* with all of the connotations of potential façade and falsehood. In Latin, the term implies self-presentation; that is, the face one presents to the world. Surprisingly, the philosophical concept of "person" developed in the context of the theo-political debates surrounding the Trinity (One God in Three Persons) and the Incarnation of the Second Person of the Trinity (the hypostatic union of two natures— divine and human—in one *person*).

During the 5th century the hotly contested views held by differing Christian camps, based mostly on philosophical positions, ended with a political fiat engineered and promulgated as the Nicene-Constantinopolitan Creed first stated at the Council of Chalcedon in 451 CE. Squabbles and debates had to end in order to restore social order, but dissension left what was understood by *person* unresolved.

The debate as to whether the Holy Spirit proceeded solely from the Father or from the Father and the Son caused a schism between the Eastern and Western Churches. Each held firmly to its position while labeling the opposite position as heresy. Of note: *Neither* the Old nor

203

the New Testaments mention YHWH as being triune. As there is much room for honest discussion with regard to the Trinity, so also is there ample space for sincere debate about our understanding of the human person and the concepts of SELF, Self, and self.

Boethius (c. 480-524), who wrote the *Consolation of Philosophy* (reprinted in 2000 by *The Oxford World Classics*), asserted that there was a higher power governing all and that suffering had a higher purpose. For him, the universe was ruled by divine love; true happiness was attained by "other-worldly" virtues. He provided the classic and basic philosophical definition still accepted today by personalists—*persona est naturae rationalis individua substantia* (the person is an individual substance of a rational nature). Moyn's article on Personalism explores the meaning of the definition. Here, using much of that article's language, the definition consists of two parts. The first part posits that the essential starting point is a subsistent individual—a singular, existing *suppositum* or *upostasis*. The adjective *individual* implies an existing substance in contrast to something that is accidental, like a trait or an aspect of a substance. The second element of the definition, *naturae rationalis,* qualifies the notion of individual substance. The person is an individual possessing a *rational nature*. (Boethius uses the term "rational" to mean *spiritual.*) The rational nature is what gives rise to the different qualities that distinguish the person, qualities to which the personalists attach decisive importance.

The Trinitarian concept of the person is far from the meaning the term assumes in contemporary Personalism. Boethius's definition only hints at today's understanding. The contemporary understanding is the result of a long, complex, cumulative development that results in a rich, bold, "if somewhat elusive," concept that in some respects still wholly invests the original connotations of exteriority in the early meaning of mask and role. It "comes rather to denote the innermost spiritual and most authentic **kernel** [emphasis added] of the unique individual, while retaining a radical openness to the external" (Moyn).

When Kant admonishes us to treat ourselves and others as an end and not as a means, he is implying a Personalism that enjoins us to be a gift to others, a call to be in open relationship with others as the *sine qua non* "of our own realization" (Moyn). In the June 14, 2018, *New York Times* opinion column titled, "Personalism: The Philosophy We Need," journalist David Brooks references Whitman's poem, "Personalism." (See Whitman, *Leaves of Grass,* 1855.) Brooks also cites, as a radical personalist, Peter Maurin (1877-1949), who along with Dorothy Day (1897-1980), founded The Catholic Worker Movement. Maurin is also the author of "Easy Essays," written in 1933 in verse.

Brooks unabashedly quotes Maritain, who said that our reason for being is "self-mastery for the purpose of self-giving" (Moyn). Brooks ends his opinion piece with the words of noted French poet, essayist, and editor Charles Péguy's aphorism, "The revolution is moral or not at all." In IFS, we would speak of the revolution as being SELF-led.

As the 20th century began, many thinkers advanced the concept of Personalism. One could say that the collective unconscious was sending the World Soul a warning in an attempt to avoid the dehumanizing carnage that would befall it in hitherto unforeseen proportions—World War I and the unending catastrophic wars since. Sadly, the reification of the person persists to this day. During my studies I encountered such thinkers as Soren Kierkegaard (1813-1853), Gabriel Marcel (1889-1973), Edmund Husserl (1859-1938), Martin Heidegger (1889-1976), Michel Foucault (1926-1984), Edith Stein (1891-1942), and Henri Bergson (1859-1941), all of whom directly or indirectly advanced Personalist philosophy. They were part of the revolution that advanced, loud and clear, the primacy of individual conscience. Many philosophers, poets, scientists, and religionists writers agreed with Péguy and refused to become the accomplices of those who advanced the dehumanization of the individual person. One need only recognize the extreme positions of capitalism and communism.

Viktor Frankl (1905-1997), the founder of Logotherapy, is one of my heroes, as is his contemporary Carl R. Rogers, who was born in Oak Park, Illinois, a city long associated with IFS. They both merit mention in this context.

Closer to home, the Boston Personalist School inspired a generation of counseling professionals. Harvard philosopher and psychologist Gordon W. Allport (1897-1967) promoted the psychological dimensions of Personalism in his attempt to find a focus on the person in-between Psychoanalysis and Behaviorism using his Trait Theory. The spring 2011 issue of *The Pluralist* published a noteworthy article by Andrzej Jastrzebski titled "Gordon W. Allport's Concept of the Human Person: On a possible dialogue between philosophy and psychology." Jastrzebski reminds readers that Allport saw "an ulterior power of self-directedness in the human person." During the 1960s and 1970s, Allport was a standard reference in the field of Counselor Education.

**The Trinitarian Discussion Continued**

The open discussions of the Trinitarian problem came to a sudden dogmatic halt in the late 5th century. But, the notion of personhood could not remain frozen in such a nominalist state because doing so would leave believers to either give the doctrine their own interpretations or to hide behind so-called acts of faith and declare the Trinity and the Incarnation of The Son an incomprehensible mystery that one ought not to ponder in search of a reasonable understanding. This was not a knowledge that could be arrived at by inductive or deductive reasoning. This conundrum was what so troubled Jung when he saw his father, a clergyman in the Swiss Reformed Church, capitulate to introjected doctrine, telling his questioning son that things of faith are to be believed and not understood. But the human mind cannot rest at ease in a state of avoidance, a hallmark of all anxiety disorders. To make absolute statements of personal certainty about an incomprehensible

206

phenomenon appears to me to be idolatrous in the fullest tradition of the Mosaic Second Commandment and its violation.

If, now and in the past, the concept of Personalism is considered an equivalent term to that of the *selfhood,* the definition of the concept of *person* needs expansion. One of the many interpretations of a God in Three Persons that lingered after the closure of the debate by authoritarian fiat was that the three Persons in the Trinity were the three *different* and *manifest roles* of God. I mention this as one of the early indications of the incipient idea of multiplicity in Western philosophical and psychological thought.

We ought not to ignore the multiplicity of gods—East or West. The Hebraic evolution of an understanding of One God must include the people's struggle with reconciling the practice of worshipping various local gods with their One God's struggle to come to grips with parts, aspects, or sides of Himself. Demonic possession, alluded to in the writing of the Gospels and finding its high point in the Exorcisms of the Middle Ages, is evidence of multiplicity, albeit of a negative nature. (See Russell, 1984, *Lucifer.*) Today, we recognize dissociation as the most fundamental defense (protection) against traumatization.

Alongside this excursion into a mounting intuition and eventual realization of the evidence of multiplicity is the acceptance by thoughtful philosophers and theologians of the individual as a *who,* a *person,* a *self,* a subject—not an it, not an object. The person rose above being reduced to an observable role, a measurable unit of behavior, something valued because of extrinsic factors, such as bank accounts, public fame, trappings of power, even accomplishments in business, learning, physical attributes, and so on. So also did God rise above being conceived of as a supposed distant entity—objective and remote—and eventually as an absolute monarch vulnerable to a *Lese Majeste* while sitting on His Throne. (I cannot resist the scatological allusion to a toilet seat nor to a 1798 poster of John Bull, pants down, farting on an image of George III.)

207

God was now a person; no, three persons, represented in art in human form—a father, his son, plus the son's mother. And within that trinity, a dove, as the image of the love between them all and thereby depicting a Divine Quaternity. They were ONE in relationship—the nature of God. (During the 1980s, when participating in an intensive at the Jungian Institute in Kusnatch, I encountered such a painting of the Quaternity in a wayside chapel while on a hike in the Swiss countryside. The synchronicity of the moment did not escape me, nor does the recall of the event at this time in my continuing search for the Elusive SELF.)

If we are each a person and relate to each other in love (otherwise there is no relationship), then the **me** that **I** am participates in the nature of the Triune God who is **three Persons in loving relationship.** If each of us is a person, then the Source and Cause of our being must also be a Person, but beyond our understanding, yet with whom we can relate, not forgetting that we are not the origin of our own existence. This does not address the problem of the Holy Spirit as the third person of the Trinity. And why the third? Is there a hierarchy? How does this pertain to the human psyche? Who within the psyche loves the self back to the SELF? The Self? In his 1984 book, *The Creation of Consciousness,* Edward Edinger suggests a solution by paraphrasing Jung:

> The symbolism of the Trinity refers psychologically to the creation of consciousness. Father and Son, like god and man, are opposites which collide on the cross. The Holy Spirit as the reconciling third emerges from that collision proceeding from the Father and the Son. Thus, the Holy Spirit (Paraclete) can only come after the death of the son, i.e., consciousness comes as the fruit of the conflict of twoness. (p. 21)

Edinger then continues by stating a particular relationship between Christ and Buddha:

> What Christ and Buddha have in common is the idea of being a carrier of consciousness. Characteristically, the image emerging from the West represents the standpoint of the ego [**self**], and that deriving

208

from the East speaks from the standpoint of the Self [**SELF**]. To-gether they reveal a pair of opposites. The crucified Christ and the meditating Buddha represent consciousness as agony and conscious-ness as tranquil bliss—total acceptance of the bondage to matter on the one hand and total transcendence of the world on the other. United they picture the two sides of the carrier of consciousness. (p. 22)

The "heavy burden the hero carries is *himself,* or rather *the self* [**Self**], his wholeness, which is both God and animal—not merely the empirical man, but the totality of his being, which is rooted in his animal nature and reaches out beyond the merely human toward the divine" (p. 109). Earlier in his book, Edinger reminds us, "The union of opposites in the vessel of the ego [**Self**] is the essential feature of the creation of con-sciousness" (p. 21).

Let me acknowledge that I am also omitting a discussion that would lead us far astray of our chosen theme. Suffice it to say that the Catholic Dogma of the Assumption, dogmatically defined by Pope Pius XII in 1950, is an expression of a long-held belief of the faithful expressed as the *vox populi*—the voice of the people. The dogma affirmed that Mary was taken up into heaven, body and soul. And, in 1954, the same Pontiff asserted the Coronation of Mary as the fourth person of the Qua-ternity, a belief expressed by the people and represented as such in re-ligious art. This has been interpreted by many believers as affording us a direct line of communication to the godhead. World religions are replete with such quaternities. In the case of Western Christianity, the implications are vast. Direct contact with the Trinity is possible and available via the Woman, the feminine, according to Jung. One could boldly say that contact between SELF, Self, and self is available via a receptive loving embrace, as is the contact between the Divine Persons. We can be in contact with our kernel, our core, our center. If God has parts, so do we. If God has a dark side (Satan and his minions), then so do we—our Shadow (Jung), our Lower Self (Pierrakos). We, as persons, cannot be greater than the undefinable source from whom we emanate, but we can be in contact with IT and be connected with IT.

All of the above has implications for the assertion that the body has intrinsic value in the completion of the Self.

Confronting the need to effect the union of opposites, Martin Luther King Jr. (1929-1968), student of Personalism at Boston University, advanced that "the meaning of ultimate reality is found in personality" (Moyn). Therein lies the discussion hall, the battlefield, the garden, where we debate and struggle and till the soil of Personalism. Years before, at Harvard, William James called himself a Personalist. This is evident in his Gifford Lectures that I reviewed in limited detail early on in this study. The idea that we, as persons, are parts of the absolute was not foreign to James. How large is the Multiplicity? Immeasurable? Infinite?

Centuries before the Trinitarian wars, Aristotle had considered the difference between persons and non-persons yet did not deny that all were sentient beings. As such, all sentient beings merit consideration. (See J. S. Duclos, 2018, Value, Morality, and Wilderness. [Unpublished doctoral dissertation, Boston University].) Aristotle distinguished man from other animals because **man has an inner self** that pursues truth, goodness, and beauty (the Transcendentals) and seeks answers to moral questions. In modern and postmodern times, Martin Buber influenced Gabriel Marcel, the Christian Existentialist whose work I read attentively as a student of philosophy. Buber tells us that person-to-person, self-to-self relationships are what keeps us in reality with all that is. (See Buber, 1937, *I and Thou.*)

The Personalist's creed is that we are born *persons.* Our personalities evolve. We grow into a greater and greater Self-Consciousness, Self-Awareness, and develop Self-Autonomy—or we do not. Above all, we experience ourselves as subjects, not objects. When we fall into our own objectification and into that of others, we collapse into a false self-experience. Moyn's article supports the idea that *self-presence* is the substance of personhood and that *personality* manifests the self.

Yet, there is something problematic with the above assertion, given the multiplicity of the mind. It holds a residual view of the self as a unitary being, but some confusion arises when we read that "personality signifies interiority." Our personality, the way we are in this world of interactions, the way that we manifest, might be a reflection of our essential personhood with all of the qualities of the SELF, the compassion that results from the harmonious unions of all opposites in the Psyche. However, it might also be the evidence of the usurpation of the Self by a runaway and cut-off, but well-meaning, subpersonality or part in need of compassion. Language is a necessary but inadequate helper in the effort to grasp what is ultimately beyond our grasp. Nonetheless, Self-understanding is our destiny, which reminds me of the famous lines from Robert Browning's (1855) poem, "Andrea del Sarto," as an apt analogy: "Ah, but a man's reach should exceed his grasp, / Or what's a heaven for?"

**Contemporary Spiritual Theology**

In his October 10, 2018, Daily Meditation, "The God Particle," Richard Rohr writes that "God seems to be elusive." I find this statement surprisingly in agreement with my proposition on the psychological plane. Referencing I Corinthians 3:16, Rohr says we are each a temple of God and that the Spirit of God dwells in us. He continues by saying what so many contemplatives, mystics, and poets have also said, "God is found in our innermost center." He uses the time-honored metaphor of a well. To find the elusive God, we must descend into the well within us. On the way down, we must "lay hold of the debris" that hinders our descent. We must gather this debris, "bring it up," and "deal with it courageously." I once agreed with the metaphor of the debris, but personal and clinical experience convinced me otherwise, as did my study of the works I reference in this book and of other authors to whom

211

I am most grateful. Debris is not what we find when we go inside. We find a population of dedicated helpers, some of whom bar passage to the hidden center of our well, down where the universal waters nourish all wells. Those helpers do so because of a misguided intent to keep us safe by separating us from the Source of living waters. What they need from us is compassionate understanding, gratitude, and connection that will transform them into allies and eventual facilitators of our journey to the center, which is the essentially spiritual healing process that IFS protocol offers—the Self in its search to quench its thirst for transformative authenticity one sip, one swallow, one cup, one full drenching at a time on the negotiated way to the wellhead. I have come to understand his metaphor of "debris" and "clutter" as the residuals of pain and suffering.

I adopt Rohr's statement by referencing burdened exiles and panicked protectors in the language of IFS:

If we persevere in clearing [access to] this well, we'll discover that the water of this inner well, the water in which we are swimming, is God [the SELF]. We'll find ourselves floating in God, and God moves to the outside as described in John 7: 37. [SELF leads the Self.] From our "innermost being will flow rivers of living waters, which is God's self [SELF] spilling out into our life and into the lives of those we touch."

The very phrase "God's self" offers confusion unless we understand the phrase to mean God's Image, the *Imago Dei,* the SELF energizing the self that has humbly agreed to be led by the SELF and become imperfectly and developmentally a Self.

## Universal Compassion

At this point, taking a side trip in our study fits well with a discussion arising from the wisdom of "My Wish: The Charter for Compassion," by Karen Armstrong, the internationally renowned scholar of religions, in a 2008 TED TALK. She illustrates the healing implication in a worldwide sociopolitical context, which Brooks echoes in his 2018 *New York Times* Op-Ed.

Internal Family Systems calls upon us to behave toward all of the members of our internal family in similar fashion, "to treat others as we wish to be treated," which applies to the internal and external populations of our internal and external worlds. Armstrong appealed to people who are ready to commit themselves to what they love, prize, and hold dear; to, in fact, behave with compassion toward all others. She reminded her audience that compassion implies feeling with the other, that compassion brings us into the presence of the divine, that it is The Golden Rule proclaimed by Confucius (551-479 BCE) and reiterated by Jewish religious teacher Hillel, the Elder (110 BCE-10 CE), in his insistence that we find compassion in all of the historical scriptures held as sacred by its adherents. Compassion is the message and action, adopted and adapted, by Joshua, the Carpenter from Nazareth. Armstrong interprets Compassion as that which . . .

> impels us to work tirelessly to alleviate the suffering of our fellow creatures, to dethrone ourselves from the center of our world and put another there, and to honor the inviolable sanctity of every human being, treating everybody, without exception, with absolute justice, equity, and respect.

She expands on this, saying that we are not to "confine [our] compassion to [our] group." We are not to treat others in ways in which we would not like to be treated.

What I find to be so relevant to the therapeutic practice of compassion in IFS therapy is Armstrong's invitation to go beyond simply tolerating each other and to engage in the *appreciation* of each other. Everyone is welcome. All parts are welcome. To all parts we owe a debt of gratitude. We offer Hope to all who populate the inner and outer worlds. We will know that we love each other to the extent that we weep together, that we see each other as holy, as a sacred other. This is Personalism at its finest.

## Personalism Continued

If we say that a person is unique and an irreplaceable, incomparable individual, are we talking of the self, *the me* as the center of consciousness? (See the works of Hans Urs von Balthasar [1905-1988].) If so, we have an ontological problem. What will we be talking about when self-consciousness is usurped by competing neuronal networks? An idealism in Personalism can lead us to overly spiritualize the person when adherents contend that the human person acts in the world from the inner self, as a subjective "I" with the power of self-determination (Moyn). Realism exists when the personalist says that "we are made for relationship" and that we need to possess ourselves in order to give of ourselves.

A quote from Moyn's article makes me think of the role of compassion in IFS therapy: "Without a disinterested gift of self, man cannot achieve the finality that is proper to a human being by virtue of being a person, and cannot discover his true self." This quote leaves us with these and more unresolved questions: Who is this "person" who discovers his "true self" and gives this disinterested gift of "self?" Who is this "self" the person gives? Is it the SELF—the Center, the Circumference, and Totality of the Psyche—who, out of the universal unconscious, gives birth to the self, the me, who is the center of consciousness? And is it the Self, the I, who is aware of itself that can give the gift of Self? These questions give us much to ponder, given the insufficiency of language. We have been on the trail of this search, and the quest goes on.

## Neuroscience and Psychotherapy

Here I want to take a brief excursion into the living metaphor of the "triune brain." Louis Cozolino, in his well-recognized 2002 book, *The Neuroscience of Psychotherapy,* refers to Paul McLean, known for the triune brain theory, when he writes of a "brain within a brain within a brain" (Cozolino, p. 8) and reminds us that "only the neo-mammalian

214

brain is capable of consciousness and verbal communication" (p. 9). Given that we continue to evolve from the moment of birth and that all organismic change is subject to developmental experiences, it is no wonder that "many of the most important aspect of our lives are controlled by reflexes, behaviors, and emotions learned and organized outside of our awareness (p. 12). In Michael Heller's 2012 encyclopedic book on Body Psychotherapy, he uses the term "non-conscious" for all that is and functions outside of human consciousness within the entire world of what we call body. For this reason, IFS therapy is fundamentally somatic. All aspects of our being and doing is a mind, body, psyche trinity. On a conscious level, we tell ourselves that we are, what we are, and who we are. Our "autobiographical memories are at the core of our sense of history, our conscious connections with others, and our sense of self in interpersonal and physical space" (Cozolino, p. 34).

Cozolino summarizes the work of Ulric Neisser's (1928-2012) on cognitive psychology when he says, "The self consists of the integration of five separate functions. I experience myself in time, in the environment, in relationship, in a private self-dialogue, and in my "idea of 'me'" (Cozolino, pp. 153-154). Cozolino later attempts a working definition of the self: "The self is a matrix of learning and memory organized and encoded within hidden layers of neural networks" (p. 170). He then offers an experiential definition of the *true self:*

> The true self reflects brain and bodily networks that can tolerate negative feelings and integrate them into conscious awareness. This true self is reflected in our ability to seek out what feels right for us in our activities, ourselves, and relationships with others. (p. 197)

He further explains that "the true self reflects neural integration and access across modes of information processing and an awareness of the difference between reflexive and reflective forms of language. The true self embodies an open and ongoing dialogue among the heart, the mind, and the body" (p. 198). Cozolino then mentions what Winnicott called the *false self* that . . .

215

results from expectations and impingements for which the child is developmentally unprepared. . . . The false self also reflects dissociated neural processing, lack of adequate affect regulation, and the inhibition of sensations and emotions necessary for the formation of the true self. (p. 198)

What the false self needs is to be in the presence of an emotionally regulated adult who can be fully present and thereby able to mirror the child's innate capacity for authentic self-reflection. As an IFS therapist, I advance that we are speaking of a self that is blended or taken over by unintegrated parts that we compassionately confront with our SELF-led Self. Cozolino ends his book with a statement that merits full inclusion:

Self-awareness is a relatively new phenomenon in evolutionary history. It is also just recently that we have become aware of the fact that our brains organize the totality of our experience. Psychotherapy increases neural integration through challenges that expand our experience and perspective of ourselves and the world. The challenge of expanding consciousness is to move beyond reflex, fear, and prejudice to a mindfulness and compassion for ourselves and others. Understanding the promise and limitations of our brains is but one essential step in the evolution of consciousness. (p. 319)

We are incarnate spirits, rational animals, persons. We define ourselves without having a stance outside of ourselves to provide us an objective view. When science turns it eye on the self, the Self, and the SELF, it must bow in recognition of its helplessness. Science has no direct route to the knowledge of this trinity, thus the necessity of circumambulation—a walk around, over, and under—to glimpse the triune relationship of the self, the Self, and the SELF.

This book is one such limited journey.

*That is the goal*
*that all parts enter*
*into a communion*

—Matthew Fox (1940-)

## AFTERWORD

The SELF is always present. The source of all is always present. Without the IT's *energia*, nothing exists, nothing functions. The SELF is beyond the touch of any and all other entities. SELF is within and without time, in and outside of place, before and after all that is and is not. SELF defines everything. SELF defines not only the what but also the who, the how, and the why of all that exists in the when and the where. Nothing has being without the SELF. It is in and by and through the creative omnipresence of the IT that the Elusive SELF is beyond our capacity to grasp the IT's limitless essence as one and multiple. Everything and everyone is in the IT's image and likeness. Nothing can possibly be a self-originating separate entity; not even the human person endowed with the gift of multiplicity and of evolving consciousness.

This gift that blossoms forth from the Image of the ONE SELF into a plethora of individual multiple selves reflects, of necessity, the IT"s unfathomable dimensions, creates the individual person's experience of a multilayered consciousness that arises from a universal and personal origin by whatever name we call them. Parts, subpersonalities, aspects, neuronal networks, and other terms refer to those multiple ways in which our multiplicity has its existential being and in which the SELF's multidimensional essence manifests.

Some would say that the SELF is the perfect living image of the IT's union of opposites. Nothing and no one can change IT in any way. Some would say that it is the fate, destiny, and mission of the self

217

to evolve into a Self in time and place. Others would add that the SELF is expanding and that this expansion involves the evolution of the individual self into a SELF-led Self, thus increasing the SELF Energy on our planet, in our solar system, in our galaxy, in the expanding universe until all returns to its origin—the ALL, the IT, the OTHER, the Source—now mysteriously more aware than at the moment of the first expansion. All a miracle, said Einstein.

Reading the newly available 2020 second edition of *Internal Family Systems Therapy* by Schwartz and Sweezy this late 2019 November day, as I edit the last draft of this book, I am in awe of the refinements in IFS since that first edition came out a quarter of a century ago. My thoughts have also evolved since I became a Certified IFS Therapist. Some of my earlier understanding has been confirmed and solidified but, hopefully, not congealed. For example, I see the seat of consciousness to be the **self**, the "I," the "me" that Freud experienced—a **self** that expands into a greater consciousness—the **Self**, the more that it is available to being **SELF-led**, the more that the multiplicities are differentiated (à la M. Bowen), individuated (àla Jung), and incarnated (à la Body Psychotherapy) and welcomed into the whole to contribute to the whole.

When I read Chapter Three, "The Self," in Schwartz and Sweezy's second edition, I translate the terms "self" and "Self" into the language of my proposed trinity of **self, Self,** and **SELF,** according to the context they present. An attempt to reveal my own thinking in order to engage in a greater conversation is the goal of my lengthy reflections in *The Elusive SELF.* Yet, in the end, it is the artful loving relationship of all multiplicities that makes things whole, that *sanctifies,* according to William James; that unburdens the members of the internal family for the good of all.

The **SELF** is, of its essence, compassionate. The **Self** becomes compassionate the more hospitable it is to the **energy** of the **SELF.** It is the **SELF** that is transcendent. The **Self** is Its willing disciple and servant. The **SELF's energy** can be obscured by burdened, mis-directed, and ill-informed, although well-intentioned, parts. The analogy of an eclipse might express the level and intensity of the barrier set up by the extreme state, such as an *alter* in a dissociated state. Other unintegrated parts offer varied levels of obscurity even in their benevolent roles. Like the sun, the **SELF** is never obliterated. The **ITs** light and warmth might be distanced and screened, but it is always present and sustaining. The **SELF**, in those moments, does not abandon the **self** on its developmental journey to becoming a **SELF-led Self**.

Our soul is a precious nugget, a holon of the **SELF**, the I, the person that participates in my given **Selfhood** in this life and is energized in a complete organismic process by the **SELF**. It is the **SELF-led Self** that incarnates, in actuality, the wisdom of individual and universal human behavior. When the **Self** embraces more and more of its multiplicity with the life-giving qualities of the **SELF**, and joins with other hospitable **Selves,** the myriad internal and external selves move toward a greater peaceable kingdom—the actualization of the limitless common good for all that is.

To acknowledge the **SELF** as elusive is to recognize that the SELF might be all we say it is and totally other than what we say it is. This is our protection against idolatry.

*Admitting where*
*one's knowledge ends*
*is the beginning of wisdom.*

—Source Obscure

## APPENDIX A: A LIMITED COLLECTION OF THOUGHTS AND POINTS OF VIEW

To aid readers in understanding the concepts detailed in this work, I offer the following annotated glossary of words with commentary from referenced writers. For full publishing information, see References.

\* \* \*

**Adaptation:** "A differentiation from which was the very subject of my personal organization and which becomes thereby the object of a new organization on behalf of a new subjectivity that coordinates it" (Kegan, 1982, *The Evolving Self,* p. 85).

**Affect:** "Affect is essentially phenomenological, the felt experience of a motion (hence 'e-motion')" (Kegan, p. 81).

**Belief:** (1) "Who hears may be incredulous/Who witnesses, believes" (Emily Dickinson in S. H. Buhner 2004, *The Secret Teachings of Plants,* p. 177). (2) "It is rational to believe without evidence" (James, 1896, "The Will to Believe").

**Beyond the Material:** "I thoroughly understand that there are scientists to whom the world is merely the result of chemical forces or material electrons. I do not belong to this class" (George Washington Carver in Buhner, 2004, p. 43).

**Burden:** "There is a time when a thing is a heavy thing to carry and then it must be put down. But such is its nature that it cannot be set off on a rock or shouldered off onto the fork of a tree like a heavy

220

pack. There is only one thing shaped to receive it and that is another human mind" (Theodore Sturgeon in Buhner, 2004, p. 202).

**Causality:** "Behind every cause lies countless other causes. Any attempt to trace these back to their sources only leads one further away from an understanding of the true cause. . . . Nature has neither beginning nor end, before nor after, cause nor effect. Causality does not exist. When there is no front nor back, no beginning nor end, but only what resembles a circle or sphere, one could say that there is a unity of cause and effect but one could just as well claim that cause and effect do not exist" (Masanobu Fukuoka in Buhner, 2004, p. 6).

**Character:** "We are well enough aware that some skill, some ability, usually predominates in the character of each human being. This leads necessarily to one-sided thinking. Since man knows the world only through himself, and thus has the naïve arrogance to believe that the world is constructed by him and for his sake, it follows that he puts his special skills in the foreground, while seeking to reject those he lacks, to banish them from his own totality. As a correction, he needs to develop all of the manifestations of human character—sensuality and reason, imagination and common sense—into a coherent whole, no matter which quality predominates in him. If he fails to do so, he will labor under painful limitations, without ever understanding why he has so many stubborn enemies, why he even meets himself as an enemy" (Goethe in Buhner, 2004, p. 226).

**Clinical Problems:** "They are all about the threat of the constructed self's collapse" (Kegan, p. 275, *The Evolving Self*).

**Coherence:** "The things which enter our consciousness are vast in number, and their relations—to the extent that the mind can grasp them—are extraordinarily complex. Minds with the inner power to grow will begin to establish an order so that knowledge comes easier; they will begin to satisfy themselves by finding coherence and connection" (Goethe in Buhner, 2004, p. 185).

221

**Combative Stance:** I remember a quote attributed to William James that anticipates Damasio and flows easily from Spinoza's perspective—that *"It is rational to believe without evidence."* (See James's 1896 lecture, "The Will to Believe.") Remember how James thinks from an experiential realistic pragmatism. For him, a saint translates his holiness, his spiritual life, into action for the benefit of others; and his nonviolence has limits. Damasio puts it in this way:

"I said the life of the spirit needs the complement of a combative stance. Nature is neither cruel nor benign, but our practical view can be justifiably subjective and personal. On that view modern biology is now revealing that nature is even more cruel and indifferent than we previously thought. While humans are equal-opportunity victims of nature's casual, unpremeditated evil, we are not obliged to accept it without response. We can try to find means to counteract the seeming cruelty and indifference. Nature lacks a plan for human flourishing, but nature's humans are allowed to devise such a plan. A combative stance, more so perhaps than the noble illusion of Spinoza's blessedness, seems to hold the promise that we shall never feel alone as long as our concern is the well-being of *others* [emphasis added]" (Damasio, 2003, *Looking for Spinoza,* p. 287).

And the "others" mentioned above include all of our parts. This is what James intended when he spoke of the purpose of saintliness—the flourishing of self and others.

**Compassion:** "Genuine self-compassion is a journey into the multiple parts of yourself—the good, the bad, the ugly, the confused, the abandoned—so as to make friends with those parts on the deepest levels" (Schwartz, 2015, "Facing Our Dark Side," in *Psychotherapy Networker,* p. 19).

**Consciousness:** "Consciousness signifies the presence of a mind with a self, but in practical human terms, the word actually signifies more. With the help of autobiographical memory, consciousness provides us with a self that is enriched by the records of our individual experiences" (Damasio, 2003, *Looking for Spinosa,* p. 270).

**Dharma's View of the Self:** "The Dharma's view of the self is as evolved and radical as Copernicus's view of the universe. The self, as we know it, doesn't really exist. The key phrase is *as we know it.* The self is simply not what we think it is. Once, someone asked me what I had learned in all my years of Buddhist practice, and I spontaneously answered, 'I'm not who I think I am.' We are often so identified with who we think we are that it not only determines how we live, but it limits how we can be. Our thoughts and concepts obscure reality, circumscribing us and our world" (Das, 1997, *Awakening the Buddha Within,* pp. 116-117).

**Ego:** "The ego is like a clown in a circus, always trying to stick in its oar to make it look like it has something to do with what is going on" (Sigmund Freud to Carl Jung in Kegan, 1982, p. 6).

**Energetics of Life:** "When in the exercise of his powers of observation man undertakes to confront the world of nature, he will at first experience a tremendous compulsion to bring what he finds there under his control. Before long, however, these objects will thrust themselves before him with such a force that he, in turn, must feel the obligation to acknowledge their power and pay homage to their effects" (Goethe in Buhner, 2004, p. 49).

**Equilibrium:** "The goal of psychotherapy" (Kegan, p. 272).

**Freud, as interpreted by Bruno Bettelheim.** See Part One, Chapter One, of this study: "Freud and Man's Soul." (See also Bettelheim, 1982, *Freud & Man'sSsoul.*)

**Freedom:** "A reduction of dependence on the object-emotional needs that enslave us." "Spinoza believed that an entity is free only when it exists solely by the lights of its nature and when it acts solely by its own determination" (Damasio, 2003, *Looking for Spinosa,* p. 276).

223

**Guilt:** "Guilt has to do with having a problem simply because the lie exists and one is implicated thereby. . ." (Kegan, p. 94).

**Heart:** "And now here is my secret, a very simple secret; it is only with the heart that one can see rightly; what is essential is invisible to the eye" (Antoine de Saint-Exupery in Buhner, 2004, p. 147).

**Hidden, The:** "Since nothing is so secret or hidden that it cannot be revealed, everything depends on the discovery of those things which manifest the hidden" (Paracelsus in Buhner, 2004, p. 292).

**Higher Light:** "It is by obeying the suggestion of a higher light within you that you escape from yourself and, in transit, as it were, see with the unworn sides of your eye, travel totally new paths" (Henry David Thoreau in Buhner, 2004, p. 247).

**Hope:** (1) "Hope is nothing else but an inconstant joy, arising from the image of something future or past, whose outcome to some extent we doubt" (Damasio, 2003, p. 289). (2) One of the three transcendental/theological virtues: Faith, Hope, and Charity (*Caritas*—Love for all). (3) "Hope is definitely not the same as optimism. It is not the conviction that something will turn out well, but the certainty that something makes sense, regardless of how it turns out" (Havel, 1990, *Disturbing the Peace.*) (4) "Might we better understand others in their predicament if we could somehow know how their way of living reflects the state of their hoping at this depth? — not the hopes they have or the hoping they do, but the ***hopes and hoping they are***" (Kegan, 1982, *The Evolving Self,* p. 45)?

**Human Being:** "O human, see then the human being rightly: the human being has heaven and earth and the whole creation in itself, and yet is a complete form, and in it everything is already present, though hidden" (Hildegard of Bingen in Buhner, 2004, p. 202).

**Human Spirit:** "In the human spirit, as in the universe, nothing is higher or lower; everything has equal rights to a ***common center*** which manifests its hidden existence precisely through this harmonic relationship between every part and itself" (Goethe in Buhner, 2004, pp. 33, 218).

**Incarceration:** "The scariest part of prison was falling in love with the women, the inmates. . . . They were smart and funny and beautiful and deeply kind and remorseful and in so much pain, and these same women had killed people, taken actual lives. This complexity, this ambiguity, was almost unbearable. . . . Everything was suddenly in question" (Ensler, 2006, *Insecure at Last*, p. 118).

**Individuality:** " 'Individuality' permits one to 'give oneself up' to another; to find oneself in what [Erik] Erikson has called 'a counter-pointing of identities,' which at once shares experiencing and guarantees each partner's distinctiveness, which permits persons—again Erikson's words—'to regulate with one another the cycles of work, procreation, and recreation.' Every equilibrium is a qualitative victory over isolation" (Kegan, p. 106). (See also Erikson, 1968, *Identity*.) *(Is this not the work of witnessing, retrieving, unburdening, and resourcing?)*

**Individuation Process:** "This drive toward individuation is apparently a spontaneous urge, not under the leadership of the ego, but of the archetypal movement in the unconscious, the non-ego, toward the fulfillment of the specific basic pattern of the individual, striving toward wholeness, totality, and the differentiation of the specific potentialities that are innately destined to form the particular personality in question. The unconscious is the matrix out of which these various qualities arise step by step toward differentiation in consciousness, which they approach first in symbolic guise until the ego learns to understand and incorporate them. In this unconscious matrix, then, the pattern of the wholeness of the personality lies hidden awaiting the hand of experience to stir it into activity; it is not an ego ideal formed by upbringing, but a dynamic urge emanating from the core of one's being, laden with affect and presenting itself to consciousness in terms of archetypal symbols" (Perry, 1953, *The Self in Psychotic Process,* p. 45).

**Insight:** "We all walk in mysteries. We do not know what is stirring in the atmosphere that surrounds us, nor how it is connected with our own spirit. So much is certain—that at times we can put out the feelers of our soul beyond its bodily limits, and a presentiment, an actual insight . . . is accorded to it" (Goethe in Buhner, 2004, p. 147).

**James, William:** Born in New York City in 1842. Educated in New York, Europe, Rhode Island, and Boston. Died in Chocorua, New Hampshire, in 1910, age 68.

**Joy and Sorrow:** "The neurobiology of emotion and feeling tells us in suggestive terms that joy and its variants are preferable to sorrow and related affects, and more conducive to health and the creative flourishing of our beings" (Damasio, 2003, p. 271).

**Life:** "Life is valuable by virtue of people's investment in it, or its investment in others. . . . " (Kegan, p. 99)

**Life Force:** "Life, as a whole, expresses itself as a force that is not to be contained within any one part" (Goethe in Buhner, 2004, p. 44).

**Linear Mind:** "The insistent, single point of view of the linear mind is itself a lie. All people are, in fact, born multiple personalities, all people naturally should possess multiple points of view, have multi-dimensional consciousness. The adoption of a linear, *single-minded* focus corrupts the self, forces us to forego depth of self to become one-dimensional. It forces parts into the bag by its very nature" (Buhner, 2004, p. 248).

**Love:** "He who loves God must not expect God to love him in return" (Damasio, 2003, p. 258). The same can be said of the SELF. Those who love the SELF must not expect a reward from the SELF in return, for the SELF is, as nature, objective.

**Nature:** "In Nature's presence we are all children, nothing more, and honors and names and purses lose their significance and importance

226

and are forgotten and only the awe and marvel in our hearts remain" (Luther Burbank in Buhner, 2004, p. 179).

**Organic Being:** "An organic being is so *multifaceted in its exterior, so varied and inexhaustible in its interior,* that we cannot find enough points of view nor develop in ourselves enough organs of perception to avoid killing it when we analyze it" (Goethe in Buhner, 2004, p. 67).

**Panentheism:** "The belief that the divine pervades and interpenetrates every part of the universe and also extends beyond space and time. Panentheism maintains an ontological distinction between the divine and the non-divine and the significance of both, that God includes the world as a part, though not the whole, of God's being, that God is greater than the universe, is viewed as the soul of the universe, is the universal spirit present everywhere, that transcends all things created, and that the universe is nothing more than a manifestation of God, that it is contained in God according to the Kabbalah" (Wikipedia).

**Parts:** "We spend our life until we are twenty deciding what parts of our self to put into the bag, and we spend the rest of our life trying to get them out again" (Robert Bly in Buhner, 2004, p. 239).

**Parts and Whole:** "The things that we call the parts in every living being are so inseparable from the whole that they may be understood only in and with the whole" (Goethe in Buhner, 2004, p. 39).

**Parts in the Extreme:** "But . . . attempts at division . . . produce many adverse effects when carried to the extreme. To be sure, what is alive can be dissected into its component parts, but from these parts it will be impossible to restore it and bring it to life again" (Goethe in Buhner, 2004, p. 39).

**Parts, The Shut-up:** In the following paragraphs, Buhner expands on the subject of "shut-up" parts:

"And what's more, [shut-up] parts are enraged. So when we catch a glimpse of one with our conscious mind, it scares the

227

begeesus out of us. For another truth that comes in its own time is that any part that we have locked up begins to take on tremendous energy. And the years of repression, the stored [energy] of being *'shut up!'* have taken their toll. The shut-up parts have begun to devolve, to become hairy and monstrous, to grow claws. . . . But these split-off parts are essential to our wholeness" (Buhner, 2004, p. 239).

"When you first open the bag and let a part out, it is often misshapen, frightened, and angry. It takes some time, and much bargaining, many kept promises, and much love before it once again takes on its proper form—before it is healed and whole . . . *and these parts must genuinely be liked/a genuine relationship reestablished for any reintegration to occur"* (Buhner, pp. 239-240). *"There is death in this restructuring, this reclamation of the self. For the reduced-you dies when you eat shadow, adding a new part to yourself* [emphasis added]" (Buhner, p. 241).

"And just when you think you have gone as deep as you can, when there are no more shadows to find, no more parts to be locked away, a phenomenon will thrust itself upon you—a person, place, or plant—that forces you to go deeper still. Forces you to see parts of yourself that you did not know were there, that you had no *conscious* wish to know" (Buhner, p. 244). "And this rearrangement of your internal self is stimulated and directed from the world outside you. It does not come from a top-down hierarchy of values, but is a quality, a value, that **emerges from within, from the center** outwards, when your individuality is entangled with that of the world. It comes out of a center of expressed meanings, out of interaction with the world, out of aesthesis [sensory awareness]" (Buhner, p. 245).

**Patients:** "I am of the opinion that our patients become our real instructors about the psyche throughout the years, providing we take in and digest what they tell us" (Perry, p. xiii).

**Perception:** "The human being knows himself only insofar as he knows the world; he perceives the world only in himself, and himself only in the world. Every new object, clearly seen, opens up a new organ of perception in us" (Goethe in Buhner, 2004, p. 227).

**Person:** "'Person' is understood to refer as much to an activity as to a thing—an ever-progressive motion engaged in giving itself a new form" (Kegan, p. 8).

**Phenomena:** "Individual phenomena must never be torn out of context. Stay with the phenomena, think within them, accede with your intentionality to their patterns, which will gradually open your thinking to an intuition of their structure" (Goethe in Buhner, 2004, p. 178).

**Plurality:** "No living thing is unitary in nature; every such thing is a plurality. Even the organism which appears to us as an individual exists as a *collection of independent living entities*" (Goethe in Buhner, 2004, p. 46).

**Presence:** Presence is the key that opens the pathways between us all and all that is. Ronald Siegel's sound neuroscientific concept of presense offers validation for the time-worn spiritual and psychotherapeutic practice of "being in the here and now" with the other. (See R. Siegel & R. Schwartz, 2015, The Fiction of the Self, *Psychotherapy Networker.*)

**Psychology:** "Psychology asks fundamental questions about being human: the examination is metaphysical. but we are wary of deceiving ourselves and so we 'cheat'—we look into the souls of our neighbors for verification" (Kegan, p. 2).

**Psychotherapy:** "When the counselor responds to the problem not in terms of assurance, or its resolution, or its interpretation, but in terms of the experience of having, or of being in, the problem, the counselor is offering the client a most intimate and usually unexpected companionship—not as another object in the world, but as fellow hanger-in-the-balance, *a companion to [the] very experience of knowing* (meaning-making) and a party to the re-cognition whose time has come. The counselor is offering the client a culture to grow in" (Kegan, p. 276).

"In order to change a psychic structure that has become inadequate for progressive development, the structure must be resolved and its *raw energetic content* liberated for a renewal of its form of expression" (Perry, p. 50).

**Religious Experience:** "Religious experience is human experience" (James, 1902, *The Varieties of Religious Experience.*)

**Rescue:** "We get rescued by giving what we need most. What we are waiting for has always lived inside of us" (Ensler, p. 114).

**Research:** "If some phenomena appears in my research, and I can find no source for it, I let it stand as a problem. . . . I might have to let it lie for a long time, but at some moment, years later, enlightenment comes in the most wonderful way" (Goethe in Buhner, 2004, p. 78).

**Results:** "Not through an extraordinary spiritual gift, nor through momentary inspiration, unexpected and unique, but through constant work did I eventually achieve such satisfactory results" (Goethe in Buhner, 2004, p. 173).

**Revelation:** "[Thoreau] aimed to become just, and in this struggle followed the ancient doctrine, contrary to scientific doctrine, that certain secrets of nature reveal themselves only to the observer who is morally developed" (Robert Bly in Buhner, 2004, p. 226).

**Seeing:** "Seeing better increases our vulnerability to being recruited to the welfare of others" (Kegan, pp. 16-17). "The reasons why we are drawn to others, especially to their welfare, are surely mysterious" (p. 19). James links this to saintliness.

**Self:** (1) "There is presumed to be a basic unity to personality, a unity best understood as a process rather than an entity. This process, according to [Carl] Rogers' conception, gives rise to the 'self'" (Kegan, p. 5). [Self, in IFS understanding.]

(2) [SELF is] "a pattern of wholeness that thus represents itself in archetypal form that . . .

230

- governs and structures the total psyche as the ego does its conscious content. Since it is constellated only under conditions of stress, this phenomenon *is apt to evade study* under 'normal' or experimental conditions;
- is the ruling center around which the many contrasting contents of the psyche tend to structure themselves into a pattern that is always unique; that is, the 'law of one's own being'" (Perry, pp. 45-46).

(3) As a "simple ego-like life form." "Damasio [rather boldly] calls [the tectum and dorsal tegmentum] region of the brain the *SELF*. This SELF forms the *functional 'ego'* upon which all [the] more complex representations of our selves are built [the autobiographical self]" (Solms & Turnbull, p. 110).

**Self-Examination:** See Buhner, 2004, *The Secret Teachings of Plants,* Chapter 13.

**Spinoza's Salvation:** Damasio writes, "When you are less than kind to others, you punish yourself, there and then, and deny yourself the opportunity to achieve inner peace and happiness, there and then. When you are loving to others there is a good chance of achieving inner peace and happiness, then and there. Thus, a person's actions should not be aimed at pleasing God, but rather at acting in conformity with the nature of god. When you do so, some kind of happiness results and some kind of salvation is achieved. *Now* Spinoza's salvation—*salus*—is about repeated occasions of a kind of happiness that cumulatively make for a healthy mental condition (Damasio, 2003, p. 273). This is a basis for a solid ethics that James would support.

**Spirituality:** "The way I define spirituality is a deeply held belief that we are inextricably connected to one another by something bigger than [we are], and something that is grounded in love. Some people call that God, and some people call that fishing." (See Brene Brown, 2015, *Daring Greatly*.)

**Theory and Practice:** "In theory, there's no difference between theory and practice. In practice there is" (attributed to baseball legend Yogi Berra).

**Third Thing, A:** "Whatever appears in the world must divide if it is to appear at all. What has divided seeks itself again, can return to itself and reunite. . . . In the reunion of the intensified halves, it will produce *a third thing, something new, higher, unexpected*" (Goethe in Buhner, 2004, p. 37).

**Treatment:** From the "*self open to the Energy of the SELF*" (Buhner, 2004, pp. 221-225).

**Truth:** "We can never see directly what is true; that is, [what is] identical with what is divine; we look at it only in reflection" (Goethe in Buhner, 2004, p. 228).

**Vagina Warriors:** In *Insecure at Last,* Ensler (2006) says, "They have a wicked sense of humor. . . . They know that compassion is the deepest form of memory. . . . They know that punishment does not make abusive people behave better. They know that it is more important to provide a space where the best can emerge rather than 'teaching people a lesson'" (p. 84).

**Work:** "I persist until I have discovered a pregnant point from which several things may be derived, or rather one which yields several things, offering them up of its own accord" (Goethe in Buhner, 2004, p. 176).

*The Soul is the*
*inter and intra*
*cellular filled space.*
*—Marcel Duclos, dream (7-18-2018)*

## APPENDIX B: ADDITIONAL PERSPECTIVES FROM OTHER SOURCES

For full publishing information for all of the works mentioned here, see References.

**Ho, Mae-Wan.** (1993). *The Rainbow and the Worm: The Physics of Organisms.*

"For me, the big motivating question is Erwin Schrodinger's, 'What is life?'" says Mae-Wan Ho (p. 1). Who and what is the Elusive Self is a question of comparable dimensions. To answer Schrodinger's question, Ho dares to offer a tentative definition—"life is a process of being an organizing whole." She states that life is "not a thing, nor a property of a material thing or structure." She reminds us that life must "reside in the pattern of dynamic flow of matter and energy that somehow makes the organisms alive, enabling them to grow, develop, and evolve" (p. 5).

Could we not consider the SELF a parallel? Ho agrees with French philosopher Henri Bergson's *elan vital:*

As for us humans, we are living organisms among living organisms. We, like all these, have "extreme sensitivity to specific cues from the environment," we have "extraordinary efficiency and rapidity of energy transduction," we have "long range order and coordination, and ultimately," we have "wholeness and individuality." (Bergson in Ho, p. 6)

233

So, humans are a marvel among marvels. We have a place in "the continuity between the living and non-living," which is Ho's thesis. She invites us to think without limits.

**Dourley, J. P.** (1987). *Love, Celibacy and the Inner Marriage.*

Dourley, a Roman Catholic priest and Jungian analyst, integrates theology and psychology. To nourish the discussion of the leadership of the SELF in the life of the Self, I want to glean a few more insights from him. When I look at my copy of his book, pages slipping out of the glue, struggling to keep themselves together, I find that few pages were spared my pencil—underlines, brackets, my idiosyncratic notations, one of which reads, *Unless you are true to (her) Wisdom, I will kill you* (Dream: 07-26-88). Thirty years have passed since that dream, and I cannot assure myself that I have been even partially true to Wisdom in these intervening years. That the dreamer who dreamed this dream (a voice in the blackest of black) was no "other" than the Source of all religious experience in the collective unconscious affirms Jung's philosophy. The voice that speaks to us in dreams of integration, is . . .

for Jung, the voice of the Self [SELF]. When it speaks, the dreamer must listen and yield to its wisdom as though he or she were being addressed by the voice of God. This is the Self [SELF] as the ultimate authority, as that power in the unconscious which works toward the unity of the ego [self] with its latent totality in the depth of the unconscious. The voice of the Self [SELF] seems to point to some power within us which views the ego [self] from a higher perspective, from a viewpoint of eternity. (Dourley, p. 15).

How congruent this is with James's experiential conviction. And, when we enter the internal world of IFS, we find ourselves in a very real return journey to the center of our being via a body, mind, soul discipline whose means, the integration of parts, and its end, the reign of Creative Hope, can be observed and measured. Dourley makes mention of Bonaventure's (1221-1274 CE) *Itinerarium Mentis ad Deum*

234

(The Journey of the Mind to God)—the self's return to the SELF as a Self. (See Dourley, fn. 22, p. 160.)

Dourley speaks of this journey as a "progressive unification of the opposites of the unconscious and consciousness from which the Self [Self] is born as spirit, involves the ongoing suffering of the ego [self] at the hands of the unconscious in the interest of a newly emerging Self [Self]. This dialectic of the inner priesthood and victimhood is for Jung the archetypal meaning of the Catholic sacrificial rite of the Mass" (Dourley, pp.16-17). This is the *crux* of the matter. Dourley wants to advance an understanding of religious experience as James did a century before.

Dourley writes: "For Jung, religious experience is made possible through the activation of the immense energies of the archetypes and by the ego's experience of the numinosity clothing the symbols, myths, and ritual enactments that proceed from this activation. Thus, the world religions and nightly dreams proceed from the same source, one to which each individual has access and which has access to each individual. The dreams are private revelations which, whether dramatically or gradually, lead the individual into her or his myth. Thus, when Jung identifies the practice of religion with the observation of what comes out of the unconscious, he is obviously investing the voice of the unconscious with the weight of the voice of God for the individual" (Dourley, p. 21).

This is the *Vox Dei*. The voice of the SELF or of the SELF's messengers, living beings in the psyche whom we may address, confront, welcome into our wholeness-making, our *sacrum facere,* our sacrifice on the altar of our life. Dourley, the priest-theologian-analyst is familiar with the symbolisms of the Mass. He adds the following observation:

> In [Jung's] work on the Catholic Mass he works to show that the truth of Christ as priest and victim is the truth of the flow of psychic growth as the unconscious sacrifices the ego to the demands of further growth, and the ego becomes then the place of the incarnation

235

of the divine or unconscious—which must, in turn, sacrifice itself to the ego as it enters the confines of finitude. . . . Christ [then is the] image of the Self coming through crucifixion to a resurrected and unbroken unity with the Father, the source of all. "I and the Source are one" is something that the experience of true growth drives every human to say who has undergone its terrifying demands. (Dourley, p. 22)

In the great archetypal tradition, Dourley underscores Jung's demands . . .

of the psychologist that he or she drive the pursuit beyond or deeper than the levels of consciousness, reason, and clarity. To deny the truth of the prerational and/or irrational depths of the human, and the continued power of these levels over our conscious thoughts and behavior is to truncate the human and to deny to it the further reaches of its potential for good or evil. (Dourley, p. 23)

At the risk of losing our humanity, we must give all of our internal family members, personal and universal, the utmost respect with realistic trepidation and welcoming hospitality.

**Mattoon, M. A.** (1981). *Jungian Psychology in Perspective.*

Mary Ann Mattoon tells us that . . .

Superordinate to all the components of the psyche is the Self [SELF] (fn., p. 31. [See below.]). The Self [SELF] is so all-encompassing a concept that it is difficult to characterize; hence it has been described in various ways. The phrase that seems to designate the concept best is "the total personality," conscious and unconscious. Thus, it becomes evident that the ego [self] is "subordinate to the self [SELF] and is related to it like a part to the whole" (CW9-II, para. 9). Jung also referred to the Self [SELF] as the center of the personality, comparable to the sun in the solar system—the source of all the system's energy. In this image the ego is to the Self [SELF] as the Earth is to the sun. (Mattoon, p. 31)

Footnote, page 31, reads:

*The spelling of the word self with a capital or lower-case S is a matter of disagreement among Jungians. It is not capitalized in the* Collected Works. *I have capitalized it in this book, however, to indicate its importance and to differentiate it from the concept of "self" in other psychologies* (e.g., Cattell, R. B., 1957, *Personality and Motivation Structure and Measurement;* and Rogers, C., 1959, *A Theory of Therapy, Personality, and Interpersonal Relationships*). *In these other systems, "self" usually means what Jung meant by "ego."*

In previous chapters, I have added the concept of the "Self" to highlight the IFS concept of the transformation of the ego [self] into the SELF-led consciousness we call the Self, the one who lives more fully the differentiated identity in communion with the SELF.

It is still surprising to me today, forty years after Mattoon wrote *Jungian Psychology in Perspective,* that a Jungian analyst felt the need to assert empirical evidence for the components of the Psyche. At the end of Chapter Two, "The Components of the Psyche," Mattoon writes that "the existence of the unconscious is rapidly becoming recognized as indisputable" (1981, p. 33). And yet, in this second decade of the 21st century, our Western culture acts as if the unconscious and its population play no role in the conduct of our affairs—personal, societal, political, economic, or religious—to name a few domains demonstrably affected by every manner of inner parts. Splitting and dissociation, fragments, aspects, subpersonalities, complexes, and archetypes fill our consultation rooms. They belong to the therapist and to the patient, to their families, to their communities, to their human roots. One could boldly assert that heaven and earth are present.

**Merton, T.** (Ed.). (1964). *Gandhi on Non-Violence.* New York, NY: New Directions.

In *Gandhi on Non-Violence,* editor Thomas Merton quotes Gandhi, who argues against the illusion of perfection: "A *satyagrahi* cannot wait or delay action till the perfect conditions are forthcoming. He will act with whatever material is at hand, purge it of its dross, and convert it into gold" (Merton, p. 49). This reminds me of the wisdom of the alchemists.

In the introduction, Merton presents the following quote taken from "On Being in One's Right Mind," an article by A. K. Coomaraswamy originally published in November 1942:

Thou shalt do nothing but forsake thy own will, viz., that which thou callest "I" or "thyself." By which means all thy evil properties will grow weak, faint and ready to die, then thou wilt sink down again into that one thing from which thou art mercy originally sprung. (Merton, p. 18)

How comforting to hear the same wisdom coming from across cultures, a wisdom that sings the same song of witnessing, unburdening, and re-sourcing in the *therapeutae* of the ages.

Merton does not disappoint. He also mentions the "Angelic Doctor," Thomas Aquinas, digging into the "Summa Theologica":

In Thomas Aquinas . . . evil is not only reversible but it is the proper motive of that **mercy** [emphasis added] by which it is overcome and changed into good. Replying to the objections that moral evil is not the motive for mercy since the evil of sin deserves indignation and punishment rather than mercy and forgiveness, [Aquinas] says that on the contrary *sin itself is already a punishment* "and in this respect we feel sorrow and compassion for sinners." (Merton. See Note 16. Summa Theologica, II, Ibid., q. 30, art1, ad.1, p. 12)

It is not difficult to recognize Helen M. Luke's emphasis on mercy, which I discuss in Part Two: Chapter 6, "Old Age and the IFS Thera-pist." And, the IFS therapist joins the sisterhood and brotherhood of therapists in daring to "feel the sorrow and compassion" for the suffering exiles, managers, and protectors struggling in the internal family, tumbling wounded and exhausted in the outer world. But Merton is not finished. He adds the following to make his point as duly applicable in our practical world. "In order to do this, we have to be able to *experience their sin as if it were our own*" (Merton, Note 17, Ibid., art. 2, p. 12).

What a brilliant statement of identification with the other in their ultimate vulnerability. What a profound proclamation that we are all one. What a challenge to live the mystic's realization that we share the same body, what some have called the *Mystical Body of the Christus*—no one escaping the glorious shared union of opposites.

**Guntrip, H. J.** (1973). *Psychoanalytic Theory, Therapy, and the Self.*

Guntrip writes, "To care for people is more important than to care for ideas" (p. v). Such a simple statement. Nothing grandiose. Nothing earth-shattering on the surface, but what an earthquake ready to topple the house of cards posing as monuments to irrefutable truths whatever the cost to the individual. I woke this morning thinking of the Inquisitions across time and place that forgot the primacy of the person. Guntrip was one of those rare individuals who stood his quiet ground before the Evolving Self. Making reference to Donald Winnicott, and using the humble doctor's words, Guntrip tells us,

> I would say that the infant is "a whole psyche with ego-potential at birth" and it depends on the mother's [caretaker's] relating, whether this potential is evoked and grows a real Ego or Personal Self [Self]. If not, the "true self" [Self] is not so much "put back into cold storage" but left unevoked by lack of any object-relationship in which it could grow. This is a matter of degree and artificial false selves [parts, subpersonalities] are developed on a conscious level as substitutes. (Winnicott in Guntrip, p. xi)

How aptly and succinctly does this speak of the wounded entities who are the objects of care and compassion in IFS Therapy.

Later, in his little gem of a book, Guntrip anticipates Martin Luther King Jr., whom I heard tell a standing-room-only crowd in the chapel at Boston University, the year before he was assassinated, that he would forever be a *maladjusted man* in this our society. Guntrip wrote,

> A human being may have to refuse to adapt to his human environment, and he prepares to lose his life in order to save something that is more precious to him than biological survival, his "soul," his truth to himself as an individual who means something that is of intrinsic value. (p. 107)

This is the redemptive work of all psychotherapy that does not deviate from the duty to liberate the evolving Self from the distorting forces from within and without while freeing those very forces in the process.

**Edinger, E. F.** (1995). *The Mysterium Lectures: A Journey through C. G. Jung's Mysterium Coniunctionis.*

In Lecture 7. 3., "An Alchemical Active Imagination," Edward Edinger reminds us of the following:

> We curse our complexes, don't we? They won't go away. We work and we work on them and they are still there—that element of inflammability keeps setting us on fire again and again. Despair, in this case, seems to be the gateway that leads to hearing the new element, the Voice. It's interesting that the alchemist had to reach the state of despairingly cursing Sulphur before Sulphur spoke up—before the autonomous psyche manifested itself in a way perceivable to the ego [Self]. (p. 101)

Only when the self comes to its wits and accepts its emptiness is it— as an emerging Self—able to recognize the helping hands of the SELF. In Lecture 27. 2., "The *Coniunctio*," Edinger reveals one of his profound convictions:

I am convinced that *coniunctio* means consciousness, and as I think of it, consciousness [Self] is both the cause and the effect of the *coniunctio*. We have to state it in this paradoxical way because, as I see it, the *coniunctio* is a product of both centers of the psyche—it's the product of both the ego [self] and the Self [SELF]. (p. 324)

Perhaps these are the most enlightening and bewildering two sentences that express what I have come to understand as the **Self** that is **SELF-led.** And the work of the IFS therapist is to enter into this mix under the influence of the qualities of the SELF and partner in the creation of the Self in both patient and therapist.

**Hannah, B.** (1976). *Jung: His Life and Work—A Biographical Memoir.*

In the early 1960s when I was a theology student residing at a summer camp on the shores of Casco Bay in Maine, I visited Bailey's Island via an aging lobster boat. This was before I had encountered the writings of Jung that eventually gave flesh to the abstract theology that at the time the Second Vatican Council of the Roman Catholic Church was challenging.

In 1987, I visited the cemetery in Kusnacht, Switzerland, the burial place of Jung, his family members, and some of his early associates, including Barbara Hannah, whose book I now mine for my closing comments.

At an earlier point in this long reflection and meandering search for the Elusive SELF, I touched upon themes that are featured in Hannah's book. I do so again because of her personal witnessing of Jung's engagement with the central theme that William James pondered in his Gifford Lectures.

In 1937, after Jung gave the Terry Lectures on "Psychology and Religion" at Yale, he gave a seminar in New York City that was a continuation of the Bailey Island Seminar of the previous year. At the farewell dinner, Jung "agreed to speak again in spite of his exhaustion. . . . He said that he would try to see if anything came to him to say. . . . Clearly

241

most of the speech came to him directly from the unconscious itself" (Hannah, p. 238). I interpret this to mean that Jung spoke from his SELF-led Self.

Jung's life's work was, in great part, his attempt to heal the Christianity that so afflicted, so burdened his father with irrational beliefs and practices as a pastor in the Swiss Reformed Church. (See also Dourley, 1984, *The Illness That We Are: A Jungian Critique of Christianity*; Goldbrunner, 1955, *Holiness Is Wholeness and Other Essays*; M. Stein, 1985, *Jung's Treatment of Christianity—The Psychotherapy of a Religious Tradition.)*

I include the following lengthy paragraphs without interruption as a final summation of this search for the Elusive SELF.

Jung spoke for some time about Christ as a human being and showed what a difficult problem he was faced with. As an illegitimate child, [Jesus] naturally had a life-long battle with the power devil. This is clear in the temptation in the wilderness, but he had the most unusual sense of integrity to refuse all of Satan's offers. Yet he did not quite escape them; his kingdom was not of this world, but it remained a kingdom all the same. And the strange incident of his triumphal entry into Jerusalem seems to stem from the same root. But all such convictions deserted him on the cross, when he uttered the tragic words: "My God, my God, why hast Thou forsaken me?" That was Christ's moment of utter failure, when he saw that the life he had led according to his best convictions and with such integrity had been largely based on illusion. On the cross he was deserted by his mission, but he had lived his life with such devotion that, in spite of this, he won through to a resurrected body.

Then Jung said to his audience—and this is what struck so many of them as last words—that we could only follow Christ's example and live our lives as fully as possible, even if it is based on a mistake. We should go and make our mistakes, for there is no full life without error; no one has ever found the whole truth; but if we will only live with the same integrity and devotion as Christ, he hoped we would all, like Christ, win through to a resurrected body. (Hannah, p. 239)

This is the finding of the Elusive SELF—always necessitating radical choice, daring hope, courageous mistakes, and a disturbing integrity on the way to a spiritualized body and a bodily spirit—a full incarnation manifest in and by and through the Self.

## the sound of the genuine

*now if I hear the sound of the genuine in me     and*
*you hear the sound of the genuine in you*
*it is possible for me to go down in me*
*and come up in you*

*so when I look at myself through your eyes*
*having made that pilgrimage*
*I see in me what you see in me and*
*the wall that separates and divides us*

*will disappear—*
*we will become one*
*because the sound of the genuine*
*makes the same music*

—adapted from Howard Thurman's
Spelman College Address, May 4, 1980.

# References

Ackerman, D. (1990). *A natural history of the senses.* New York, NY: W. W. Norton.

Adler, J. (2002) [2006:6]. *Offering from the conscious body: The discipline of authentic movement.* Rochester, VT: Inner Meditations.

American Psychiatric Association. (1980). *Diagnostic and statistical manual of mental disorders—DSM-III.* Arlington, VA: American Psychiatric Associates Publishing.

Anderson, F. G. (2013). 'Who's taking what?' Connecting neuroscience, psychopharmacology and internal family systems for trauma. In M. Sweezy & E. L. Ziskind. (2013). *Internal family systems therapy: New dimensions.* New York, NY: Routledge.

Anderson, F. G., Sweezy, M., & Schwartz, R. C. (2017). *Internal family systems skills training manual.* Eau Claire, WI: PESI Publishing & Media.

Aquinas, T. (1922). *Summa theologica* of St. Thomas Aquinas. Part II. London, England: Burns, Oates, & Washbourne.

Armstrong, K. (1993, 2004). *A history of god.* New York, NY: Ballantine Books.

Armstrong, K. (TED2008). My wish: The charter for compassion. Retrieved from http://www.ted.com>talks>up-next.

Augustine. (1997). *The confessions of Saint Augustine (of Hippo).* (M. Boulding, Trans.). Hyde Park, NY: New City Press.

Augustine. (1979). *On the trinity.* (Book III). (J. A. Zinn, Trans.). Peabody, MA: Paulist Press.

245

Bachelard, G. (1994). *The poetics of space.* (M. Jolas, Trans.). Boston, MA: Beacon Press.

Beahrs, J. O. (1982). *Unity and multiplicity: Multilevel consciousness of self in hypnosis, psychiatric disorder and mental health.* New York, NY: Brunner/Mazel.

Bettelheim, B. (1982). *Freud & man's soul.* New York, NY: Alfred A. Knopf.

Binet. A. (1892). *Alterations of personality.* (H. G. Baldwin, Trans.). New York, NY: D. Appleton.

Blavatsky, H. P. (1889). *The voice of silence.* (W. Q. Judge, Trans.). New York, NY: Theosophical Society.

Boadella, D. (1997). *Wilhelm Reich: The evolution of his work.* Chicago, IL: Regnery.

Boethius. (c. 524). *Consolation of philosophy.* Available through Oxford World Classics. Oxford, UK: Oxford University Press.

Bonaventure. (1259, 1956). *Itinerarium mentis ad deum* (The journey of the mind to God). (P. Boehner, OFM, Trans.). New York, NY: The Franciscan Institute Publications.

Bosnak, R. (1988). *A little course in dreams.* Boston, MA: Shambhala.

Boulding, M. (Trans.). (1997). *The confessions of Saint Augustine of Hippo.* New York, NY: Vintage.

Bromberg, P. (1994). Speak! That I may see you: Some reflections on dissociation, reality, and psychoanalytic listening. In *Psychoanalytic Dialogues, 4,* 519-548.

Brooks, D. (2018, June 14). Personalism: The philosophy we need. In *The New York Times,* p. A25.

Brown, B. (2012). *Daring greatly: How the courage to be vulnerable transforms the way we live, love, parent, and lead.* New York, NY: Penguin.

Brown, H. F. (1895). *John Addington Symonds: A biography.* (No longer in print.)

Browning, R. (1855). Andrea del sarto. In *Men and Women.* (See *The Harvard Classics.* New York, NY: P. F. Collier & Son.)

Buber, M. (1937). *I and thou.* New York, NY: Simon and Schuster.

Buhner, S. H. (2004). *The secret teachings of plants: The intelligence of the heart in the direction perception of nature.* Rochester, VT: Bear & Co.

Caird, J. (1880). *An introduction to the philosophy of religion.* New York, NY: Macmillan.

Coe, G. A. (1900). *The spiritual life: Studies in the science of religion.* New York, NY: Eaton & Mains.

Conger, J. P. (1994). *The body in recovery: Somatic psychotherapy and the self.* Berkley, CA: Frog Books.

Coomaraswamy, A. K. (November, 1942, Summer-Autumn, 1983). On being in one's right mind. In *Studies in comparative religion, vol. 15.* Nos. 3 & 4. Retrieved from http://www.studiesincompara-tivereligion.com.

Cooper, D. A. (1997). *God is a verb: Kabbalah and the practice of mystical Judaism.* New York: Riverhead Books.

Couissiner, M. (1863). *Le Catechism en image* [The catechism in pictures]. Reprint (2010) available from Kissinger Publishing, White-fish, MT.

Cozolino, L. (2002). *The neuroscience of psychotherapy.* New York, NY: W. W. Norton.

Damasio, A. (2003). *Looking for Spinoza: Joy, sorrow, and the feeling brain.* London: Harvest Press.

Das, Lama Surya. (1997). *Awakening the Buddha within.* New York, NY: Broadway Books.

De Caussade, J.-P. (2009). *The sacrament of the present moment.* San Francisco, CA: HarperSanFrancisco.

De Chardin, P. T. (1959). *The phenomenon of man.* New York, NY: Harper Perennial.

Dhorme, E. (1984). *A commentary on the book of Job. (Le livre de Job,* 1926, H. Knight, Trans.). New York, NY: Thomas Nelson.

D'Olivet, A. F. (1913). *The golden verses of Pythagoras: And other Pythagorean fragments.* (M. Duclos, Trans., 2018). New York: Samuel Weiser, Inc. Retrieved from http://www.sacred-texts.com/cla/gvp/ index.htm.

Dorn, G. (1602, 1951). *Theatrum chemicum, Volume 7,* iii-viii, p. 272.

Dourley, J. P. (1984). *The illness that we are: A Jungian critique of Christianity.* Toronto, ON: Inner City Books.

Dourley, J. P. (1987). *Love, celibacy and the inner marriage.* Toronto, ON: Inner City Books.

Dourley, J. P. (1981). *The psyche as sacrament: A comparative study of C. G. Jung and Paul Tillich.* Toronto, ON: Inner City Books.

Duclos, J. S. (2018). Value, morality, and wilderness. [Unpublished doctoral dissertation, Boston University].)

Edinger, E. F. (1984). *The creation of consciousness: Jung's myth for modern man.* Toronto, Canada: Inner City Books.

Edinger, E. F. (1972). *Ego and archetype: Individuation and the religious function of the psyche.* Boston, MA: Shambhala.

Edinger, E. F. (1995). *The mysterium lectures: A journey through C. G. Jung's mysterium coniunctionis.* Toronto, Canada: Inner City Books.

Eliot, T. S. (1943). Little gidding. In *Four Quartets.* New York, NY: Harcourt, Brace.

Ensler, E. (2006). *Insecure at last: Losing it in our security-obsessed world.* New York, NY: Penguin Random House.

Erikson, E. H. (1950). The eight ages of man. In *Childhood and society.* New York, NY: W. W. Norton.

Erikson, E. H. (1968). *Identity: Youth and crisis.* (New York, NY: W. W. Norton.

Erikson, E. H. (1998). [Extended version]. *The life cycle completed.* New York, NY: W. W. Norton.

Evans, R. (1957). Jung on film. See Jung, C. G.

Ficino, M. (1998). *Three books of life: A critical edition and translation.* (C. V. Kaske & J. R. Clark, Eds.). Tempe, AZ: Arizona Center for Medieval and Renaissance Studies (ACMRS).

Finley, J. (02 November 2018). Searching for love. Retrieved from http://www.cac.org/searching-for-love-2018-11-02/.

Frankl, V. E. (1989). 3d ed. *The doctor of the soul: From psychotherapy to logotherapy.* New York, NY: Vintage Books.

Freud, S. (1927, 1989). *The future of an illusion.* New York, NY: Norton & Norton.

Freud, S. (1926, 1978). *The question of lay analysis: Conversations with an impartial person.* New York, NY: Norton & Norton.

Friedman, R. E. (1995). *The hidden face of God.* New York, NY: HarperCollins.

Gazzaniga, M. S. (1998). *The mind's past.* Oakland, CA: University of California Press.

Gendlin, E. T. (1978). *Focusing.* New York: NY: Bantam Dell.

Goertzel, B. (1997). *From complexity to creativity: Exploration in evolutionary, autopoietic, and cognitive dynamics.* New York, NY: Bantam Books.

Goldbrunner, J. (1955). *Holiness is wholeness and other essays.* (S. Goodman, Trans.). New York, NY: Pantheon Books.

Goldbrunner, J. (1964). *Individuation: A study of the depth psychology of Carl Gustave Jung.* Notre Dame, IN: University of Notre Dame Press.

Greene, E., & Goodrich-Dunn, B. (2004). *The psychology of the body.* Philadelphia, PA: Lippincott Williams & Wilkins.

Guggenbuhl-Craig, A. (1980). *Eros on crutches: Reflections on amorality and psychopathy.* Dallas, TX: Spring Publications.

Guntrip, H. J. (1973). *Psychoanalytic theory, therapy, and the self.* New York, NY: Basic Books.

Hanh, T. N. (1975). *The miracle of mindfulness.* Boston, MA: Beacon Press.

Hannah, B. (1976, 1991). *Jung: His life and work: A biographical memoir.* New York, NY: Perigree Books.

Hartley, L. (Ed.). (2009). *Contemporary body psychotherapy: The Chiron approach.* New York, NY: Routledge.

Havel, V. 1990. *Disturbing the peace: A conversation with Karel Huizdala.* New York, NY: Vintage.

Heller, M. C. (2012). *Body psychotherapy: History, concepts, and methods* (M. A. Duclos, Trans.). New York, NY: W. W. Norton.

Herbine-Blank, T., Kerpelman, D. A., & Sweezy, M. (2016). *Intimacy from the inside out: Courage and compassion in couple therapy.* New York, NY: Routledge.

Herzog, E. (2001). *Psyche and death: Death-demons in folklore, myths and modern dreams.* Dallas, TX: Spring Publications.

Hill, D. (2015). *Affect-regulation theory: A clinical model.* New York, NY: W. W. Norton.

Hirsch, E. (1999). Soul in action. In *How to read a poem: And fall in love with poetry.* San Diego, CA: Mariner.

Ho, M.-W. (1993). *The rainbow and the worm: The physics of organisms.* Singapore: World Scientific.

Huss, P. (108?). The Psychological Use of the Gospels, Lecture. Psychology and Clinical Studies. Andover Newton Theological School. Boston.

Ignatius. See Rickeby, J., in Further Reading.

James, W. (1907, 1979). *Pragmatism: A new name for some old ways of thinking.* Cambridge, MA: Harvard University Press.

James, W. (1890). *The principles of psychology.* New York, NY: Henry, Holt.

James, W. 1902). *The varieties of religious experience: A study in human nature.* London, England: Longman, Green.

James, W. (1997). *William James: Selected writings.* New York, NY: Book-of-the-Month Club (BOMC).

James, W. (1896). *The will to believe and other essays.* London, England: Longmans, Green.

Jastrzebski, A. (2011, Spring). Gordon W. Allport's concept of the human person: On a possible dialogue between philosophy and psychology. In *The Pluralist. 6*(1), pp. 71-86.

Johnson, L. T. (2015). *The revelatory body: Theology as inductive art.* Grand Rapids, MI: William B. Eerdmans.

Johnson, R. A. (1986). *Inner work: Using dreams and active imagination for personal growth.* New York, NY: Harper and Row.

Jung, C. G. (1951). *Aion: Researches into the phenomenology of the self.* In *The Collected Works of C. G. Jung, Volume 19* (Part 2). Princeton, NJ: Princeton University Press.

Jung, C. G. (1961). Archetypes and the collective unconscious. In *The Collected Works of C. G. Jung, Volume 9.* Princeton, NJ: Princeton University Press.

Jung, C. G. (1979). *The collected works of C. G. Jung.* Princeton, NJ: Princeton University Press.

Jung, C. G. (1957). Jung on film: The Richard Evans interview. Available online at gnosis.org/gnostic-jung/Jung-on-film-html.

Jung, C. G. (1957). *Memories, dreams, reflections.* New York, NY: Pantheon Press.

Jung, C. G. (1960). Psychology and religion. (The Terry Lecture Series). New Haven, CT: Yale University Press.

Jung, C. G. (1958). Psychotherapists or the clergy. In *Psychology and Religion: West and East, Volume 11* (Bollingen series, 20). Princeton, NJ: Pantheon Books.

Jung, C. G. (1976). Symbols of transformation. In *The Collected Works of C. G. Jung, Volume 5.* (Bollingen series, 20). Princeton, NJ: Princeton University Press.

Kegan, R. (1982). *The evolving self.* Cambridge, MA: Harvard University Press.

Keleman, S. (2018, Fall/Winter). *International body psychotherapy journal.* Retrieved from http://www.eabp.org/publications-Journal. php.

Keleman, S. (1975). *Your body speaks its mind: Expanding our selves.* Berkley, CA: Center Press.

Krueger, D. W. (2002). *Integrating body self and psychological self: Creating a new story in psychoanalysis and psychotherapy.* New York, NY: Brunner-Routledge.

Kurtz, R. (1990). *Body-centered psychotherapy: The Hakomi method.* Mendocino, CA: LifeRhythm.

Lear, J. (2008). *Radical hope: Ethics in the face of cultural devastation.* Cambridge, MA: Harvard University Press.

Levine, P. A., & Frederick, A. (1997). *Waking the tiger: Healing trauma.* Berkeley, CA: North Atlantic Books.

Levine, P. A., & Kline, M. (2006). *Trauma through a child's eyes: Awakening the ordinary miracle of healing.* Berkeley, CA: North Atlantic Books.

Lewis, T., Amini, F., & Lannon, R. (2000). *A general theory of love.* New York, NY: Random House.

Lidz, T. (1976). [Revised edition.]. *The person: His and her development throughout the life cycle.* New York, NY: Basic Books.

Luke, H. M. (1931, 1987). *Old age: Journey into simplicity.* New York, NY: Parabola Books.

Macy, J. (2007). *World as lover, world as self: Courage for global justice and ecological renewal.* Berkeley, CA: Parallax Press.

Malan, D. (1979). *Individual psychotherapy and the science of psychodynamics.* London: Butterworth.

Maslow, A. (1970). *Motivation and personality.* New York, NY: Harper & Row.

Maslow, A. (1954, 1964). *Religion, values, and peak experiences.* New York, NY: Harper & Row.

Mattoon, M. A. (1981). *Jungian psychology in perspective*. New York, NY: The Free Press.

Maurin, P. (1933). Easy essays. In *The Catholic Worker*. Retrieved from http://www.catholicworker.org.easyessays.

McGichrist, I. (2009). *The master and his emissary: The divided brain and the making of the western world*. New Haven, CT: Yale University Press.

Meier, C. A. (1986). *Soul and body: Essays on the theories of C. G. Jung*. San Francisco, CA: The Lapis Press.

Merton, T. (1964). (Ed.). *Gandhi on non-violence*. New York, NY: New Directions.

Middelkoop, P. (1985). *The wise old man: Healing through inner images*. Boston, MA: Shambhala.

Miles, J. (1995). *God, a biography*. New York, NY: Alfred A. Knopf.

Moore, T. (1983). *Rituals of imagination*. Dallas, TX: The Pegasus Foundation.

Moore, T. (1994). *Soul mates: Honoring the mysteries of love and relationship*. New York, NY: Harper Perennial.

Moyn, S. (2011). Personalism, community, and the origins of human rights. In *Human Rights in the Twentieth Century* (S.-L. Hoffmann, Ed.). New Haven, CT: Yale Campus Press.

Oldenberg, H. (1882). *Buddha: His life, his doctrine, his order*. (W. Hoey, Trans.). London, England: Williams & Norgate.

Paulhan, F. (1894, 1909). Les caractères. In *Revue de metaphysique et de morale*. F. Alcan (Ed.). *2:*591-605. Paris, France.

Perry, J. W. (1953). *The self in psychotic process: Its symbolism in schizophrenia*. Dallas, TX: Spring Publications.

Pierrakos, J. (1997). *Eros, love & sexuality: The forces that unite man and woman*. Mendocino, CA: LifeRhythm.

Robillard, C., & Duclos, M. (2003, 2005). *Common threads: Stories of life after trauma*. (See Xlibris Corporation, 2003; CreateSpace, 2005.)

Robillard, C., & Duclos, M. (2011). *Cultivating hope with abuse survivors.* Londonderry, NH: The Safe Place Seminars.

Robillard, C., & Duclos, M. (2011). *Necessary illusions: Musings of a man and woman.* Londonderry, NH: The Safe Place Seminars.

Rogers, C. R. (1959). *A theory of therapy, personality, and interpersonal relationships as developed in the client-centered framework,* New York, NY: McGraw-Hill.

Rohr, R. (2018, July 7). Economy. Daily meditations. Retrieved from http://www.cac.org/Richard-rohr/daily-meditations.

Rohr, R. (2019, May 10). God is relationship. Daily Meditations. Retrieved from http://www.cac.org/Richard-rohr/daily-meditations.

Rohr, R. (2018, October 10). The God particle. Daily Meditations. Retrieved from http://www.cac.org/Richard-rohr/daily-meditations.

Rohr, R. (2018, September 20). Healing addiction. Daily Meditations. Retrieved from http://www.cac.org/Richard-rohr/daily-meditations.

Rohr, R. (2018, July 29). The one and the many. Daily Meditations. Retrieved from http://www.cac.org/Richard-rohr/daily-meditations.

Rohr, R. (2018, September 19). The soul's objective union with God. Daily Meditations. Retrieved from http://www.cac.org/Richard-rohr/daily-meditations.

Rohr, R. (2018, September 12). Theosis. Daily Meditations. Retrieved from http://www.cac.org/Richard-rohr/daily-meditations.

Rohr, R. (2018, September 11). Trinity. Daily Meditations. Retrieved from http://www.cac.org/Richard-rohr/daily-meditations.

Ross, C. A. (1997). *Dissociative identity disorder: Diagnosis, clinical features and treatment.* New York, NY: John Wiley & Sons.

Ross, C. A. (1994). *The Osiris complex: Case studies in multiple personality disorder.* Toronto, Canada: University of Toronto Press.

Rothschild, B. (2002). *The body remembers: The psychophysiology of trauma and trauma treatment.* New York, NY: W. W. Norton.

Russell, J. B. (1984). *Lucifer: The devil in the Middle Ages.* Ithaca, NY: Cornell University Press.

Schore, A. N. (1994). *Affect regulation and the origin of the self: The neurobiology of emotional development.* New York, NY: W. W. Norton.

Schwartz, R. C. (1997). *Evolution of the internal family systems model.* New York, NY: Guilford Press.

Schwartz, R. C. (2015). Facing our dark side. In *Psychotherapy Networker.* Retrieved from http://www.psychotherapynetworker.org/.

Schwartz, R. C., & Sweezy, M. (2019). 2nd ed. *Internal family systems therapy.* New York, NY: Guilford Press.

Schwartz, R. C. (2018, May 15). Webinar, Internal family systems (IFS) therapy: A revolutionary & transformative treatment of PTSD, anxiety, depression, substance abuse—and more! Retrieved from https://www.pesi.com/. . ./internal-family-systems-therapy-ifs-with-richard-schwartz.

Schwartz, R. C. (2008). *You are the one you've been waiting for.* Oak Park, IL: Trailheads.

Schwartz, R. C., & Falconer, R. R. (2017). *Many minds, one self: Evidence for a radical shift in paradigm.* Oak Park, IL: Trailheads Publications.

Sieck, M. (Ed.). (2007). *Relational somatic psychotherapy: Collected essays of Robert Hilton.* Santa Barbara, CA: Sieck and the Santa Barbara Graduate Institute.

Siegel, D. J. (2015, May/June). The colors of tomorrow. In *Psychotherapy Networker.* Retrievedfromhttp://www.psychotherapynetworker. org/.

Siegel, D. J. (2010). *The mindful therapist.* New York, NY: W. W. Norton.

Siegel, R. D., & Schwartz, R. C. (2015, January/February). The fiction of the self: The paradox of mindfulness in clinical practice. In *Psychotherapy Networker.* Retrieved from http://www.psychotherapynetworker.org/.

Siegel, R. D., & Schwartz, R. C. (2015). *An historic moment: Interpersonal neurobiology (IPNB) meets Internal Family Systems (IFS).* [DVD]. Boston, MA: The Center for Self-Leadership.

Singer, J. (1974). *Boundaries of the soul: The practice of Jung's psychology.* Garden City, NY: Doubleday.

Solms, M., & Turnbull, O. (2002). *The brain and the inner world: An introduction to the neuroscience of the subjective experience.* London, England: KARNAC.

Starbuck, E. D. (1911). *The psychology of religion.* London, England: Edwin Diller.

Stein, M. (1985). *Jung's treatment of Christianity—The psychotherapy of a religious tradition.* Wilmette, IL: Chiron.

Stern, D. (1984). *The present moment in psychotherapy and everyday life.* New York, NY: Norton.

Sweezy, M., & Ziskind, E. L., (Eds.). (2013). *Internal family systems therapy: New dimensions.* New York, NY: Routledge.

Unknown. (1981). *The cloud of unknowing.* (J. Walsh, Trans.). New York, NY: Paulist Press.

Unknown. (c. 1350). *Theologia Germanica.* Reprinted by Martin Luther. (1518). New ed. 1980. Mahwah, NJ: Paulist Press.

Vivekananda, Swami. (1896). *Raja yoga.* Retrieved from http://www.en.wikisource.org/wiki/.The_Complete_Works_of_ Swami_Vivekananda/volume_1/Raja-yoga.

Von Franz, M.-L. (1980). *Alchemy: An introduction to the symbolism and psychology.* Toronto, ON: Inner City Books.

Watkins, J. G., & Watkins, H. H. (1997). *Ego states: Theory and therapy.* New York, NY: W. W. Norton.

Whitman, W. (1855). A clear midnight. In *Leaves of Grass.* Self-published.

Whitman, W. (1855). Personalism. In *Leaves of Grass.* Self-published.

Williams, C. (1938). *He came down from heaven and the forgiveness of sins.* Oxford, England: Oxford University Press.

256

Winnicott, D. (1965). *The maturational processes and the facilitating environment: Studies in the theory of emotional development.* London: Hogarth Press.

Xie, J. (2018). Ongoing. In *Eye level.* Minneapolis, MN: Graywolf Press.

Ziegler, A. J. (1983). *Archetypal medicine.* Oakland, CA: University of California Press.

## Further Reading

Aposhyan, S. (2004). *Body-mind psychotherapy: Principles, techniques, and practical applications.* New York, NY: W. W. Norton.

Aurelius, M. (1997). The meditations of Marcus Aurelius. In *The Harvard Classics.* (Dover Thrift Editions. William Kaufman, Ed., Mineola, NY: Dover Publications.)

Caldwell, C. (Ed.). (1997). *Getting in touch: The guide to new body-centered therapies.* Wheaton, IL: Quest Books.

Cattell, R. B. (1957). *Personality and motivation structure and measurement.* Oxford, England: World Book.

Cousins, E. (1978). *Bonaventure.* Mahwah, NJ: Paulist Press.

Damasio, A. (1994). *Descartes' error: Emotion, reason, and the human brain.* New York, NY: Penguin Books.

Davies, J. B. (1996). Reasons and causes: Understanding substance users' explanations for their behavior. In *Human Psychopharmacology, vol. II,* 539-548.

Davis, W. (2014). The endo self: A self model for body-oriented psychotherapy. In *International Body Psychotherapy Journal. 13 (1),* 31-51.

Emerson, R. W. (1841, 1995). The oversoul. In *Emerson's essays.* New York, NY: HarperPerennial.

Felitti, V. J., Anda, R. F., Nordenberg, D., Williamson, D. F., Spitz, A. M., & Marks, J. S. (2019, June). Relationship of childhood abuse and household dysfunction to many of the leading causes of death in adults: The adverse childhood experiences (ACE) study. In *American Journal of Preventative Medicine. 56, 6.* 774-786.

Fox, M. (2011). *Christian mystics: 365 readings and meditations.* Novato, CA: New World Library.

Gazzaniga, M. S. (1989). Organization of the human brain. In *Science, 245,* 947-952.

Goulding, R. A. (2002). *The mosaic mind: Empowering the tormented selves of child abuse survivors.* Oak Park, IL: Trailheads.

Grand, S. (2000). *The reproduction of evil: A clinical & cultural perspective.* Hillsdale, NJ: The Analytic Press.

Guerney, E. (1887). *Tertium quid: Chapters on various disputed question.* London, England: Kegan, Paul, Trench.

Homes, R. W. (2003). *IFS Spirituality and Self.* In *Journal of Self Leadership. 3, 1.* 1-5.

Jacobson, E. (1938). *Progressive relaxation.* Chicago, IL: University of Chicago Press.

Johanson, G., & Kurtz, R. (1991). *Grace unfolding: Psychotherapy in the spirit of the Tao Te Ching.* New York, NY: Bell Tower.

Josephs, L. (1995). *Character and self-expression.* Northvale, NJ: Jason Aronson.

Lowen, A. (1975). *Bioenergetics: The revolutionary therapy that uses the language of the body to heal the problems of the mind.* New York, NY: Penguin Books.

MacLean, P. D. (1990, January). *The triune brain in evolution: Role in paleo-cerebral functions.* New York, NY: Springer Science and Business Media.

McConnell, S. (Forthcoming 2020). *Somatic Internal Family Systems Therapy: Awareness, Breath, Resonance, Movement and Touch in Practice.* Berkley, CA: North Atlantic Books.

Meyendorff, J. (1959). *St. Gregory Palamas and orthodox spirituality.* Yonkers, NY: St. Vladimir's Seminary Press.

Meissner, W. W. (1992). *Ignatius of Loyola: The psychology of a saint.* New Haven, CT: Yale University Press.

Mones, A. G. (2014). *Transforming troubled children, teens, and their families.* New York, NY: Routledge.

Nichols, M. P., & Schwartz, R. C. (1998). *Family therapy: Concepts and methods.* Boston, MA: Allyn and Bacon.

Ogden, P., Minton, K., & Pain, C. (2006). *Trauma and the body: A sensorimotor approach to psychotherapy.* New York, NY: W. W. Norton.

Perls, F. (1969). *Gestalt therapy verbatim.* Santa Barbara, CA: Gestalt Journal Press.

Perls, F. (1969). *In and out the garbage pail.* Santa Barbara, CA: Gestalt Journal Press.

Pierrakos, E. B. (1957, October 11). The higher self, the lower self, and the mask. Retrieved from http://pathwork.org. [Pathwork Guide Lectures. The International Pathworks Foundation].

Rickaby, J. (Trans.). (1915). *The spiritual exercise of Ignatius of Loyola.* London, England: Burns.

Rogers, C. R. (1961). *On becoming a person: A therapist's view of psychotherapy.* Boston, MA: Houghton Mifflin.

Rogers, C. R. (1967). *Person to person: The problem of being human: A new trend in Psychology.* Boston, MA: Houghton Mifflin.

Rogers, C. R. (1964). *Religion, values, and peak experiences.* Boston, MA: Houghton Mifflin.

Rogers, C. R. (1980). *A way of being.* Boston, MA: Houghton Mifflin.

Rohr, R. (2011). *Falling upward: A spirituality for the two halves of life.* San Francisco, CA: Jossey-Bass.

Rohr, R. (2013). *Immortal diamond: The search for our true self.* San Francisco, CA: Jossey-Bass.

Rohr, R. (2009). *The naked now: Learning to see as the mystics see.* New York, NY: The Crossroad Publishing Company.

Rohr, R. (2019). *The universal Christ: How a forgotten reality can change everything we see, hope for, and believe.* New York, NY: Convergent.

Rohr, R. (2018, October 18). Suffering love. Daily Meditations. Retrieved from http://www.cac.org/Richard-rohr/daily-meditations.

Rosenberg, J. L., Rand, M. L., & Asay, D. (1985). *Body, self, and soul: Sustaining integration.* Atlanta, GA: Humanics.

Spiegel, L. (2007). *Internal family systems therapy with children.* New York, NY: Routledge.

Thurman, H. (1980, May 04). The sound of the genuine. Spelman College address. Retrieved from uindy.edu/eip/files/reflection4.pdf.

Weiss, H., Johanson, G., Monda, L., & Reed, M. (2015). *Hakomi mindfulness: Centered somatic psychotherapy.* New York, NY: W. W. Norton.

Wheelwright, J. (Ed.). (1968). *The reality of the psyche: Awaken in the dream.* New York, NY: G. P. Putnam's Sons.

White, E. (1927, 1980). *The apocryphal New Testament.* (M. R. James, Ed.). *'And ye shall know yourselves that ye are in God and God in you. And ye are the City of God.'* London: Oxford-Clarendon.

Whitmont, E. (1983). *Return of the goddess.* London, England: Routledge & Kegan Paul.

Wills, F., & Sanders, D. (1997). *Cognitive therapy: Transforming the image.* Thousand Oaks, CA: Sage Books.

*SI ENIM COMPREHENDERIS*
*NON EST DEUS*
*NON EST RE*

CPSIA information can be obtained
at www.ICGtesting.com
Printed in the USA
LVHW041644240422
717099LV00006B/159

9 781652 406136